Laȝamon's Brut

Laȝamon's Brut *and the Anglo-Norman Vision of History*

KENNETH J. TILLER

Associate Professor of English,
University of Virginia's College at Wise

UNIVERSITY OF WALES PRESS
CARDIFF
2007

Published by the University of Wales Press

University of Wales Press
10 Columbus Walk
Brigantine Place
Cardiff
CF10 4UP

www.wales.ac.uk/press

ISBN 978-0-7083-1902-4

British Library Cataloguing-in-Publication Data.
A catalogue record for this book is available from the British Library.

Printed in Great Britain by Antony Rowe Ltd, Wiltshire

*For Gillian
and my parents*

Contents

Acknowledgements

My interest in Laȝamon's *Brut* dates back to graduate school where I was introduced to the text by the late Professor Janemarie Luecke, CSC, during a course in Middle English literature. The *Brut* was a difficult text to work with at that time, as the only readily available primary text was Brooks and Leslie's two-volume diplomatic edition of the Otho and Caligula manuscripts. As a result, perhaps, there was little secondary material to work with. In the intervening years, in part due to the dual-language edition of the work by Ray Barron and Carole Weinberg and to Rosamund Allen's translation, scholarly interest in Laȝamon has justly grown. More scholars and critics have begun to appreciate the work of this remarkable Early Middle English writer. Yearly Laȝamon sessions at Kalamazoo and meetings of the International Laȝamon's *Brut* society – held about once every three to four years – illustrate the growth of interest in Laȝamon studies. The collegiality and academic exchanges of these gatherings have made my work in the field much more rewarding.

This work has grown out of my dissertation at the University of Notre Dame, under the direction of Professor Dolores Warwick Frese. I express my sincere thanks to Professor Frese for her friendship and insightful comments on the earliest drafts of this project. Thanks also to Professor Jonathan D'Arcy Boulton for his valuable support as co-director of the dissertation. Earlier versions of sections of chapters 2 and 4 appear, respectively, as 'Romancing history: masculine identity and historical authority in Layamon's *Brut*', in *Layamon: Contexts, Language and Interpretation*, Rosamund Allen, Lucy Perry, and Jane Roberts (eds), King's College London Medieval Studies 19 (2002); and as 'The truth "bi Arðure þan kinge"': Arthur's role in shaping Lawman's vision of history', in *Arthuriana*, 10, 2 (2000), a special edition edited by Elizabeth Bryan on theoretical approaches to the *Brut*. My gratitude goes out to these publications for permission to use sections of the articles. I wish to express special thanks to all members of the International La3amon's *Brut* society, and in particular to Professor Elizabeth J. Bryan and Professor James E. Noble for their ongoing support of and important feedback on my efforts on the *Brut*. I am further grateful for the kind attention of the staff and readers of the University of Wales Press – especially Duncan Campbell for encouraging me in this project, and Claire Powell and Sarah Lewis for continuing Duncan's efforts on behalf of this project. Special thanks are due to Sarah Lewis for consistently following up on the progress of the manuscript and for great patience throughout this process. Thanks also to the Press's anonymous reader for helpful criticism and suggestions. I am grateful for a summer research grant from the Faculty Development Committee at the University of Virginia's College at Wise to revise this work. I also thank my colleagues in the department of Language and Literature at the University of Virginia's College at Wise, with special gratitude to Professor Emeritus of English Richard H. Peake and to Academic Dean and Professor of German Amelia J. Harris, for institutional and moral support. Warmest thanks go to Professor Catherine Mahony of the University of Virginia's College at Wise and to her husband, the late Professor Jack Mahony, for intellectual companionship and for the many invigorating conversations that have helped sharpen my thinking.

My last and deepest thanks I reserve for my wife and colleague, Gillian Huang-Tiller. Her keen critical eye, forthright commentary and patience have, more than anything else, helped bring this project to fruition. 'Heo leornede hire lære leofliche on heorten.'

Introduction: *Laʒamon's* Brut *and the translation of twelfth-century history*

History as translation

Unlike modern readers, who expect history to relay reliable information exactly as it occurred, medieval readers (and listeners) approached history for a written record of the workings of God in the world, for an explanation of and justification for current events, or even for a good story. In this regard, history of the period is similar to 'creative' or 'fictional' literature, so much so that Nancy Partner can cite the 'rich' tradition 'of history as serious entertainment'.[1] However, this 'entertainment' was not structured without the ideological and aesthetic concerns of the historian. Robert W. Hanning refers to the historian's 'precommitments to the past', 'traditions of expression and analysis' and 'historical, ideological, or ethical themes [that] dominate and organize the complete [historical] work'.[2] These studies tell us that history in the medieval period was a more broadly conceived genre than it is today. This is not to say that there was no such thing as 'historical truth' or 'verifiable history' during the period, only that such conceptions were based on other things than 'facts'. 'True' history during the period was often dependent upon adherence to other texts and textual traditions.[3] For instance, twelfth-century insular historians based their understanding of historical 'truth' on fidelity to Bede's *Historia Ecclesiastica* – a fidelity that remained constant until Geoffrey of Monmouth offered a competing narrative.[4] All interpreted texts and re-presented them for new contexts, often dramatically altering the meaning or 'sentence' of the original, according to ideological or religious predispositions. Because it involved the re-working and reconceptualizing of text, the task of the medieval historian in twelfth-century England paralleled that of the translator, and the

writing of history – especially of the foundational history – constitutes
an act of translation.

Translation, with its roots in Latin *trans* (across) and *lato* (to bear or
carry), usually refers to the replication of one text in another language;
the writing of history, transferring material from one text to another
(and from one language to another), constitutes the same sort of act.
Ernst Curtius has argued that *translatio* forms the basis of medieval
European historical thought:

> The word *transferturi* ('is transferred') gives rise to the concept of *translatio*
> (transference) which is the basis for medieval historical theory. The renewal
> of Empire by Charlemagne could be regarded as a transferral of the
> Roman *imperium* to another people. This is implied in the formula
> *translatio imperii*, with which the *translatio studii* (transferral of learning
> from Athens or Rome to Paris) was later coordinated.[5]

To medieval writers, *translatio* carried with it the task of establishing
meaning, by which I mean that it was a hermeneutic process of reading
the will of God in the text. Translation and interpretation were scarcely
distinguished, as Ruth Morse has observed.[6] Rita Copeland has further
identified medieval *translatio* as embodying both a hermeneutic and a
rhetorical function; according to Copeland, translation was a practice
'inscribed within a large disciplinary nexus, a historical intersection of
hermeneutical practice and rhetorical theory'.[7] Historical writing,
carrying both interpretative and rhetorical functions, also operates at
this intersection.

The writing of history as translation is most striking in foundational
histories, or histories of conquest and settlement. In such histories, the
translation of texts of the conquered people, such as the insular Britons,
involves the concurrent translation of the culture in which the text is
produced for the new dominion. Often, such activity includes appropriation and translation of historical texts of precursor cultures regarded
as worthy of emulation, even if no direct contact is involved; here, the
Roman practice of translating Greek myth and history – and with it
Greek culture – served as a model. For example, the multiple mythical
'histories' of medieval Europe, such as Charlemagne and the Frankish
kingdom, that linked peoples to the ancient Trojans (and by extrapolation, to the Romans) provided a link for the new dominion with an
illustrious semi-mythical past. Consequently, the *translatio imperii*, the
transference of the imperial authority formerly lodged in Rome to

another political entity, came to be intimately linked with the *translatio studii,* the transferral of education and culture from one centre to another, including the programmatic translation of texts from the language of the former central power into the language of the new one. In other words, the concept of *translatio* served as a master metaphor for the process of transferring imperial power from one entity to another, parallel to the establishment of new centres of culture and education. Tangentially, the work of Christian exegetical translators of the first, second and third centuries – translating Old Testament history so that it predicted New Testament revelation – paralleled Roman translation of Greek literature.[8] All of these factors in turn play into later Anglo-Norman practices of translating history.

Prior to the Conquest, understanding of the *translatio imperii* and *studii* characterized practices in King Alfred's Anglo-Saxon kingdom. Although the ninth-century Alfred neither saw his kingdom as the inheritor of Roman authority nor sought to incorporate Graeco-Roman myth and history into Anglo-Saxon history, he did recognize the importance of translation to cultural progress. His written justification for translation, in the introduction to the English translation of Saint Gregory's *Pastoralis Regula,* shows a clear relationship between translation and cultural achievement:

Ða gemunde ic hu sio ær wæs on Ebriscgeðiode finden, ond eft, ða hie Creacas geliornodon, ða wendon hie hie on hiora agen geðiode ealle, ond eac ealle oðre bec. Ond eft Lædenware swæ same, siððan hie hie geliornodon, hie hie wendon ealla ðurh wise wealhstodas on hiora agen geðiode.[9]

[Then I call to mind how it once was among the Hebrew texts, and afterwards, when the Greeks learned them, they translated them into their own language, and all the other books. And afterward the Latin people did the same once they had learned the texts; they turned all, through their wise interpreters, into their own language.]

Alfred's respect for the Latin language and the Latin religious text is sincere, as is his regret that few people in his day could read them. Alfred sincerely laments the decline of Latin literacy among the English, especially among the English clergy, and proposes the translation of biblical texts to remedy the situation. In this sense, the passage signals a genuine love of the texts. Yet there is a subtext that, since the Greeks and 'Latin people' achieved greatness in part through their translation of precursor texts, Anglo-Saxon England has the same potential if it follows the same course of action. There is an element of mastery embedded in the Old English term, *wenan*, for translation; it connotes not only *to translate* or *to restore*, but also *to change, alter* or *direct*, thus conveying implications of the possession of text, a connotation it shares with the Latin *transfero* or *verto*.[10] We can thus see that Alfred's intentions may be more complex than first meets the eye. Robert Stanton argues that neither a strictly 'aggressive' nor a 'faithful' model of translation can be ascribed to Alfred's translation programme, because it embodies elements of both appropriation and servitude.[11] Alfred's learning programme reflected to a great extent the linked tropes of *translatio imperii* and *translatio studii* characteristic of the Roman and Carolingian Empires. By translating important religious and historical texts, the English gave their language the same status as that of their precursors.

It should be evident, at this point, that the practice of 'translation' means more than 'copying' the material of one text into another language. Modern and contemporary theorists of translation have shed some light on the translator's relationship to the source text. They have asked whether translation extends and expands the life of the source text, giving it new vitality in new contexts, or if the original is lost in the process of translation. Walter Benjamin, for instance, articulates the task of the translator and advocates the view that to translate is to give life to the original, not through the literal translation of meaning, but through its intent, syntax and 'spirit'. Benjamin's translator 'lovingly and in detail incorporate[s] the original's mode of signification, thus making both the original and the translation recognizable as fragments of a greater language'.[12] Like Benjamin, George Steiner perceives the translator as intuitively reproducing the 'spirit' of the original, and perhaps even improving upon it: 'Where it surpasses the original, the real translation infers that the source text possesses potentialities, elemental reserves as yet unrealized by itself.' For Steiner, 'Fidelity is not literalism or any technical device for rendering "spirit" [. . .] The translator, the exegist, the reader is *faithful to* his text, makes his response responsible, only when he endeavours to restore the balance of forces, of integral presence, which appropriative comprehension has disrupted.'[13] Both see translation as a supplement to and an expansion of the source text, while both recognize that the task of the translator involves more than 'translating', as it is conventionally understood. Because the writing of history always engages origins and sources, their views of translation allow us to see how the historian – who reconceives past events and early texts for new contexts – serves as a translator.

What I have sketched so far is a necessarily brief overview of medieval (and some modern) translation practices and their relationship to history and, more importantly, to the writing of history. This relationship would seem especially acute in a society such as post-Conquest England, where competing British, English and Norman narratives had to be reconciled into a single vision of English history through translation. Curiously, however, discussions of medieval *translatio* tend to ignore this period in English history, and usually offer only brief references to Alfred's translation programmes. This tendency may have developed, in part, because of Britain's separation from Europe and the need to discuss a separate *translatio imperii* and *translatio studii*, tangential to the European ideal of re-establishing the Roman *imperium*. It may also result from the unusually complex paradigm for the transmission of culture and language: grounded in the binary relationship between Latin and *the* vernacular, most medieval translation theories lack a vocabulary for discussing the complex interplay of Latin and the vernaculars of the Norman French, the English and the Celtic people simultaneously occupying the British Isles. They cannot, for instance, account for the often-conflicting blend of admiration and contempt displayed by Anglo-Norman historian-translators toward their English material; theirs was not a simple case of translating the work of a superior culture to enrich their own or one of 'civilizing' 'barbaric' material, but a nuanced engagement with a people they found similarly developed, yet often surprisingly 'Other'. Further, because these theories tend to concern themselves exclusively with the transmission of Latin text into the vernacular, they are often ill-equipped to discuss the complicated transfer of text from English into Latin and, some generations later, into French. They also lack the vocabulary for considering *transvernacular* translation, as in the exchanges between French and English that intensified during the Angevin period (1154–1216). Neither do they provide a context for examining the asymmetrical power relationships between the English vernacular, Anglo-Norman French and Latin, which formed translation and historiographic practices of the period: Copeland, for instance, focuses entirely on translations from Latin into the European vernaculars; Morse, likewise, concentrates mainly on the Latin-to-vernacular path of translation. Furthermore, although they are informed by the political and cultural dimensions of translation, even medieval theories of the subject often do not take into account the differences a linguistic-based social hierarchy made; that is, how do circumstances differ when *two* vernaculars, one the 'power' vernacular (French) and one of the underclass (English or Welsh), coincide? In other words, they tend not to question whether it makes a difference if the translator is translating from a position of power and prestige, or if he or she is working from the position of a dominant or subaltern group.

To shed some light on translation practices during this difficult period, I have turned to post-colonial translation theories of the past few decades. Although a set of theories situated in the context of modern European expansionism might seem inapplicable to medieval texts – and many medievalists have cautioned against an overenthusiastic reception of post-colonial theories by medievalists – it is an approach that medievalists (including many cited herein) have found fruitful. Bruce Holsinger has recently made the case for interrelationships between medievalism and post-colonial theory, arguing that post-colonial theories in fact owe their existence to medieval texts and the writings of medievalists.[14] That the uneven social structure of Anglo-Norman England might, in a general sense of the term, present a colonial milieu is something scholars and critics have recently noted. J. C. Holt has observed that 'for the French, England was a land of adventure and opportunity, a land of new freedom and initiative', in other words, a colony.[15] The post-colonial context of Anglo-Norman England provides a particularly useful way of discussing translation methods, for translation, as Tejaswini Niranjana tells us, 'as a practice shapes, and takes shape within, the asymmetrical relations of power that operate under colonialism'.[16] Certainly, such a power dynamic was operative in England during the generations preceding the Norman Conquest, when the use of English as a primary language stigmatized a speaker as a member of the underclass, and of the Celtic languages, such as Welsh, as beyond the margins of dominant society. In a colonial environment, however, the conflict is often complex, characterized by combinations of curiosity, desire, repulsion and outright hostility. Dealing mainly with specific post-colonial settings of the twentieth century, including India, Quebec and Africa, scholars and theorists, such as Niranjana, Susan Basnett, Harish Trivedi and Sherry Simon, have articulated the political dimensions of translation and how ideas of translation are affected by – and affect – attitudes toward language and toward translation. Simon, for instance, comments on the imperialistic nature of colonialist approaches to translation: '"Translation" refers not only to the transfer of specific texts into European languages, but to all the practices whose aim was to compact and reduce an alien reality into the terms imposed by a triumphant Western culture.'[17] Translation of non-European (Indian, Asian or African) texts into European languages, in other words, provides the European readership with a model of the other – or Other – culture that confirms European cultural superiority. The translation of text becomes part of a larger process of translating cultures.

With the caveat that Anglo-Norman England was not a 'colony' in the strict sense of the term, the same sort of asymmetrical social relations that existed in the colonies, and still exist in the former colonies of Europe, existed then and affected translation as practised in twelfth-century England, especially regarding the status of the Anglo-Saxon vernacular. Although Holt may be correct in arguing that Anglo-Norman England functioned as a 'colony' of French-speaking Normandy, the Normans did not present themselves as 'colonists' of the territory, neither did William I annex it to his duchy of Normandy (had he done so he would have held it in the name of the French king rather than ruled it as a sovereign). Unlike the English colonists of the modern period, the Normans sought to represent themselves as English, redefining (translating) England on their terms, and at the same time translating themselves as the new English. In terms of language, the Normans instituted Latin as the only official language of court and church. Of course, the pre-Conquest English had a clerical class fluent in Latin, and Latin was an official medium of legal, ecclesiastical and intellectual exchange before the Conquest. However, it coexisted with English. What was lost with the Norman invasion was an extensive tradition of vernacular English secular and sacred works, epitomized by the writings of Ælfric, that made books of the Bible and hagiographic narratives accessible to English speakers. Although still used in daily communication by the English, this rich written tradition disappeared, and with it, the prestige of the language. Holt notes that 'the Norman Conquest murdered the written Anglo-Saxon language as surely as it demolished the Old Minster at Winchester'.[18] In the decades following the Conquest, Alfred's *translatio imperii* was reiterated by the Anglo-Normans in their adaptations of Anglo-Saxon history, as they elaborated notions of divine providence gleaned from Anglo-Saxon historical texts into a pattern of rises and falls that had culminated in the Conquest. As a consequence, the native English were effectively marginalized from their own history, no longer active participants but passive recipients, with the Normans enacting what Benjamin calls 'bad' translation by metaphorically denying life to the original.[19] By grafting English

historical texts – Bede and the *Anglo-Saxon Chronicle* in particular – on
to their own historiographic model, these historical translators made
the Anglo-Normans the legitimate inheritors of the English historical
tradition begun by Bede, theirs the fifth in a divinely ordained series of
insular conquests.

Colonial and post-colonial theories provide a context for discussing
the asymmetrical power relationship that existed between English and
Latin, and later between English and French and Latin. In particular,
the presence of a hegemony speaking a foreign language, a language
that would, within two generations of the Conquest, come to symbolize
power and prestige, so much so that many of the indigenous population
began to learn it.[20] This hegemony, further, took a conqueror's interest
in the written histories of the conquered and subsequently began to
translate them for their own use, again absorbing the other text into its
own vision of history. In this regard, the situation can be seen as analogous
to a colonial one, even though it lies outside the confines of nineteenth-
and twentieth-century European colonization of Asia and Africa, and even
though the linguistic situation is not a perfect parallel. However, many
of the complexities associated with colonialism, especially regarding
relationships with indigenous inhabitants, characterize the decades
following the Conquest. Like colonial translators, Anglo-Norman writers,
especially historians, engaged in the process of representing the indigenous
inhabitants as deserving their fate as conquered people, a phenomenon
documented as part of the drive by colonizers to represent the 'alien
reality' of the colonized.

Anglo-Normans worked for assimilation into England, but what they
desired was to be English on Norman terms. To this end, they reconstructed
the land itself according to European political and ecclesiastical models:
hence, the Norman cathedral with its Anglo-Saxon foundation; the motte-
and-bailey castles that dominated the English landscape; the systems
of vassalage and primogeniture; and the textualization of the land that
constituted the Domesday Book. Holt's comments on Domesday make
explicit the already implicit association of the Domesday Book with
changes in the English landscape: '*Domesday* was made like a pyramid
or like the mottes of the Normans' castles, in layers.'[21]

In this sense, England indeed became a 'copy' of Normandy, while
yet remaining a separate entity, with dramatic changes to the English
people, their land and their language. Regarding the land, Anglo-
Norman constructions that both marked the English landscape and
signified Norman authority reflect this process of assimilation and

translation, chief of which was the castle: in the first thirty-four years after the Conquest, there were ninety castles recorded in the English landscape, twenty-five of them royal constructions.[22] Each served as a concrete symbol of Anglo-Norman territorial dominance, just as the Anglo-Norman historical text became a symbol of Norman dominance over insular historiography. The edifice of the Anglo-Norman cathedral serves as perhaps an even more appropriate emblem for Anglo-Norman history, especially in its ambivalent relationship to its Anglo-Saxon precursor. With its Norman superstructure over an Anglo-Saxon foundation, it paralleled the Anglo-Norman historiographic palimpsest, written over English historical narrative.[23] At the same time, the structure celebrates the very institution it displaces, through the honourable translation of the bodies of Anglo-Saxon saints and – as in the case at Winchester – using the stones of the Anglo-Saxon edifices for the new cathedrals; similarly, historians celebrated the English historian Bede in the act of absorbing his work into theirs. As conquered territory, post-Conquest England can be seen as part of a colonial, and later post-colonial, system.[24] The Norman ascendancy restructured England itself, following to an extent the Continental model of culture, government, religious institutions and architecture.[25] The people were further assimilated into this new model of Englishness, including (though not limited to) the adoption of Norman names and manners. The situation paralleled ways in which modern colonies were constructed as translations. According to Bassnett and Trivedi, regarding the European colonization of both the West and the East, 'Europe was regarded as the great Original, the starting point, and the colonies were therefore copies, or "translations" of Europe, which they were supposed to duplicate'[26] This observation shows how the original European imperialists invert the translation paradigm, translating the colonized into their own unified vision. To some extent at least, Anglo-Norman England was constructed as a copy of the Norman 'original', continental France, in such institutions as the legal practices of serfdom and of holding all lands in lordship. Holt tellingly compares Norman architectural structures to the building projects of colonial India during the nineteenth century that replicated English structures; he cites the 'great railway terminals which the Victorians built in India' as symbols of territorial domination.[27] Like the railway terminal, the castle symbolizes the colonizer's power by transforming the landscape into a replica of the colonizers' homeland.

   Like the Domesday Book, William I wearing the crown at Winchester, or the frequent translation of English saints into Norman cathedrals, the Anglo-Norman historical text was both a continuation of Anglo-Saxon history and a commemoration of the defeat and suppression of the Anglo-Saxon people.[28] As such, the reaction of the Anglo-Saxon people might be expected to display both pride and dismay at the enshrinement of their saints, along with the perpetuation of their historical traditions. Anglo-Norman history (as chapter 1 illustrates) commemorates such Anglo-Saxon heroes as Hengest, Cerdic and Edward the Confessor, but in a broader historiographic rubric that stresses English culpability for their conquest and suppression. Whatever the varied reaction of the insular Saxons, the resulting effect is the layered appearance of Anglo-Norman historical texts, reflecting the palimpsest ethnographic composition of the island itself, evident in the descriptions of insular languages given by Henry of Huntingdon and William of Malmesbury. They identify the various languages of the island associated with the different invasions and settlements. Historical translation, in these instances, is thus overtly linked to conquest.

With the land itself as the object of the translation, the history of the conquerors becomes the natural sequel to the precursor culture's historical narrative, and the history of the precursor culture accordingly becomes a validating part of the history of the conqueror. The repeated conquest and reconquest of Britain led to a belief that continual conquest was endemic to the isle, and hence must be the result of divine judgement. This view was extrapolated to include the conquest of England (as the land came to be known under the Angles and Saxons) in Anglo-Norman histories. Thus, when Henry translated narratives of Bede's *Historia Ecclesiastica* and the *Anglo-Saxon Chronicle*, he reinterpreted conquests of the isle as part of a larger providential historiography of repeated sin and purgation that he termed the 'Five Plagues of Britain', according to which each subsequent invasion of the British isles – the Romans, the Scottish–Pictish alliance, the Anglo-Saxons, the Danes, and finally, the Normans – was a visitation of 'ultio divina' (divine vengeance).[29] In the process, these historians absorbed the precursor culture's historical narratives into their own versions of history. Thus, the jeremiadic and providentialist narratives of Gildas and Bede become forerunners to the latest Norman Conquest. Partner, in her extensive commentary on Henry of Huntingdon and his methods of amplification of earlier insular history, observes the importance of an interventionist God to Henry: 'The Divinity, as an actor in human history, is a distant architectural God in the early books, building the slow alternations of sin and retribution; in the contemporary books, He becomes nearer and irritable, inclined to be partisan, and quick to send portents and meaningful death, especially during the unstable hatreds of Stephen's reign.'[30] The discourse of apostasy and sinfulness applied to earlier inhabitants of the island served the ends of Anglo-Norman historians to justify the conquest and domination of England, without offering unqualified praise to the Normans. The Conquest may have been regrettable, but it was deserved; the Normans, for their part, are susceptible to the same pattern of sin and retribution characteristic of all rulers of the island. Immediate pre-Conquest English writers, such as Wulfstan the Elder, provided a ready-made master-narrative of providential purgation for historical translators, which reinforced the matrix. Wulfstan's warning of impending judgement against the English referred, of course, to renewed Danish invasion, but it would have been easy – even natural – to reinterpret the Norman occupation as fulfillment of his apocalyptic prediction. The historiographic portrait of the pre-Conquest English church as morally decadent, if not outright heretical, can be seen as part of a strategy for reconstructing the English as colonized subjects to justify and legitimate the Conquest. As an apostate or degenerate people, the native English were themselves reconstructed as colonial subjects, presented as what Naranjani calls 'pictures of the decadence or depravity of "us natives"'.[31]

The paradigm of historiography–translation–conquest characterizes the situation of historical writing in post-Conquest England, as the need of the Anglo-Norman ascendancy for a legitimate historical pedigree led to the extensive translation of Old English historical texts into Latin historical narrative – and in later generations, into French (the 'power' vernacular) – to anchor Anglo-Norman legitimacy in a revised version of insular history.[32] In effect, Latin (for the first generation of Anglo-Norman historians) and French (for the later Angevin writers) gave 'English' history a sense of dignity and prestige, putting them on a par with classical and continental historians. For these historians, historical composition served two purposes: it preserved the memory of the past in a rapidly shifting cultural landscape, and at the same time reworked the Anglo-Saxon past to provide legitimacy for the Anglo-Norman ascendancy. To this end, historians worked, not to suppress the past, the Anglo-Saxons and their contributions to insular history, but to rearrange the details of this history so that the Anglo-Norman ascendants became the logical – and legitimate – extension of it. For the largely non-Latinate Anglo-Saxons (whose pre-Conquest forebears may have depended upon English translation for religious and historical instruction), translation involved their exclusion from continued participation in insular history.

The proliferation of historical texts during the first decades of the twelfth century can therefore hardly be dismissed as innocent curiosity on the part of Anglo-Norman historical authors about their newly conquered and radically altered land. The result of this activity was an English history in Anglo-Norman terms that displaced the English from their own history. Anglo-Norman historians gave the English a past, but no present and no future. Perhaps even below their conscious register, Anglo-Norman historians legitimized the Conquest by grafting Anglo-Norman history onto Anglo-Saxon history, thus rendering the Normans as its flawed but rightful inheritors.

The relationship of Anglo-Norman historians to the English language of the conquered often shows a degree of respect, but a stronger sense of foreignness and otherness. English, in turn, came to be associated with membership in the subaltern or underclass. Orderic's Latinizing of his own name as *Ordericus Vitalis* provides an apropos example of the diminished state of the English language. Concerning the status of language in colonized societies, Naranjani further notes that among the colonial Indians, a desire for the 'English book' emerged; eight hundred years earlier, we find the English subjects begging for – and writing for themselves – the Norman *Latin* book. Language, in fact, can be seen as the marker in Anglo-Norman historiography of the difference separating 'us' and 'other'. Holt, for instance, documents local *miracula* stories in the twelfth century that featured cures for the dumb in which the victims – always English – recover their voices in French.[33] The ability to use Latin or French distinguished the English with whom the Normans and their followers could identify from the Anglo-Saxon monolingual 'barbarians' from whom they sought to distance themselves, and who deserved the yoke of imperialism.

The English language thus became, for Anglo-Norman historian-translators, a symbol of the 'barbaric', even of the 'strange' or 'other'. As further evidence of the way English was received in post-Conquest England, one of the major Anglo-Norman historians of the twelfth century, William of Malmesbury, outlined his process of translating vernacular materials through a decidedly gastronomic metaphor; he pledges to 'exarata barbarica Romano sale condire' (season the crude [English] materials – literally scratches or scrawlings – with the salt of Rome).[34] Embodying the ambivalent motives of aggression and desire characteristic of colonial translators, William's culinary model of historical translation serves as a model for the linguistic substitution that occurred in the twelfth century, as in Henry's translation of the *Brunanburh* poem of the *Anglo-Saxon Chronicle*. Henry approaches the *Bruananburh* as a foreign-language text, in spite of his own English heritage: 'De cuius prelii magnitudine Anglici scriptores quasi carminis modo proloquentes, et *extraneis tam uerbis quam figures* usi translatione fida donandi sunt' (The English writers describe the magnitude of these deeds in a sort of song, using *foreign words and figures of speech*, which must be translated faithfully).[35] The 'foreignness' of the language marks the isolation of the English from their own history within their own realm. Henry nonetheless makes a good-faith effort to translate the text faithfully, promising to capture the dignity of the original: 'ex grauitate uerborum grauitatem actuum et animorum gentis illius' (from the gravity of the words the gravity of the acts and thoughts of this people).[36] Henry's translation of the Anglo-Saxon poem concludes with a recapitulation of the initial conquest of Britain; the Anglo-Saxon original leaves the relationship of Anglo-Saxon success and resettlement implicit:

> Brytene sohtan,
> wlance wigsmiþas   Wealas ofercoman,
> eorlas arhwate, earde begeatan.

[The famous war-smiths sought Britain, overcame the Welsh, noble earls, seized land.]

Henry translates this passage as 'postquam huc venerunt, trans mare latum, Saxones et Anglo, Brittones pulsi: clari Martis fabri, Walenses vicerunt, reges fugaverunt, regna susceperunt' (this had not happened since there came over the sea, Saxons and English, to strive with the Britons; having crossed the sea, the famous craftsmen of Mars vanquished the Welsh, drove away their kings and seized the kingdom). The kennings are replaced by matter-of-fact terms for the rulers. More importantly, the paratactic Anglo-Saxon phrases, with single-verb phrases serving multiple subjects and with grammatical relations left to the reader's surmise, are replaced by Latin hypotactic phrases that establish the implied causality of the Anglo-Saxon original. Henry's grammatical relations reflect his broader picture of his historiographic structure of the event, which depicts the Anglo-Saxon conquest of Britain as an antetype for the Norman Conquest, a single culture-shaping battle which displaced the (sinful) indigenous inhabitants to make way for new occupiers. Henry's treatment discloses a desire both to represent the Anglo-Saxons as dramatically Other – and hence part of an unrecoverable past – in terms of language, and to depict them in terms understandable to the Anglo-Norman dynasty.

Anglo-Norman historians can thus be seen to enact a form of historical colonization when they translate English historical texts, engaging in a textual conquest parallel to William I's territorial conquests. In both the textual and political situations, the conquerors seek to establish themselves as legitimate heirs to the land and to its historiographic traditions, concealing in the process the ruptures and suppressions that have given them this status. These historians thus become translators, carrying out the agon of translation and concealment identified by Willis Barnstone:

> The source should be buried. If the burial is complete, with nothing showing, then the shadow of translation is forgotten. Bloom's central thesis of anxiety of influence and his maps of misreading apply to every aspect of the translation syndrome of denial.[37]

By concealment of precursor texts, I do not mean that historians denied their indebtedness to their source texts, which they clearly did not. They freely acknowledged and admired Bede and their other English sources, as the previously cited examples illustrate. Rather, I maintain that by grafting these earlier texts onto their own fluid historical narratives, Anglo-Norman historian-translators gave insular history the appearance of a seamless whole. In so doing, they translated Anglo-Saxon history along the lines of a preconceived historiographic master-narrative that re-presented the Norman dynasty as both a continuation of and an improvement upon the previous Anglo-Saxon dynasty. This 'conquest' of Anglo-Saxon history provided the new dominant class with its own historical pedigree.

By adding new material to the translated fragments and applying an architectonic narrative pattern based on elaborate notions of divine providence, Anglo-Norman historical writers created the appearance of a unified and original work. They effected this reshaping of English history through a fusion of classical rhetoric and Christian providentialism. They used the translation of English historical texts to prove that the Anglo-Saxons had deserved their fate as conquered people, but also to preserve the cultural memory of the English people, and to do so in a way that would be acceptable and palatable to the Norman ascendancy. In this way, English history was fused with the history of the Anglo-Normans, as twelfth-century historical translators grafted accounts of post-Conquest events onto the accounts of Bede and the *Anglo-Saxon Chronicle* according to a mode of emplotment based on divine providence. Thus, when Henry translated Bede and sections of the *Chronicle*, he re-interpreted conquests of Britain as part of a larger matrix of the providential 'Five Plagues'. In the process, these historical translators subordinated the precursor culture's historical narratives to their own versions of history.

The complex relationship between colonizer and colonized thus offers insight into Anglo-Norman historiographic translation practices. The main difference between their practices and those of 'colonialist' trans-lators, in the strict sense of the term, is that in colonial translation discourse there is a concerted effort to maintain a distinction between dominant culture and the dominated, who become reinscribed as Other. In contrast, the Normans appropriated English identity and apparently identified themselves as 'English' as early as the twelfth century.[38] The overarching consequence of such activities was the reconstruction of an English identity in Norman terms, wherein the epitome of the English ecclesiastic or nobleman was a Latinate French-speaking man of at least partial French descent. This reconstruction of English identity paradoxic-ally excluded most of the ethnic English. In a strict colonizer–colonized situation, translation of indigenous text into the language of the colonized serves as a way of imposing dominant culture on a subordinate (or sub-altern) group. In Anglo-Norman England, translation of English history into Latin historical narrative became a strategy for recovering English history and enlisting it in the service of Anglo-Norman historiography. This paradoxical promotion of English history and exclusion of the English people is starkly evident in historical texts such as Henry's, which speaks of the extinction of the English while offering an ongoing history of England. It is worth noting, further, that examination of English texts from the perspective of colonial and post-colonial translation theory calls into question the totalizing and monadic notion of 'Western' culture often used by practitioners of this theory; such examination reminds us that, among other things, English – the quintessentially hegemonic language of the twentieth century – was once the language of the colonized and occupied.

However, the translation of history is not a one-sided affair; it is hardly possible to absorb the history of a culture or group of people without oneself being subtly altered in the process, as 'foreign' history becomes indigenized. For example, in the process of transforming himself from the Duke of Normandy (a vassal of the King of France) into the (legitimate) King of England, William and his followers were subtly altered by the English history they inherited; they were Norman, but by virtue of the new historical tradition, also English – hence the desire to preserve continuity and to smooth over ruptures between their dominion and the previous Anglo-Saxon kingdom. As such, translation also enacts a double movement, as the source text may transform the translator and readers of the new text. As Warren observes: 'Translation [. . .] can enact or resist colonialist success, or both.'[39]

In the chapters that follow, I outline how this double movement takes the form of changes to the conqueror-translator and challenges to his authority, originating from the source text, from the conquered land and from the defeated people. The two-sided dynamics of translation, in which the translator is both conqueror and servant of the source text, is similarly articulated in Steiner's dialectical depiction of the translator's relationship with the translated text. For Steiner, assimilation of the source text and of the culture it encodes carries with it an explicit threat to the translator: 'But we may be mastered and made lame by what we have imported [. . .] Societies with ancient but eroded epistemologies of ritual and symbol can be knocked off balance and made to lose belief in their own identity under the voracious impact of premature or indigestible assimilation.'[40] In other words, through exposure to other languages and the differing cultural signs that each encodes, translation may change the translators, and, therefore, must be approached cautiously. Steiner's consumptive–digestive model of translation seems aptly to explain the process in Anglo-Norman translation techniques. Implicit in William of Malmesbury's metaphor for historical translation is a similar gastronomic analogue for the threat posed by the translated text. William may find the English text 'indigestible' in its native form and may accordingly seek to appropriate it, using an overtly aggressive translation process. In other words, the 'barbaric' Anglo-Saxon texts threaten to make him a bit more 'Saxon', or they may challenge his perceived cultural or moral superiority over the former inhabitants of the isle. This process also suggests the 'cannibalistic' paradigm proposed by Else Ribeiro Pires Veira 'as a complex metaphor undergoing metamorphoses in different contexts and critical perspectives'.[41] That is, the 'consumption' of Anglo-Saxon material alters both the texts and their translators. This model suggests a complex mixture of aggression and desire; the resulting process of translation fundamentally reshaped the English land, language and people.

I do not suggest by these readings that all Anglo-Norman writers had the same ideology and purpose; in fact, some of the writers I discuss were of mixed English and Norman parentage. Their aims often differ.

Some, such as William of Jumièges and Guy of Amiens – writing in the generation after the Conquest – clearly intend to denigrate the Anglo-Saxons and celebrate the Norman conquerors. Others, such as 'Florence' or John of Worcester and the anonymous translator (or author) of the *Vita Haroldi*, work overtly to rehabilitate the reputation of the Anglo-Saxons by questioning claims of Anglo-Norman legitimacy and by promoting the prestige of Anglo-Saxon religious and secular leaders.[42] Still others, such as Gaimar, William of Malmesbury, Orderic, Henry of Huntingdon, Wace and, of course, Geoffrey of Monmouth, have more complex and ambivalent attitudes about English and Anglo-Norman relations and ways of representing the respective peoples. 'Formed by Colonial experience, Geoffrey's *HRB*,' as Warren observes, 'equivocates between admiration and condemnation of the history of conquest.'[43] In his complex reading of conquest, Geoffrey, like his peers William, Orderic and Henry, wrote under the pressures of Norman colonialism and saw both gain and loss in the changes he witnessed and recorded. In one way or another, however, each of these writers contributed to the rise of a Norman-inspired prose Latin historiography, which lowered the prestige of the English language and alienated the non-Latinate English laity from its own history. The phenomenon is indicative of the rise in prestige of the outside languages and the desire of some indigenous writers to identify themselves and their writing with the conquering and colonizing cultures.

It might be argued that such a loss was of little consequence, because most of the population were illiterate. However, the importance of language to the English sense of themselves as a people is illustrated in post-Conquest English writings that bemoan their subjection and the displacement of their language. Although no systematic attempt to institute a 'national' language occurred in the multilingual society of twelfth-century England, the English language suffered neglect as a literary and ecclesiastical language because of the prevalence of non-English clergymen, introduced by William. Evidence for the consequences of this loss in England can be found in the anonymously written *Worcester Fragment*; contemporary in place and time to the *Brut* and using similar alliterative metre, this short alliterative verse expresses the corrosive effects of a loss of language:

> [Nu is] þeo leore forgoten, and þet folc is forloren.
> Nu beoþ oþre leoden þeo læ[reþ] ure folc,
> And feole of þen lor þeines losiæþ and þæt folc forþ mid.

[Now is the knowledge forgotten, and the people are forlorn. Now other people [or other languages] teach our people, and much of the lore is lost and the people with it.][44]

Admittedly, the ambivalence over the semantics of *leod* – a term La3amon uses frequently in its threefold meaning of people, land and language, and which forms a major premise of my own study – clouds the issue of language somewhat: is the anonymous poet complaining that the English people receive instruction in a language they cannot understand, or that non-English people, unfamiliar with their customs and learning, are mismanaging their spiritual affairs? In either case, given the emphasis on verbal teaching in this passage, it is difficult not to believe that *leod* involves at least an element of language. These lines make evident, then, that the loss of English as the dominant language of court and church was recognized by at least some of the English as having serious and deleterious effects on the people. In his discussion of the *Fragment* – the only major study of the text – Steven Karl Brehe recognizes the relationship between the loss of language, culture, and religion: 'the English viewed the cultural rupture they suffered after the conquest as a spiritual loss'.[45] In other words, language was recognized as a key component to the religious well-being of the community. Beyond the spiritual aspect of the lament, the fragment shows a strong sense of ethnic identity – *ure folc* and *opre leoden* – and an equally strong sense of how language and shared knowledge contribute to this identity. The poem further suggests, contrary to the claims of some historians, that language and ethnic barriers perpetuated the ethnic distinction between 'Norman' and 'English'. The wounds from 1066 were not completely healed by the end of the twelfth century. (It is also worth noting that the *Fragment* belies conventional views of Norman-appointed clerics as being more devout or erudite than their Anglo-Saxon counterparts.) The *Worcester Fragment* further marks the protests of a colonized population of alienation from its own religious traditions. Monika Otter, in her discussion of the textuality and fictionality of twelfth-century histories, argues that in spite of evidence of cooperation between Normans and English in the twelfth century, there are enough instances of conflict to create at least a perception of Norman hostility.[46] One hundred years (perhaps) after the late twelfth-century *Worcester Fragment* and the probable composition date of the *Brut*, Robert of Gloucester would still identify the land as under the rule of the 'Normans', a people distinct from the Saxons:

& þus was in normannes ond. þat lond ibroðt iwis.
ðat anaunter ðif euermo. keuering þer of is.
Of þe Normans beþ heyemen. þat beþ of englelonde.
& þe lowemen of Saxons. as ich vndersonde.

[And thus was the land indeed brought into the hands of the Normans, so
that one wonders if there is any recovering from it. The Normans are the
high men of England, the low men, the Saxons, as I understand it.]

Although Warren regards Robert's reference to 'Normans' at such a late
date as 'tendentious', it reveals that ethnic tensions persisted long past
King John's loss of Normandy.[47] English writers and speakers, apparently,
were not universally willing to accept an 'English' identity established
on Anglo-Norman terms.

How does such textual evidence square with the near-consensus
among scholars that distinctions between Norman and English became
largely irrelevant sometime during the twelfth or thirteenth centuries?[48]
The problem with assessing questions of ethnic or cultural identity from
the perspective of the conquerors alone – and in many instances
historians and literary historians have few alternatives – is that it fails to
take into account how such a change to the concept of the 'English' was
received by the insular Anglo-Saxons. Here, post-colonial translation
theory offers some perspective into the complexities of the linguistic
situation in the two centuries following the Conquest. Specifically, it
asks, even if members of the Anglo-Norman ascendancy began to regard
themselves as 'English' as early as the late twelfth and early thirteenth
centuries, does it follow that the English were ready to accept them as
such, or that such realignment necessarily solved all political, cultural,
and linguistic tensions regarding English and Norman, as well as those
involving other insular ethnic groups? Such theories also provide a
vocabulary for discussing the writings of suppressed peoples in the
language of the subaltern. It is in this complex cultural and linguistic
context that I propose to examine the work of the historian-translator
Laȝamon, who works from Latin and French into English and reverses
the predominant pattern of translation associated with the Anglo-
Norman *translatio studii*. In the process, I argue, Laȝamon exposes
the ruptures that have occurred in the transfer of power from British
to English to Anglo-Norman culture and narrates the development of
history as a translation of text, land and people; he ultimately asserts
the English language as an apt vehicle for history and for 'serious'

discourse. From this perspective, the linkage between the historical text as temporal conquest and military conquest as territorial translation can be seen from the perspective of the English post-colonial experience, in its translation of Normans into Anglo-Normans and in its translation of the English from active producers of history to passive recipients of another culture's history.[49] This late twelfth-century (or early thirteenth-century) historical poem calls attention to a linguistic conception of history based on translation, and links territorial conquest to the trans-linguistic writing of history.

In the context of twelfth-century historical translation, the *Brut* sheds considerable light on the linguistic and ideological assumptions that inform conceptions of history. As a loose translation of Wace's French historical poem the *Roman de Brut* (1155), it provides a fitting example of the complexities of medieval historical translation. As the first English historical text of the Angevin period (1154–1215) and one of the rare translations into English of the first and second centuries after the Norman Conquest, it reasserts the dignity of the English language and, perhaps more significantly, documents the role of language and trans-lation in shaping insular history. La3amon's choice of the alliterative long line preserves a recognizably English poetic form; its rather solemn alliterative beat helps shape what Martin Shichtman refers to as the poet's 'tragic' or 'elegiac' vision of history.[50] On the level of translation, through a complex association between translators of text and con-querors of territory, La3amon establishes an implicit link between the territorial advances of the Norman conquerors and the efforts of Anglo-Norman historical authors to translate English historical texts and traditions as part of a new historiographic matrix. Ultimately, the *Brut* exposes the writing of history as a linguistic process, an act of *translatio* that establishes its own legitimacy by appropriating the historical texts of others.

From the perspective of Anglo-Norman historiographic translation, La3amon's translation of a text in the language of the conquerors into that of the conquered, and his reversal of the dominant path of trans-lation, can hardly be dismissed as an 'innocent' translation, especially in the linguistically charged milieu of post-Conquest England. Critics, however, have been slow to assess the historiographic implications of La3amon's role as historian and translator. Only recently have they begun to take a serious look at the implications of La3amon as translator of Wace's *Roman de Brut* (1154). Françoise Le Saux, for example, offers a systematic analysis of La3amon's pattern of omissions, expansions and additions to Wace, citing Laȝamon's 'upgrading' of the character of the Britons.[51] Daniel P. Donoghue notes the cultural ramifications of Laȝamon as a translator, observing that, to give the text an 'English' quality, Laȝamon goes beyond

> the linguistic exercise of translating from Norman French to an archaistic English. He consistently changes Wace's modern Norman arms and fighting style to something more reminiscent of pre-conquest Anglo-Saxons, even to the extent of transforming chivalric knights into Germanic foot soldiers.[52]

Donoghue here recognizes the cultural significance of Laȝamon's translation methods. What criticism of the *Brut* has yet to account for, however, is Laȝamon's self-conscious presentation of this text as a translation, and the overtly political ramifications of this translation process. As a result, Laȝamon's role in promoting a cultural response to Anglo-Norman historiography and to the exclusion of the English language as a vehicle for history and poetry has gone unexamined. Nonetheless, the complexity of Laȝamon's *Brut* as an English reworking of the French *Roman de Brut* and Laȝamon's own role as a historical translator in dialogue with his historical precursor-texts articulate a poetics of history for the post-Conquest Anglo-Saxons. In so doing, Laȝamon's textual performance reveals the translation process as an inherently political act, an activity that transforms its English target audience into history-producing subjects, even as it transfers its source text from Anglo-Norman French into early Middle English. The *Brut* thus becomes as much a history of translation as a translation of history, a continual power-struggle between translator and translatable text.

Compared to other historical texts of his period, Laȝamon's *Brut* places observably greater emphasis on the transference of information across linguistic and cultural boundaries. In the *Brut*, the power dynamics inherent in historical translation – the power of the translator and of the translated text itself – are brought to the surface as Laȝamon's brief autobiographical introduction expresses his engagement with language and history. From the very beginning, Laȝamon identifies himself as a literate priest – 'þer he boc radde' (l. 5) – whose vision of history is to be dependent foremost upon the written word. Further, he highlights his trilingual literacy; each of his source texts must be translated. One (at least) is in Latin; one is in French; and if the third is in English, it is an earlier dialect that would require translation into the English of twelfth- or thirteenth-century Worcestershire.[53] With the knowledge of the linguistic situation in England in mind, the language Laȝamon employs in dealing with his sources merits reconsideration, for it reveals a conception of historical translation based on domination and resistance, and scepticism about the prospects of any 'true' history. History, it turns out, may be a matter of language, an ingenious translation of one historical tradition into another.

Critical issues in Laȝamon studies

The text of the *Brut* survives in two manuscript versions, MS Cotton Caligula A.i.ix and MS Cotton Otho C.xiii, both dating from around 1250–60. From its thirty-five-line prologue (twenty-five lines in Otho), we learn that its author Laȝamon was a priest, that his residence was at Areley Kings – about ten miles north of Worcester – at the parish church (Caligula), or with an unnamed 'good knight' (Otho), and that he read books. He further tells us that, at some point in his life, he decided to write a history of the earliest inhabitants of Britain, using three separate sources: Bede's *Historia Ecclesiastica* – presumably the English translation though scholarship is somewhat divided here – an unidentified Latin text by 'Seinte Albin and ðe feire Austin' (MS Caligula, ll. 17–18) and a French text, recognizable as Wace's *Roman de Brut*.[54] The date at which this writing took place remains uncertain, which makes reconstructing the poem's context difficult. Scholars usually assign a date of composition somewhere between 1189 and 1216, based on Laȝamon's use of the preterite *wes* in reference to King Henry and Queen Eleanor; Henry II died in 1189, and by 1216 England had a new King Henry and Queen Eleanor. However, E. G. Stanley has made a compelling case for a much later *terminus ad quem*.[55] On the other hand, Laȝamon's use of the preterite in reference to himself in lines 1 and 2 – 'an preost *wes* on leoden Laȝamon *wes* ihoten' / He *wes* Leounaðes sone' – discounts, in my opinion, the generally accepted 1189 *terminus a quo*. Either the living Laȝamon chose to refer to himself in the preterite, perhaps as an envoy to a later reader, or the prologue was changed after his death; in neither case does the verb tense tell us anything about Henry's or Eleanor's status during the prologue's composition.[56] Although Laȝamon does switch to the present tense a few lines later – '*nu biddeð* Layamon' – this change is more likely to be a stylistic shift from the autobiographical prologue to the history or poem proper, rather than an attempt to draw a distinction between a still living poet and a dead king.[57] Further, I believe that critics have been too dismissive of the philological objections raised by H. B. Hinckley regarding Laȝamon's use of the preterite that further call into question the accepted basis for the 1189 *terminus a quo*.[58] Laȝamon would have needed time to acquire, digest and translate the *Roman de Brut* – a minimum of perhaps ten years, but probably longer. What we are left with, then, is a period of around eighty years – from around 1170 to 1250 – when the *Brut* could have been composed, a vast swath of time, and very problematic, given the transitional nature of English social and political life during this period. External clues provide some insight into the date of the text: Le Saux notes Laȝamon's reference to the relics of Saints Columkille, Brendan and Bride (Bridget), 'discovered' in 1185. Of course, it is possible that Laȝamon is referring to an already extant tradition of the Irish relics, and even if it is a direct reference to the discovery, it proves only that this particular portion of the *Brut* was composed after 1185. More convincing is Le Saux's assertion that the prologue's reference to the 'high king' Henry indicates composition prior to 1216; had it been written later, there would have been some attempt to differentiate the two 'Henries'.[59] Concerning Laȝamon's use of language as a clue to dating the text, moving the *terminus ad quem* very far into the thirteenth century means that, at some point, Laȝamon's 'archaic' lexicon starts to become a problem. For example, his fairly consistent use of the Old English dual pronoun case seems difficult to explain in a thirteenth-century text, even if we allow for a measure of deliberate archaizing; it is less of a problem if we envision a twelfth-century *Brut*. Furthermore, a cursory examination of the *Brut* shows that its vocabulary and syntax bear more resemblance to more reliably dated twelfth-century texts, such as the later *Laud* chronicle entries, the *Poema Morale*, *The Owl and the Nightingale* and, of course, the *Worcester Fragment*, than to works of the mid to late thirteenth century, such as *Havelok*. Splitting the difference between 1185 and 1216, therefore, I propose the traditional composition date of *c*.1200, with the understanding that the date could vary by at least fifteen years either way. This date, as chapter 2 illustrates, places Laȝamon within a context of historiographers who were beginning to question previously accepted assumptions about the nature of providence and history, and English writers acutely aware of the cultural significance of language.[60]

Although reconstructing a specific historical context for the *Brut* is difficult, not only because of uncertainty over the date of the text, but also because of our lack of knowledge of the author and his immediate circumstances (other than what the prologue tells us), it is possible to situate the text in a historiographic milieu of increasing scepticism regarding Anglo-Norman providential models. Given the paucity of texts in English during La3amon's period, another difficulty in examining La3amon's translation methods is the lack of a model for critics of the *Brut*, as well as for La3amon himself. The few translations from French into English were mainly poems (such as *The Owl and the Nightingale*) or homiletic tracts, and in the twelfth century there were few of these. In historiographic matters, English was left out of the paradigm of vernacular-and-Latin altogether; this exclusion characterizes current scholarly discussions. La3amon cannot be said to *mise en roman* the materials of his source texts, as could French historians such as Gaimar, Wace and the vernacular prose historians of France and Flanders.[61] What the *Brut* accomplishes is, in fact, a disruption of the accepted dichotomy between 'Latinate' and 'vernacular' by asserting the value, through example, of the third, marginalized vernacular of the conquered. It is, however, a legitimate question whether or not La3amon consciously wished to express that the language he used was, in fact, Anglo-Saxon. After all, he fails to identify it as such in the prologue, mentioning the *English* book of Bede as if it were written in another foreign language, on a par with French and Latin. Neither does he overtly identify his task as the translation of text into English or *Sæxisc*. Nonetheless, La3amon does refer to the English (or Saxon) language as 'ure tonge' in the *Brut*. Elsewhere, he translates the few English words and phrases found in Wace – *wesseil*, *drinceheil*, and *Nim eure sexes* – into his own West Midlands dialect, indicating awareness that the Saxon of Wace's Hengest was the English of his own ancestors. I accept the methodological difficulties presented by the *Brut*. Nevertheless, there are some important conclusions we can draw: La3amon's society was hierarchical and class conscious, and language use still marked one as a member of an upper or lower class. Although many of the Anglo-Norman ascendants had learned English and could use it, they still saw themselves as different from the 'English' underclass and, more importantly, many of the English were apparently unwilling to accept an England drawn on Anglo-Norman lines. I believe that the context of the late twelfth-century hierarchical and linguistically complex society of Worcester (the West Midlands) offers a fruitful site for examining this text, the developing conceptions of history, and the ways in which language and translation contribute to the complex reconstructions of the British past.

   In highlighting the linguistic circumstances of twelfth-century England, La3amon ironically calls attention to a fourth vernacular that he silences and excludes himself, namely Welsh, a language spoken in Laȝamon's neighbourhood and one that provides the basis for the history he composes. Indeed, such critics as Le Saux have argued persuasively that Welsh stories and traditions influenced Laȝamon. This exclusion from his tripartite paradigm is troubling and may perhaps be related to the English status as a conquered people that had, in their own time, been conquerors and colonizers. Their earlier marginalization and exclusion of the Britons, along with appropriation of their narratives and traditions, would appear to have been repeated in the Norman Conquest. Laȝamon's response, I argue, is complex and – to borrow Daniel Donoghue's term – ambivalent. He embraces the British legends and traditions, and seems at times sensitive to the resemblance between Britain under the English and England under the Normans. On the other hand, he subjects the Britons to the same sort of linguistic erasure that the English literary tradition had suffered two generations before his time. The ways in which Laȝamon works through these dilemmas to a great extent forms his historiographic understanding and further situates him in the context of post-colonial England.

Laȝamon's prologue further indicates that he was writing what he considered a history, claiming to glean the 'soðere word' (l. 27) (truer word or words) from his source material. The text was received as a work of history: the heading attached to it by the Caligula compiler reads 'Incipit hystoria Brutonum' (the Otho features the non-committal heading 'Incipit prologus libri Brutonum'); the text is followed in the manuscript codex by a chronicle tracing English history from the Norman Conquest to the thirteenth century. This reception appears to have carried through the Renaissance. The first written mention of Laȝamon outside the *Brut* manuscripts was made in 1639 by James Ussher, Archbishop of Armagh, who used it to trace the orthography of the names of the archbishops sent from Rome to King Lucius.[62] Elizabeth Bryan notes that the Elizabethan Society of Antiquaries used the text 'again and again for evidence about the history of English national institutions'.[63] In spite of its early reception, critics and scholars of this century have been reluctant to take Laȝamon's claim to historiographic legitimacy seriously. Antonia Gransden omits Laȝamon from her magisterial survey of insular historians, whereas R. William Leckie mentions Laȝamon toward the conclusion of his work, only to belittle his historical knowledge.[64] Criticism has tended to focus on philology, on the influence of Old English poetry on the *Brut*, or on Laȝamon's individual style. The consequences of this oversight have been neglect of Laȝamon's engagement with the historiographic and cultural contexts

in which he worked. Francis Lytle Gillespie (1916), for example, observes
Laȝamon's historical conception of his text – 'Layamon did not conceive
of his *Brut* as a "mere story".[65] His purpose was to write history'
(p. 374) – but privileges a strictly 'literary' reading of the *Brut*:
'[A]lthough he [Laȝamon] thought of himself as a historian, his is a poetic
rather than a critical nature, and his allegiance to imaginative veri-
similitude is certainly equal to his desire for historical truth' (p. 375).
Although G. J. Visser (1935) identifies Laȝamon as 'one of the first
writers in English to give us the early history of the Britons and their
great leader, King Arthur', he never considers the implications of the
term 'history'.[66] Similarly, Henry Cecil Wyld limits his discussion to
Laȝamon's 'intensity of feeling, the wealth of imagery, the tender
humanity, the love of nature, the chivalrous and romantic spirit'.[67] Håkan
Ringbom, who does not distinguish between 'chronicle' and 'history',
addresses the generic question of history and poetry as a way of
excluding the *Brut* from any version of historical scope: 'Lawman's
poem purports to be history, and by the nature of its material it might
be classified as a chronicle. However, even the style of its immediate
source, the *Roman de Brut*, contains many elements not typical of a
chronicle, and Lawman's treatment of the material is even further
removed from the chronicle style.'[68] Without explaining what is meant
by 'chronicle style', it is difficult to see where or how Laȝamon departs
from it. Like most of his predecessors, Ringbom adopts a limited
modern understanding of 'history', and so fails to see the importance of
Laȝamon's engagement with this mode of discourse. Even more recent
criticism of the *Brut* is still limited by a rigid distinction between 'poetry'
and 'history', characteristic of earlier scholarship. Carolynn Vandyke
Friedlander (1979) observes that the *Brut*'s narrative patterns 'strengthen
the impression that history is cyclic', but does not situate the *Brut* in any
specific historiographic context.[69] Like Friedlander, most other critics
have taken rather lightly Laȝamon's presentation of his text as history.
The consequences of this oversight have been not only a mis-
understanding of Laȝamon's *Brut* in its appropriate context, but also an
incomplete picture of insular historiography during the Anglo-Norman
and Angevin periods. As Lee Patterson has observed, concerning
Chaucer, overemphasis on the individual or idiosyncratic practices of a
writer, at the expense of the public or social aspects, blinds readers to
the interconnectedness of the writer's interior 'self' and the exterior
world:

Since the nineteenth century Chaucer criticism has focused almost exclusively on the question of character; just as the dominant liberal ideology has privileged the individual, so has the largely liberal tradition of academic criticism valued Chaucer for his depiction of a selfhood that is understood as at once historically particular and transhistorically recognizable [. . .] But what is not considered is the possibility that it is in fact always in the process of being constructed, that it is an open site for negotiating the problematic relationship between outer and inner, historical particularity and transhistorical generality.[70]

The tendency of early critics to generalize about Laȝamon may also have led to conventional views of Laȝamon as a 'barbarian' (Loomis), a naive country priest (Tatlock), or the forgotten 'last poet' of the Anglo-Saxons (Borges).[71]

However, under the influence of modern and postmodern historiography, critics have recently re-examined the implications of Laȝamon's historiography. Le Saux argues for a serious claim to historical authority in the *Brut*: 'These lines [the first five lines] state that the poet had three written sources, which he found after extensive travel; three books in three different languages – English, French, Latin – which provided the basis for a work of "soðere word", that is, a work of some scientific pretensions. In this instance, history' (l. 15). One of the first critics to apply recent historiographic theory to the *Brut*, Martin Shichtman, uses Hayden White's concept of metahistorical emplotment to examine Laȝamon and Wace in an intriguing and thorough, if occasionally over-determined, reading of the character of Gawain in the texts. In writing a tragic history for a defeated people, Shichtman argues, Laȝamon 'produces a tragic history, cognizant of the smallness of all men, even the greatest, in a world that is fallen, transitory, meaningless'.[72] Jeff Rider similarly notes Laȝamon's deliberate questioning of the boundaries between 'fiction' and 'history'. He reads the character of Merlin as evidencing the power of fictional language to order the progression of history: 'Merlin exemplifies human greatness creating history and its own destiny [. . .] Merlin is the linchpin of history. He reveals history, he shapes it, and yet he is its creature.'[73] By highlighting Merlin's role in the shaping of history – and hence of fiction – Rider's Laȝamon can be seen to subvert the dominant Anglo-Norman version of history. Both Shichtman and Rider contribute a great deal to our understanding of Laȝamon as historiographer – and much to reverse his dismissal by readers such as Leckie; yet, neither addresses the fundamental issue of language and how La3amon dramatizes the methods of translation that form conceptions of history. Daniel Donoghue, in what is arguably one of the most important pieces of La3amon criticism of the 1990s, systematically examines the *Brut* in the context of the dominant historiographic patterns of twelfth- and thirteenth-century England.[74] Tackling the difficult question of La3amon's status as an ethnically English poet writing the history of his ancestral enemies, Donoghue sees ambivalence on La3amon's part as inevitable, but finds partial resolution in the historiographic pattern of divine providence: 'The players in his [La3amon's] history (primarily the Angeln and the Brutten) are defined not by nation but by race, and the unifying principle of his history is not nationhood but divine providence, as interpreted by historiographic typology begun by Gildas and continued through Bede and Geoffrey of Monmouth.'[75] His study is thus of immense value in placing La3amon in a historiographic context and in noting the importance of his role as a translator. However, he takes a rather monadic view of 'the historiographic typology of divine providence', a construct that – as the ensuing chapters will demonstrate – has vastly different meanings for different cultural and historical situations, as well as for different people. Furthermore, the view that the *Brut* expounds providential history at all has been challenged.[76]

Kelley Wickham-Crowley, for instance, concludes that prophecy and oral and written modes of discourse construct an open-ended view of history, in which an individual's choice counters the demands of providential judgement. Wickham-Crowley's study succeeds in setting La3amon in a specific context, as a priest near the Marches of Wales, and identifies the important connection between land and people. She thus lays the groundwork for an examination of the *Brut*'s dialogic relationship with other historical texts, even though her assertion that 'Christianity and a man's individual responsibility'[77] resolve the political ambivalence does not tie up all of the loose ends in the *Brut*, such as the Christian-versus-Christian violence of the latter portions of the narrative. Otter likewise sees human action – in the case of the *Brut*, the actions of the poet-historian – as central to La3amon's representation of the historian and of history:

> [La3amon's] self-presentation as priest and poet, as well as the affective coloring of that presentation, is crucial. In the prologue, the priest-turned-historian is surveying his 'territory', with an unmistakable, almost sensuous affectus. Like Geoffrey's Brutus, Denis's Edmund, or William the Conqueror

in Fouke, he immediately proceeds to make this land his own by leaving his mark on it – in this case, with a quill. Through this image, La3amon casts himself as a clerkly narrator, as a facilitator or mediator who researches the sources and makes learned materials available to a less literate, even illiterate audience.[78]

Warren, one of the first to read the *Brut* in post-colonial terms, sees in the text a 'pedagogy of history' for La3amon's readers: 'readers perpetuate a refrain that marks out the territory of English culture'.[79]

As useful as these recent studies have been, I believe, it is also imperative to examine the process of linguistic substitution that makes up La3amon's interpretation of history. La3amon not only translates insular history, he dramatizes history *as* a translation. In engaging vernacular readers in the process of perpetuating English history – learning and reciting 'runes' – he invites them to scrutinize the claims of all histories, oral and written, to 'truth'. The *Brut* thus works, at least on one level, to expose the power-plays that historiographic models mask and to depict the consequences of these models on dominated people. Focusing on instances of translation – be it of text, land, or people – within the *Brut* and on internal evidence of La3amon's views of translation, I argue that La3amon exposes the writing of history as the displacement of cultures and of their historical traditions. My approach is necessarily somewhat synchronic, as I examine the *Brut* in the context of a specific body of Anglo-Norman historical texts that sought to create a unified version of insular history in order to legitimize the claims of the new Norman rulers of England. Drawing upon the established link between medieval translation theory and rhetoric and hermeneutics – identified by Copeland and others – I propose that the *Brut* presents a poetics of history as the translation of language, land and people; significantly, each of these three factors is signified by the Anglo-Saxon term *leod*. By shifting the orientation of history from divine providence to language, La3amon engages the historical master-narratives of his day, exposing ways in which the writing of history appropriates the historical traditions of other cultures, excluding them from their own history. La3amon, like many of his contemporaries at the turn of the thirteenth century, saw the messages to be gleaned from history as indeterminate and open to interpretation; as a result, the predictable cycle of providential historiography that characterizes the major historical texts of the mid-twelfth century gives way to varied and less certain interpretations.

To provide a context for my reading of the *Brut*, chapter 1 discusses
the twelfth-century notion of divine providence as a master-narrative
that served to legitimize Anglo-Norman dominance of England and the
appropriation of English history – especially Bede's *Historia Ecclesiastica* –
as part of a divinely ordained cycle of conquest and defeat. Through
this construct, Anglo-Norman historians alienated the native English
from their own history, casting them as the passive objects of a foreign
culture's history. Outlining the milieu of post-colonial England, chapter 1
then discusses the variant mode of historiography, initiated by Geoffrey
of Monmouth in his *Historia Regum Brittanniae*, that countered the
claims of providential historiography by refracting it into a multitude of
competing ways of reading and recording history; by making the providential mode only one voice among many, Geoffrey suggests that history
may ultimately be a matter of human interpretation. I then discuss variant
voices of the period and conclude with a specific examination of Laȝamon's
engagement with providential historiography.

Chapter 2 examines the actual translation of text within the *Brut*,
beginning with Laȝamon's prologue. The prologue, I argue, is a synopsis
of Laȝamon's views on historiography and translation through the
motif of seizing and gazing upon source texts. Laȝamon expresses the
relationship of conqueror-translator to text in implicitly (and often
explicitly) gendered terms. In his admiration of the feminized source
text, Laȝamon voices the almost paradoxic concern that the translator
may become translated and that the historian's authority, like that of
the ruler, remains tentative. Laȝamon uses the paradigm of romance,
with its blend of aggression and seduction, to dramatize this process.
Chapter 3 discusses the translation of the land as the next step in the
translation of historical texts and traditions. I pay particular attention
to foundational narratives, with their depictions of conquest and resettlement; these, I maintain, serve as tropes for the translation process.
In the *Brut*, the people, the land, and the language – all of which are
signalled by the Anglo-Saxon term *leod* – become victims in the process
of translation and textual appropriation.[80] The chapter begins with an
examination of the career of the eponymous founder of Britain, Brutus,
as a representative of the historian-translator whose territorial conquests
mirror the historian's temporal conquests. Of particular concern in this
chapter are the repeated acts of naming and renaming places, which for
Laȝamon come to signify the process of insular history, with its textual
layers and recurrent acts of substitution and displacement. Chapter 4
concentrates on translation of the people, especially on the translation

of the ruler's body as representative of the collective body of the people. Rulers come to symbolize both translators of historical text and the translatable text itself. The successful ruler translates text, and the defeated ruler is himself translated. In contrast, the ruler who escapes his own defeat (and thus avoids being utterly vanquished) comes to represent the untranslatable trace of the texts of the colonized, lingering beyond the confines of history as a continual threat to the power of the translator. Much of this chapter concerns Laȝamon's depiction of Arthur, who, as both the translator-conqueror and text to be translated, serves as a microcosm for the strengths and limitations of historiographic translation. Arthur's struggle to resist the territorial displacement of the Britons by foreign invaders and the replacement of British history by foreign history comes to reflect Laȝamon's own answer to the Anglo-Latin historiographic paradigm of the period – a paradigm that depended upon the appropriation and reinterpretation of English historical material. At the same time, however, Arthur comes to represent the historical text. Configured by Laȝamon as a literal 'speaking book', Arthur – a 'banquet' for poets and warriors – becomes a metaphor for the very historical narrative he has initiated. In Laȝamon's hands, Arthur becomes both historian and historical text liable to conquest and translation, an emblem for the English people and language in their unique position of conquerors and conquered. The conclusion of the *Brut* leaves the process of translation indeterminate, thus preserving a space for the displaced people and their languages – English and Welsh – to reassert their voices as active participants in their own history.

Laȝamon's self-conscious historio-linguistic construct exposes the translation of history as displacement of cultures and appropriation of their historical traditions. As a history of translation itself, then, the *Brut* ultimately dramatizes the English language's suppression and lays the foundations for its re-emergence. It calls for a reassessment of the English language and English ethnic identity in the face of Anglo-Norman and Angevin literary traditions that threaten to eclipse both. I do not believe that Laȝamon's concern is with heritage – whether one's ancestors arrived with Brutus, Hengest or William – but, rather, with language and with the ways in which translation shapes history. With his interest in language, Laȝamon looks forward to, and participates in, the revival of the English language's prestige in the thirteenth and fourteenth centuries. Understanding the importance of language and translation to Laȝamon's *Brut* thus provides a broader and more complete picture of insular historiography at the end of the Angevin period.

Notes

1 Nancy Partner, *Serious Entertainments: The Writing of History in Twelfth-century England* (Chicago, 1977), p. 4.
2 Robert W. Hanning, *The Vision of History in Early Britain* (New York, 1966), p. viii.
3 Evelyn Birce Vitz observes that medieval *vrai* (truth) 'often can only be said to refer to the faithfulness of the text to another text, or to a literary tradition' (*Medieval Narrative and Modern Narratology: Subjects and Objects of Desire* (New York, 1989), p. 113.
4 See William Leckie Jr., *The Passage of Dominion: Geoffrey of Monmouth and the Periodization of Insular History in the Twelfth Century* (Toronto, 1981).
5 Ernst Curtius, *European Literature and the Latin Middle Ages* (Princeton, 1953), pp. 28–9.
6 'Where we would separate translation (finding an equivalent word or phrase in a different language) from interpretation (explaining the sense in the same or another language), earlier practice saw the activities as part of one spectrum' (Ruth Morse, *Truth and Convention in the Middle Ages* (Cambridge, 1991), p. 199).
7 Rita Copeland, *Rhetoric, Hermeneutics, and Translation in the Middle Ages* (Cambridge, 1995), p. 1.
8 A degree of this sort of appropriation is implicit in Saint Jerome's dictum on translation as leading the meaning of a text 'captive': 'sed quasi captiuos sensus in suam linguam uictoris iure transpsuit' (by right of victory he led away the sense captive into his own language). Although not central to my purpose, it is worth noting that Christian translators offered a second model for biblical translation based on fidelity to the text. Rita Copeland cites the dichotomy between the classical-Ciceronian model of translation into Latin, where the translator seeks to displace the source text along with the source language, and a patristic or Hieronymian model, which stresses conservation of the immanent meaning of the biblical source. According to Copeland, these conflicting drives inform medieval translations, as elements of Roman aggression often subvert the translator's ostensive fidelity to the source text (*Rhetoric, Hermeneutics, and Translation*, pp. 49–50). Both aspects of translation seem to inform Jerome's concept.
9 *King Alfred's West-Saxon Version of Gregory's* Pastoral Care, ed. Henry Sweet, EETS 45, 50 (London, 1872).
10 See J. R. Clark Hall, *A Concise Anglo-Saxon* Dictionary (Toronto, 1960 [1894]), p. 402. Douglas Robinson discusses the etymological implications of translation as 'turning' in *The Translator's Turn* (Baltimore, 1991).
11 Robert Stanton, 'The (m)other tongue: translation theory and Old English', in Jeanette Beer (ed.), *Translation Theory and Practice in the Middle Ages*, (Kalamazoo, 1997), pp. 33–46). Stanton further claims that 'Such a mediated engagement with the text would seem, on the face of it, to rule out any explicit motive of '"Ciceronian" contestation or displacement on Alfred's part. Second, we cannot attribute to Alfred a purely "Hieronymian" outlook, whereby he would aim to conserve, or replicate, an immanent meaning.

Alfred's translation practice, and that of his colleagues, is too loose to allow such an interpretation' (p. 38). Stanton believes that 'Alfred's translation program should be judged against his own justification for it. He perceived a grave deficiency in Latin literacy at the time, and his English translations were meant to make available important works that people should have been able to read in Latin but could not. His ultimate aim was the resuscitation of the ideal of wisdom among his royal officials and clergy' (p. 39). It is, nonetheless, possible to discern echoes of the *translatio imperii* in Alfred's project, as he clearly sees translation of religious text as a hallmark of a 'great' civilization.

12 Walter Benjamin and Steven Rendall (trans.), 'The translator's task', *TTR: Traduction, Terminologie, Rédaction: Études sur le texte et ses transformations*, 10, 2 (1997), 151–65 (158).

13 George Steiner, *After Babel: Aspects of Language and Translation* (London, 1975), p. 302.

14 According to Holsinger, 'the disciplinary, institutional, and methodological histories of what we somewhat sloppily call "theory" are intertwined with those of our own disciplines in numerous ways that we have yet to address; the notion that medievalists have been anachronistically superimposing theoretical models on a past to which they are utterly foreign is thus far from accurate. In fact, I would propose that many such theoretical discourses emerged from an intensive engagement with medieval texts and with the writings of medievalists contemporaneous with the theoretical avante-garde of earlier decades' (Bruce Holsinger, 'Medieval studies, postcolonial studies, and the genealogies of critique', *Speculum*, 77 (2002), 1195–227 (1222)).

15 J. C. Holt, *Colonial England 1066–1215* (London, 1994), p. 1.

16 Tejaswini Niranjana, *Siting Translation: History, Postcolonialism, and the Colonial Context* (Berkeley, 1992), p. 2.

17 Sherry Simon, 'Introduction', in Simon and Paul St.-Pierre (eds), *Changing the Terms: Translating in the Postcolonial Era* (Ottawa, 2000), p. 11.

18 Holt, *Colonial England*, p. 13.

19 Benjamin further considers 'the task of the translator to release in his own language that pure language imprisoned in a work in his re-creation of that work. For the sake of pure language he breaks through decayed barriers of his own language' ('The task of the translator', p. 80ff.). In contrast, in a failed translation, the translator fails to break these barriers and absorbs the original into his own language.

20 Refuting charges that the application of post-colonial theories to medieval studies is 'anachronistic', Holsinger has argued for the neglected role of medievalism in fashioning post-colonial discourse: 'Even while we have been preoccupied with uncovering colonialist practices in the Middle Ages, revealing the role of medievalism in orientalist discourses of the nineteenth and twentieth centuries, and demonstrating the persistence of medievalist fantasies in the languages of postcolonial theory and global capitalism, we have overlooked the vital role that medieval studies performed in the emergence and shaping

of postcolonial studies as a field of critical inquiry' ('Medieval studies, post-
colonial studies, and the genealogies of critique', p. 1207).

[21]   Holt, *Colonial England*, p. 26. Holt previously observes that the 'castle was
an instrument of domination – a blunt instrument. The great church was an
equally blatant assertion of power' (Ibid., p. 6).

[22]   Ibid., pp. 5–6.

[23]   See Lindy Grant, 'Architectural relations between England and Normandy,
1100–1204', in David Bates and Anne Curry (eds), *England and Normandy in
the Middle Ages* (London, 1994), pp. 117–29.

[24]   The extent of architectural and cultural influence, of course, remains debatable.
Some argue that the Normans transported their art and culture to Anglo-
Saxon England, while others maintain an English basis for Anglo-Norman
culture. E. C. Fernie notes, 'The thoroughness with which Norman culture
replaced Anglo-Saxon in at least one sphere is evident in the lack of standing
Anglo-Saxon material in the major churches the first two generations after
1066. Contrariwise, the extent to which the Normans were influenced by their
being in England is indicated by the greater scale of their buildings compared
with anything they built in Normandy, and their love of the exotic in planning
and details which again have no parallels in Normandy ('Church architecture
in Norman England', *England and Normandy in the Middle Ages*, pp. 103–15
(p. 115)).

[25]   The extent to which Norman law was transported from Normandy and the
extent to which it represents a codification of English law is a topic of hot
debate.

[26]   Susan Bassnett and Harish Trivedi, 'Introduction: of colonies, cannibals, and
vernacular', in Bassnett and Trivedi (eds), *Post-Colonial Translation: Theory
and Practice* (New York, 1999), pp. 1–18 (p. 4). Robert M. Stein also notes
the role of translators in fixing the identity of England and of the English:
'As a political experience becomes more and more unthinkable (as I will
argue in a moment, literally monstrous), William [of Malmesbury] completes in
imagination a process of social simplification only just begun as policy. For
William, the conquest levels a diversity of peoples into a conqueror and a
conquered, two *gentes* (peoples or nations or bloodlines) and two peoples only,
each occupying the same space. The Celts, never treated seriously in William's
narrative, disappear altogether. The Danes are described as merely
temporary visitors even if they manage to install a king from time to time.
The Mercians, Northumbrians, East Anglians, and the rest become by 1066
simply English. The second is the simplification of the contested space itself.
Geographical diversity is rewritten under the pressure of ideological purity,
and in the course of William's narrative England becomes a totality
imagined as sacred space, a material demonstration and guarantee of God's
presence even though (or just because) it is "situated almost out of the world"'
('Making history English', in Tomasch and Gilles (eds), *Text and Territory:
Geographical Imagination in the European Middle Ages* (Philadelphia, 1998),
pp. 98–9).

[27] Holt, *Colonial England*, p. 7.

[28] For a summary of Norman building activities, see Holt, *Colonial England*, pp. 10–12.

[29] Henry of Huntingdon, *Historia Anglorum*, p. 8.

[30] Partner, *Serious Entertainments*, p.27.

[31] Naranjani, *Siting Translation*, p. 4.

[32] 'The difference between French and Latin', according to Holt, 'became one of rank, rather than race. French was for the landlords and officers, English for the peasants and privates' (*Colonial England*, pp. 14–15).

[33] Ibid., p. 15.

[34] William of Malmesbury, *Historia Res Anglorum*, p. 4.

[35] Henry of Huntingdon, *Historia Anglorum*, 310; v.19 (italics mine).

[36] Ibid.

[37] Willis Barnstone, *The Poetics of Translation: History, Theory, Practice* (New Haven, 1993), p. 95. Copeland notes that 'A chief maneuver of academic hermeneutics is to displace the very text that it proposes to serve. Medieval arts commentary does not simply "serve" its "master" texts: it also rewrites and supplants them' (*Rhetoric, Hermeneutics, and Translation*, p. 3).

[38] See John Gillingham, *The English in the Twelfth Century* (Woodbridge 2000), especially chapter 8, 'Henry of Huntingdon and the twelfth-century revival of the English nation' (pp. 123–44).

[39] Michelle R. Warren, *History on the Edge* (Minneapolis, 2000), p. 14.

[40] Steiner, *After Babel*, p. 299.

[41] Else Ribeiro Pires Veira, 'Liberating Calibans: readings of antropofagia and Haroldo de Campos' poetics of transcreation', in *Post-Colonial Translation*, pp. 95–113 (p. 95).

[42] See Stein, Otter et al.

[43] Michelle R. Warren, 'Making contact: postcolonial perspectives through Geoffrey of Monmouth's *Historia regum Britannie*', *Arthuriana*, 8, 4 (1998), pp. 115–34 (116).

[44] I quote from Stephen Karl Brehe's transcription of the piece in his article, 'Reassembling the *First Worcester Fragment*', *Speculum*, 65 (1990), 521–36. Brehe further observes, 'The cultural rupture suffered by the English under the Normans is illustrated by the linguistic rupture within line 20: The first verse says, 'Nu sæiþ ure Drihten *þus.*' In the second verse the Lord speaks, but in another tongue' (Latin) (p. 535).

[45] Ibid., p. 534.

[46] Monika Otter, *Inventiones* (Chapel Hill, 1996), p. 22.

[47] Warren, *History on the Edge*, p. 110.

[48] Emily Albu, for instance, describes 'Normanness' as 'an intermediary stage on the way to other identities – French or English, Italian or Sicilian or Levantine' (*The Normans in their Histories: Propaganda, Myth and Subversion* (Suffolk, 2001), p. 221).

[49] Applying border theory to historiography of the period, Warren comments that 'Historiography thus takes place in a temporal border, ambivalent and bound by temporal conflict' (*History on the Edge*, p. 15).

50   Martin Shichtman, 'Gawain in Wace and Layamon, a case of metahistorical evolution', in Laurie Finke and Martin Shichtman (eds), *Medieval Texts and Contemporary Readers* (Ithaca, 1987), pp. 103–19 (p. 105).
51   Françoise H. M. Le Saux, *Layamon's* Brut: *The Poem and its Sources* (Cambridge, 1989).
52   Daniel P. Donoghue, 'Laȝamon's ambivalence', *Speculum*, 65 (1990), 537–63, (546).
53   Donald Bzdyl, in his translation of the *Brut*, proposes that the prologue may have been written by someone else; see also Kelley Wickham-Crowley, *Writing the Future, Laȝamon's Prophetic History* (Cardiff, 2002), pp. 14–15.
54   All references to MS Caligula are from *Layamon's Brut or Hystoria Brutonum*, eds and trans. W. R. J. Barron and S. C. Weinberg (Harlow, 1995). References to Otho are from *Laȝamon's* Brut: *Edited from British Museum MS. Cotton Caligula A. IX and British Museum MS. Cotton Otho C. XIII*, eds G. L. Brook and R. F. Leslie, 2 vols, EETS os 250, 277 (Oxford, 1963–78). Except as noted, translations are mine, although Barron and Weinberg were consulted, along with Rosamund Allen's translation of the *Brut*, *Lawman's Brut* (London, 1992), and Sir Frederick Madden's 1847 edition of the *Brut*.
55   See E. G. Stanley, 'The date of Laȝamon's *Brut*', *Notes and Queries*, 213 (1968), 85–8. Allen favours a date between 1204 and 1227, with Laȝamon perhaps beginning during the interdict, when parish priests would have had an abundance of free time for writing history. 'Introduction' to *Lawman's Brut*, pp. xviii–xvix.
56   Nonetheless, the 1189 date enjoys widespread acceptance, perhaps owing to a desire to fix the text historically. Barron and Weinberg, for instance, maintain that 'The use of the past tense in the reference to Eleanor as Henry's queen in the prologue suggests that the poem was written after the death of Henry II in 1189, possibly after Eleanor's death in 1204' (p. ix). An earlier composition date, of course, would complicate arguments that the Caligula MS preserves a deliberately archaic idiom. In contrast, H. B. Hinckley's argument for a much earlier date of composition, founded on historical and linguistic grounds, has received little attention. 'The date of Layamon's *Brut*', *Anglia*, 56 (1932), 43–57.
57   Such third-person prologues are not uncommon in twelfth-century French history and poetry, though Laȝamon's third-person biography is somewhat unusual; Gaimar, Wace and Marie de France routinely refer to themselves in the third person. Marie's prologues also use the preterite tense to refer to the author.
58   Hinckley, 'The date of Layamon's *Brut*', 43–57. To summarize, to the point of oversimplification, the argument, Hinckley claims that Laȝamon's use of the preterite refers only to the past action of Wace's presentation of the *Roman de Brut* to Queen Eleanor, not to their status as living or deceased persons. In light of Laȝamon's self-reference, also in the preterite, Hinckley's argument merits revisiting. See also Le Saux (ed.), *The Text and Tradition of Laȝamon's* Brut (London, 1994), p. 4. However, Hinckley's suggestion of a composition date in the early to mid 1160s seems a bit ambitious.

[59] Le Saux, *Text and Tradition of Laȝamon's* Brut, pp. 8–9.

[60] I refer, of course, to the anonymous author of the *Worcester Fragment*, and also to the 'tremulous hand' of Worcester, a likely contemporary of Laȝamon with an intense interest in manuscripts in the Anglo-Saxon language.

[61] See Gabrielle Spiegel, *Romancing the Past* (Berkeley, 1993).

[62] Sir Frederick Madden, *Laȝamon's* Brut, *or Chronicle of Britain*, 'Preface', p. vii.

[63] Elizabeth Bryan, *Collaborative Meaning in Medieval Scribal Culture: The Otho Laȝamon* (Ann Arbor, 1999), p. 129.

[64] See Antonia Gransden, *Historical Writing in England c.550 to c.1307* (Ithaca, 1974). Leckie attributes Laȝamon's concluding sections about the English conquest of Britain to his alleged confusion over dates (R. William Lockie Jr., *The Passage of Dominion* (Toronto, 1981), pp. 117–19).

[65] Francis Lytle Gillespie, 'Layamon's *Brut*: a comparative study in narrative art', *University of California Publications in Modern Philology*, 3 (1916), 361–510.

[66] G. J. Visser, *Laȝamon: An Attempt at Vindication* (Assen, 1935), p. 1.

[67] Henry Cecil Wyld, 'Laȝamon as an English poet', *Review of English Studies*, 6 (1930), 1–30 (2). Refuting Wyld, but echoing his impressionistic manner of interpretation, R. S. Loomis states, 'this man of God was a barbarian at heart. He belongs to a milieu where the softening influence of woman-worship and courtesy were unknown' (*Arthurian Literature in the Middle Ages* (Oxford, 1959), p. 107).

[68] Håkan Ringbom, *Studies in the Narrative Technique of* Beowulf *and Lawman's* Brut (Åbo, 1968), p. 59.

[69] Carolynn Vandyke Friedlander, 'Structure and themes in Layamon's *Brut*', *Modern Philology*, 76 (1979), 219–230 (229).

[70] Lee Patterson, *Chaucer and the Subject of History* (Wisconsin, 1991), pp. 15–16.

[71] See, respectively, Loomis, *Arthurian Literature in the Middle Ages* (q.v. note 5); J. S. P. Tatlock, *The Legendary History of Britain* (Berkeley, 1950); and Jorge Louis Borges, *Selected Non-Fictions*, eds Esther Allen et al. (New York, 1999).

[72] Shichtman, 'Gawain in Wace and Layamon', p. 107. Shichtman sees Wace's Gawain as a 'romance hero', one who should be characterized as embodying 'transcendence of the world of experience' (pp. 107–8), and Laȝamon's Gawain as tragic, 'dark and brooding . . . he stoically endures a savagely cruel existence. He is the hero of a defeated English people, a people who, though they must struggle to retain even their national language, persist in producing a poetry filled with intensity' (p. 108).

[73] Jeff Rider, 'The fictional margin: the Merlin of the *Brut*', *Modern Philology*, 87, 1 (1989), 1–12 (2).

[74] Further, the idea of providential history in the *Brut* remains a debatable issue. Bryan, for instance, argues that the Otho manuscript of the *Brut* employs a series of marks and glosses to evoke the providential model of secular history', *Collaborative Meaning*, p. 127.

[75] Donoghue, 'Ambivalence', pp. 537–8.

[76] See especially James Noble, 'Laȝamon's "ambivalence" reconsidered', in Le Saux, *Text and Tradition*, pp. 171–82; and Lesley Johnson, 'Reading the past

in La3amon's *Brut*', in ibid., pp. 140–61. According to Johnson, La3amon follows Geoffrey of Monmouth in resisting a providential interpretation of history, and the *Brut* differentiates itself from its predecessors by its self-conscious orientation 'within [. . .] an emphatically textual environment' (p. 147). Noble asserts that the *Brut* exhibits a nationalist, anti-Norman vision of insular history, understandable by modern critics if we take into account La3amon's differentiation between two groups of Saxons: the treacherous and ultimately unsuccessful invaders who oppose Arthur and his ancestors, and who are identified with the Normans, and the later immigrants, who occupy the island peacefully after its depopulation by plague.

[77] Kelley M. Wickham-Crowley, *Writing the Future* (Cardiff, 2002), p. 19.
[78] Otter, *Inventiones*, p. 90.
[79] Warren, *History on the Edge*, p. 87.
[80] Warren notes that this term 'collocates ethnicity, political association, land and language'; *History on the Edge*, p. 89.

1

Providential historiography and the translation of insular history

The providential view of human history derives originally from the histories and prophecies of the Old Testament, in books such as *Jeremiah* or the *Chronicles*, where the misfortunes that befell the Hebrews were interpreted as divine punishment inflicted upon an erring populace. Generally, it involves reading secular history as the manifestation of a divine plan. Providentialism dominated Christian historiography from late antiquity well into the modern period. Medieval providential historiography developed from the early years of Christian Rome, where competing Christian and pagan visions of Roman history brought historiography to the forefront.[1] Although alternative Christian historiographic models, such as the Boethian Fortuna, were available to medieval historians, the traditionalist model of divine providence as the visible will of an interventionist God, who rewards and punishes His 'chosen people' (*verus Israel*), formed the dominant means of interpreting secular history at least until the middle of the twelfth century.[2] In historical narrations of conquest and foundation, providential historiography provides an apt way of interpreting, explaining and justifying the fall of kingdoms and the displacement of peoples. History, Gabrielle Spiegel reminds us, has the power 'to lend to ideology the authority and prestige of the past, all the while dissimulating its status *as* ideology under the guise of a mere accounting of "what was"'.[3] As a means of recounting 'what was', providential historiography offered justification for conquerors of territory and consolation for defeated cultural groups. In insular history, providentialism provided a way of explaining the repeated invasions and conquests of the British Isles as visitations of divine judgement on its inhabitants, and as the transference of *verus Israel* status to a new group of invaders and colonizers. Robert W. Hanning notes how use of the 'new Israel' topos by Gildas and Bede characterizes the Britons and, after their downfall, the Saxons, as God's chosen people (Hanning, *Vision*).

It would be a mistake, however, to regard all providential histories as part of a monolithic master-narrative. Although the general notion of a God who intervenes in human affairs may be said to dominate medieval historiography, historians did not share the same absolute view of divine punishment. For instance, Bede read the fall of the Britons to the invading Anglo-Saxons as a punishment for British sinfulness and as the preparation for the rise of the more Rome-allied English church. Four hundred years later, in the wake of the Norman Conquest, Anglo-Norman historians, such as Orderic Vitalis, William of Malmesbury and Henry of Huntingdon, would reinterpret the event as only the first movement in a cycle of rises and falls, in which the mantle of divine favour passed from the Britons to the English, and thence to the Normans. Historians of the latter half of the twelfth century and the early decades of the thirteenth, such as Florence of Worcester and William of Newburgh, would further modify providential history, often inverting the concept of conquest as sign of divine favour and defeat as proof of sinfulness.[4]

As a revision of past histories, insular providential history – the transformation of oral and written accounts of events into coherent narrative – bears strong affinity with translation, the transference of text from one language or one discursive mode into another. History depends upon the arrangement and interpretation of the accumulated facts and the ways in which these facts are construed – or reconstrued – into what Hayden White terms a mode of emplotment.[5] Thus, when Orosius explains the premature death of an early Latin ruler as divine judgement, when Bede refers to divine afflictions befalling intransigent British clerics, or when Henry of Huntingdon refers to God's judgement against the English people, each historian, in effect, translates a fragment of history into an exemplum of the workings of divine providence, recording the event according to a preconceived narrative pattern. In her discussion of medieval historical topoi, Ruth Morse makes the connection between history and translation explicit.[6] As the interpretation of secular events, then, writing providential history constitutes an act of translation, whether it occurs between languages (interlingual) or within the same language (intralingual). Under this model, the Britons and Saxons were in turn subjects and objects of translation, as people were translated from active producers of history into marginalized subjects, and the land itself literally translated from Britain to England.

This chapter offers an overview of the development of providential history in Britain/England to provide a context for my later examination of the *Brut*. I first discuss the use of providence by the English historian Bede to give divine sanction to the rise of the English church and people and the displacement of the Britons. I then examine the use of Bedan providence by Anglo-Norman historians as a template for reconstructing insular history as a cycle of divinely ordained rises and falls. Through providential history, these historians came to terms with the more recent conquest of England and gave the Norman ascendancy a useful history. I next turn to the challenge to providential historiography posed by later histories, beginning with Geoffrey of Monmouth's *Historia Regum Britanniæ*. I conclude with an overview of Laȝamon's unique treatment of providence as a mode of translation.

Bede and the colonization of Britain: the Historia Ecclesiastica *as historiographic translation*

It is difficult to overstate the importance of the seventh-century Northumbrian monk Bede's *Historia Ecclesiastica* in twelfth-century England. Bede provided not only a record of early English events for his Anglo-Norman successors, but also a paradigm for interpreting insular history and, more subtly, for appropriating precursor texts into different historiographic contexts. In establishing the basis for Anglo-Norman insular historiography, Bede may accurately – and ironically – be called the father of Norman historiography. Incorporating hagiography, dream visions and *miraculi*, such as the narrative of Caedmon, into its historiographic narrative, the *Historia* documents the fall of the Britons, the rise of the English kingdoms, the subsequent conversion of the English to Christianity, the establishment of an English church, and the ongoing acts of English clergy and rulers up to his own period. Because of his authority, insular historians of the twelfth and thirteenth centuries relied on Bede almost exclusively for information on early insular history. Indeed, modern historians rely on the *Historia Ecclesiastica*, frequently and justly praising its author's adherence to detail.[7]

It is important to keep in mind, however, that Bede's central concern is the *ecclesiastical* history of England, even though the text served (and continues to serve) as the chief source of information on early Anglo-Saxon secular and religious history. In spite of his celebrated accuracy, Bede's vision of history is filtered through the lens of the providential

master-narrative, based on the Orosian-Eusebian model of divine providence, and through his own appropriation of his British precursor-text,
the *De Excidio Brittaniae*, by the sixth-century monk Gildas, an eyewitness to the early phases of the Saxon invasions. By appropriation, I
do not mean that Gildas provides a different model for Bede when
recounting events in British history. When referring to British history,
Gildas follows a similar Orosian–Eusebian concept of Christian history
as a visible and recordable record of divine providence.[8] However, by
appropriating Gildas, Bede revises the original providential narrative so
that it predicts and justifies the rise of the English. While both religious
writers incorporate biblical typology in their representations of insular
history, and both see the role of divine intervention in the punishment
of a sinful nation, Gildas had no intention to document the *fall* of the
Britons, something that occurred after his lifetime and that he, in fact,
sought to prevent. More of a polemicist than an historian, Gildas saw
events in British history as providentially directed, but only as a warning
for the British leaders, who still have the chance to change their national
destiny. Bede, in contrast, amplifies and alters the role of providence to
align events with the rise of the English people as the new *verus Israel*.

For example, when Bede cites British sinfulness as the effective cause
of their downfall – 'cum quibus et luxuria crescere, et hanc continuo
omnium lues scelerum comitari adceleravit, crudelitas praecipue, et
odium veritatis amorque mendacii' (whereof the people grew to loose
and wanton living, and straight from this ensued a plague of all manner
of lewdness, especially cruelty, hate of truth and love of lying) – he reaches
this conclusion through amplification of Gildas' earlier account of the
Britons as possessed by 'odium veritatis cum assertoribus amorque
mendacii cum suis fabricatoribus' (hatred of truth and its messengers
with a love of lying and liars).[9] Although Bede echoes Gildas in his
portrayal of British resistance to foreign invasions as dependent on
divine aid, he does so with considerable extrapolation. Where Gildas
writes, 'non fidentes in homine, sed in deo' (not with faith in man but in
God),[10] Bede translates, 'alios vero numquam, quin potius confidentes in
Divinum ubi humanum cessabat auxilium, de ipsis montibus speluncis
ac saltibus continue rebellabant' ([b]ut others would never do so
[surrender to the invaders] but, rather, trusting in God where man's help
failed them, from the caves in the mountains and brakes where they
lurked, continually resisted').[11] Furthermore, Bede follows Gildas in his
use of biblical typology as a speculum through which to interpret insular
history; however, his amplifications present an extended providential

view of the fallen Britons. In the *De Excidio*, a catastrophic fire takes on the lineaments of a biblical tribulation:

> Conovebatur namque ultionis iustae praecedentium scelerum cause de mari usque ad mare ignis orientalie sacriligeorum manuexaggeratuus, et finitimas quasque civitates agrosque populans non quievit accensus donec cunctum paene exeurens insulae superficium rubra occiedentalem trucique oceanum lingua delemberet. In hoc ergo impetus Assyrio lim in Idaem comarando completur quoque in nobis secundum historiam quod propheta deplorans ait.[12]

> [In just punishment for the crimes that had gone before, a fire heaped up and nurtured by the hand of the impious easterners spread from sea to sea. It devastated town and country round about, and, once it was alight, it did not die down until it had burned almost the whole surface of the island and was licking the western ocean with its fierce red tongue. So it was that in this assault, comparable with that of the Assyrians of old on Judaea, there was fulfilled according to history for us also what the prophet said in his lament.]

Like Gildas, Bede uses the biblical motifs of the Fall of Jerusalem and the onset of the Babylonian captivity as an antetype for the more recent insular fire. In both instances, the fire signifies purgation of the landscape as part of a divine judgement against the Britons. Both further illustrate the use of Old Testament types and biblical exegesis, which, as Hanning and others have noted, informs providential historiography.[13] However, Bede's account places more emphasis on the collective nature of the punishment inflicted upon the British people (*populi*):[14]

> Siquidem, ut breviter dicam, accensus manibus paganorum ignis, iustis de sceleribus populi Dei ultones explicit, non illius impar qui quondam a Chaldaeis successus Hierosolymorum moenia immo aedificia cuncta consumpsit. Sic enim et hic agente impio victore, immo disponente iusto Iudice, proximas quasque civitatis agrosque depopulens, ab orientali mari usque ad occidentale, nullo prohibente, suum continuavit incendium, totamque prope insulae pereuntis superficiem obtexit.[15]

> [To speak briefly, the fires once kindled by the pagans proved to be God's judgement on the sins of the nation, just as the fires once kindled by the Chaldaeans destroyed the walls and buildings of Jerusalem. For as the just Judge ordained, these heathen conquerors devastated the surrounding cities and countryside, extended the conflagration from the eastern to the

western sea and without opposition overran nearly all of the perishing
island.]

In comparing these two scenes, it is important to remember that Gildas
never saw his task as documenting the 'passage of dominion' (which was
not to occur until long after his death), nor did he conceive of himself
as a historian. His task – to warn his contemporary British rulers of
impending disaster – was much more immediate than that of the
historian. As such, he never refers to the transfer of *verus Israel* status
from the Britons to the Saxons. For Gildas, the Saxons remain hated
by man and God.[16] In Gildas' typological scheme, the Saxons are
likened to the Assyrians or Chaldaeans (Babylonians) – instruments of
punishment used by God to warn or correct His own people, but not
themselves 'chosen people'. Gildas uses the history of Britain and of the
Britons as the context for his invective against the moral deterioration
of his contemporaries. Directed at a cultural group suffering the same
sort of judgement faced by the biblical Israelites, but still in control of
its land and its destiny, the *De Excidio* serves more as prophetic warning
than as history. Bede's addition of the element of reading or interpretation (*explicit*) in the above passage conveys his own role as translator
of Gildas and of an historian who reads God's word in the text of the
world. Bede also explicitly identifies the Saxons as pagan, centring the
religious struggle to an even greater extent, and also withholding Gildas'
moral judgement on the Saxons – predicting the virtuous pagan topos
of the *Beowulf* poet. Bede's alterations, though subtle, transform the
sequence into a prelude for the transfer of *verus Israel* status from the
Britons to the Anglo-Saxons.

Bede's conception of the historical Britons as morally weak and deserving of divine punishment depends upon his intralinguistic translation
of Gildas' invective against the Britons as 'nec in bello fortes sint nec in
pace fideles' (neither brave in war nor faithful in peace),[17] a characterization Gildas uses to explain their failure to resist outside invaders or
to maintain the Christian faith in the face of adversity. For example,
Bede uses Gildas' account of the Britons' inability to defend themselves
against Scottish and Saxon marauders to predict their inability to refute
the claims of the British-based Pelagian heresy. Original to Bede, the
account of the heresy's spread and of the Britons' inability to refute it is
designed to mirror the Gildan account of the timorous Britons sending
first to the Romans and then to the Angles and Saxons for military
assistance against the insular Scots and Picts. Bede's narrative of the

heresy associates the insular Britons with apostasy and spiritual weakness, predicting and justifying their exclusion from insular history. In coming to their assistance, the Roman missionary Germanus – whose name fortuitously echoes both the Roman conqueror-saviours of Britain and the Germanic Angles – vanquishes the Pelagians' spiritual *tempestatem* after first overcoming a literal tempest at sea. Germanus' metaphoric conquest over doctrinal dissent extends into the actual military realm as well, as he leads the Britons to victory over the pagan Saxons and Picts, a Beowulfian *ecgðræce* (sword-storm) in Alfred's English version of the *Historia*.[18] Although Bede omits the Gildan 'bello/pace' quote, he seems to have found in Gildas' polemic a ready model for the torpid response of the Britons to either military or spiritual challenges, and hence for their providentially ordained expulsion.[19]

Depicting the Britons as providentially condemned by God further involves paralleling the military conquests of the Saxons with the ecclesiastical triumphs of the Roman Catholic Church, as conversion operates on a trajectory similar to that of conquest and colonization. The signal act of conversion is, as Nicholas Howe observes, linked with the military conquest of the island through the trope of translation: 'conversion becomes a matter of translation'.[20] Bede draws an implicit connection between the Saxon conquest itself and the successful Christian mission of Augustine of Canterbury in a successful 'conquest' of the pagan Angles and Saxons.[21] The parallel relationship of these narratives reminds the reader of the contrast between ephemeral military conquest and eternal Christian conquest, but it also justifies the new military and ecclesiastical institutions of Anglo-Saxon England.[22] By interweaving the ecclesiastical narrative with his intralinguistic translation of Gildas, Bede provides justification for the expulsion of the Britons from the insular landscape and from the temporal landscape of insular history. Bede's engagement with Gildas, then, involves reading the subsequent history of Anglo-British struggles as the fulfilment of Gildas' jeremiadic warnings.

The transfer of 'chosen people' status, which marks the final exclusion of the Britons, occurs at the historical incident of the conversion of the English. Bede presents this passage immediately following his narration of the Germanus episode – with Germanus serving as a sort of antetype to Augustine of Canterbury, who arrives to convert the Anglo-Saxons.[23] After lamenting the pagan status of his own Anglo-Saxon ancestors and condemning the Britons for not participating in their conversion, Bede, for the first time in his historical narrative, identifies the Germanic invaders as the 'chosen people':

Sed non tamen divina pietas plebem suam, quam praescivit, deseruit, quin
multo digniores genti memorate veritatis, per quos crederet, destinavit.[24]

[But the goodness of God did not desert his people whom he had ordained,
but he destined more worthy people as heralds of the truth, through whom
they might be brought into the faith].

In the first mention of the *verus Israel* status being passed to the Saxons,
Bede marks the passage from British to English dominion in a rather
subtle way.

Here, Bede establishes a historiographic boundary between British and
Saxon history. It is no coincidence that Bede refers to Gildas directly for
the first and only time in the *Historia* in the same section where he marks
the transfer of divine favour to Gildas' ancestral enemies. The designation
of Gildas as *historicus eorum Gildus* [their historian Gildas] – a title
Gildas never claimed for himself – recontextualizes the *De Excidio* as a
historical document, and hence provides a degree of authority for the
events it relates. The pronominal *eorum* also establishes an ethnographic
boundary between Bede (now *our* historian) and the Britons (with *their*
historian). It further establishes British rule as part of an irrecoverable
past. From this point in the narrative, the present and future belong to
the insular English. In asserting this boundary, Bede asserts the divine
right of the English to insular sovereignty. What Bede omits from
Gildas is often notable, such as Gildas' reference to the Britons as the
praesentem Isreaelum (current Israel) receiving correction from God.[25] In
this regard, his methods reflect colonialist representations of 'the natives',
and translations of their texts and traditions to fit the needs of a new
hegemony.[26] With the English having been granted divine favour, British
history is abruptly translated into English history. Bede's translation of
Gildas thus reduces the British historical text to a chapter in English
history, translating the Britons themselves into objects of Anglo-Saxon
history.

It is tempting at this point to see in this section of Bede a 'colonialist'
translation, representing the texts of the conquered Other in terms
acceptable to the new conquerors. However, Bede's shared religious
sympathies compel him to consider the British Christians his fellows, at
least as long as their adversaries are pagans: thus, he refers to the Britons
as *cives* (countrymen) and the Saxons as *hostes* (enemies) during his
narrative of Ambrosius' struggles against the Saxons. Elsewhere he refers
to his Saxon forebears as barbarians, even though he does omit Gildas'
more strident invectives against them. By postpositioning his identification

of the English as 'his' people until the narrative of their conversion, Bede avoids the potential dilemma of documenting the success of a pagan people in a *Christian* history: the Saxons prevail only when they receive God's favour; Bede's own English identity is subsumed into his role as Latinate Christian historian, his Englishness visible only on the margins of the texts. It emerges in such instances as the Cædmon episode, which Kathleen Biddick reads as a sort of 'border' performance, occurring on the boundaries of Latin-Christian and English identity.[27] Biddick characterizes such events as 'Bede's blush', a moment of consciousness about the deprecation of his own vernacular language in the documentation of Christian history. Another such performance involves the translinguistic pun Bede attributes to Pope Gregory during his famous encounter with Deirian English slave-boys: the *Angli* (angels) to be plucked *De ira dei* (from the anger of God) translates English terms for racial and territorial identity (*Ænglen* and *Deira*) into those associated with the Latin ecclesiastical tradition. The pun works only in the multilingual reality of Anglo-Saxon England; the dual meanings dramatize the subjects' and Bede's dual ethnic and religious identity. More importantly, it emblematizes the role of translation in constructing the history of the conversion, documenting the entry of Latin into English daily life through the Church. In this sense, the Pope's wordplay becomes an allegory for the ensuing linguistic and religious conversion that creates Christian England.

The pattern of appropriation Bede establishes in his treatment of Gildas would recur at least once during the Anglo-Saxon period, in the eleventh-century Wulfstan the Elder's 'Sermo Lupi Ad Anglos', written forty-two years prior to the Battle of Hastings, during the depredations by the Danes. Wulfstan's sermon warns his audience that their sins exceed those of the earlier Britons, and that, consequently, the same fate awaits them unless they mend their ways. Wulfstan not only echoes but cites directly Gildas' jeremiadic harangues against the Britons:

An ðeodwita wæs on Brytta tidum, Gildas hatte, se awrat be heora misdædum, hu hy mid heora synnum swa oferlice swyðe God gegræmedan ðæt he let æt nyhsta Engla here heora eard gewinnan and Brytta dugeðe fordon mid ealle.

[A wise man named Gildas lived in the days of the Britons. He wrote about their misdeeds, how they so often provoked God with their sins that He next allowed the English host to win the land and completely destroy the British army.][28]

For Wulfstan, the authority of Gildas lent credence to a vision of history as cyclical and providentially guided. Howe notes the significance of Gildas to Wulfstan's historiographic vision; through his reading of Gildas, Wulfstan 'has mastered insular history'.[29] Like the insular Britons of Gildas' prophetic text, the English are on the verge of bringing about their own destruction.

> and soð is ðæt ic secge, wyrsan dæda we witan mid Englum ðonne we mid Bryttan ahwar gehyrdan; [and] ðy us is ðearf micel ðæt we us beðencan [and] wið God sylfne ðingian georne.[30]

> [And I speak the truth, we know of worse deeds among the English than we have heard of anywhere among the Britons; and therefore, it is of great urgency that we bethink ourselves and eagerly call on God Himself.]

That Wulfstan was envisioning an invasion from Scandinavia – which would in fact happen in 1016 – rather than from Normandy – which would happen fifty years later – was of little consequence; his negative characterization of the eleventh-century Anglo-Saxons would later provide a context for explaining the Norman Conquest according to the providential model. It is a logical extension of the *Sermon* to see in the Norman Conquest the fulfilment of Wulfstan's prophecy and a recurrence of the providential motif introduced by Bede.

Anglo-Norman appropriation of Bedan historiography

Three hundred and fifty years after the death of Bede, William I assumed domination over England, following his victory at Hastings. His claim, though decisively won by force of arms, rested on two spurious legal claims: his relation by marriage to the descendants of Alfred the Great, and Edward the Confessor's alleged choice of him as heir, reinforced by Harold Godwinson's legendary oath of support for his kingship – of dubious historicity and equally dubious legal merit.[31] Historians would provide for William what circumstances lacked. To answer the legal and moral deficiencies of William's ascendancy, to satisfy (and perhaps flatter) the Norman overlords, and to explain the catastrophic conquest and occupation of England, a generation of Anglo-Norman historians (Anglo-Norman often by birth and political affiliation) fashioned a poetics of history that both legitimized Norman rule and smoothed over continuing conflicts, by construing the Conquest as the providentially ordained punishment for the sins of the English. In dealing with the more immediate history of the Conquest and the radical reordering of the English territorial, ethnographic and historiographic landscape that occurred in its aftermath – a period of unprecedented cultural and linguistic change that Stein calls 'unthinkable' political experience – these historians crafted a vision of insular history that explained and justified both the recent Norman conquest and the more remote Anglo-Saxon conquest as phases in an ongoing cycle of divinely ordained purgation and conquest.[32] Translating intralingually from Bede's *Historia* and interlingually from the *Anglo-Saxon Chronicle*, they construed the two conquests so that they resembled each other, giving a repeated cyclical pattern to the concept of providence. Hanning observes that '[t]races of a cyclical view of history appeared, although situated within a larger framework that remained Christian'.[33] The new model served a number of rhetorical ends for these historians. It undoubtedly pleased the Norman ascendants, even as it reminded them of the dangers attendant upon conquerors. It gave some consolation to the English, in that their defeat was moral and not military.

Therefore, Anglo-Norman historians accepted the Norman invasion as a divine judgement against the English people. To an extent, such readings of the events of Hastings derive from the earliest accounts of the battle: Guy of Amiens, in his *Carmen de Hastingæ* (c. 1068), depicts the land as providentially granted to William as vengeance for Harold's fratricidal slaying of Tostig, a fanciful reading of divine judgement:

Inuidus ille Caïn fratris caput amputat ense,
Et caput et corpus sic sepeluit humo
Hñc tibi preuidit qui debita regna subegit:
Criminus infesti quatinus ultor eas.[34]

[The envious Cain struck off his brother's head, and thus buried head and body in the ground. He who subdued the destined realms foresaw the mission for you: that you should go to avenge that crime.]

For Guy, providence serves as justification for whatever means William practises to achieve his ends. Thus, Tostig's pillaging of the Northlands is objectionable, whereas William's similar activities in Kent are laudable because of his divine appointment; they serve as punishment for the unspecified *perfidiae* of the English countrymen, who suffer death and displacement at the hands of William's soldiers: 'Nec mirum, regem quia te plebs stulta negabat; Ergo perit iuste, uadit et ad nichilum'

(151–2) (No wonder, for the stupid people denied that you were king! Therefore they perished justly and went to destruction). Although Guy's use of divine providence as a trope is extreme in his flattering portrayal of William and the Norman invaders, the interpretation of the Conquest as divine judgement against the English proved influential to later generations of historians. Orderic Vitalis writes that the southeastern coast of England is left undefended 'nutu Dei'; with the characteristic ambiguity of the period, however, he adds that the slaughter at Hastings affords God the opportunity to punish 'innumeros peccatores' in both armies.[35] In this sense, Orderic differs dramatically from earlier accounts, such as Guy's, in his inclusion of Normans as objects of divine judgement. Nonetheless, Orderic states that the whole of England is subdued by 'the will of God'.[36] The abrupt, violent and apparently irreversible passage from Anglo-Saxon to Norman French rule was a calamity attributable only, as Henry of Huntingdon terms it, to 'Dei nutu factum . . . ut veniret contra improbos malum' (6.1) (The work of God, who brings evil to the reprobate). Even the *Anglo-Saxon Chronicle* account admits that 'ða Frencyscan ahton wælstowe geweald, eall swa heom God uðe for folces synnon' (The French had possession of the place of slaughter, as God granted them because of the peoples' sins).[37] The notion that the English sinned as a nation and hence lost their independence was, then, circulated through several historical sources throughout the eleventh and twelfth centuries.

However, circumstances confronting the second generation of post-Conquest Anglo-Norman historians, many of mixed Norman and English ancestry, were more complex regarding the most recent conquest of the island. These historians had to come to terms with the cultural crisis created by the Norman ascendancy and, to an extent, counter the complete denigration and erasure of Anglo-Saxon history threatened by French historian-poets, such as Guy of Amiens and his unequivocal paean to William and the Normans. As such, they may have wished to assert and preserve English contributions to insular history, as if to remind the Normans that the victims of their conquest had been conquerors in their own time and thus deserving of respect. Unlike Bede, for whom the previous inhabitants of the island – the Britons and their Celtic Christian church – were remote memories, Anglo-Norman historians confronted two distinct cultures occupying the same insular space. Further, many of them claimed Anglo-Saxon heritage and had predictably mixed reactions to the Norman regime and to its revisions of insular history. Biddick's metaphor of 'go-between' for the Latinate English historian is perhaps even more applicable to Anglo-Norman historians than to Bede, for the colonial circumstances under which they wrote involved translating English history for a non-English colonial class wielding political as well as ecclesiastical authority.[38] Further, the mixed parentage of many of the historians – such as William of Malmesbury and Henry of Huntingdon – gave them literal as well as metaphoric 'hybrid' status; the 'blushes' of William, Henry and Orderic, therefore, may have been somewhat less deep than Bede's. Reinterpretation of Bede and of the previous English historical materials served the conflicting rhetorical ends of their English and Norman parentage. Anglo-Norman historians reorganized and reinterpreted past events to form a new text with new ideological subtexts, while maintaining the impression of a set of predictable laws for history.[39]

Bede's importance for Anglo-Norman historians, however, involves not only his material about early insular history, but his way of reading changes in insular power as the transference of *verus Israel* status to a new group of conquerors. The main tropes Bede uses to depict the early Britons as having lost their divine mandate – especially the language of apostasy and heresy, applied to the indigenous (or, more accurately, indigenized) people to justify their displacement from the land and from active participation in insular history – apply to Anglo-Norman narratives of insular history, especially to their depictions of the Anglo-Saxons as having lost their status of *verus Israel*. Even cursory examination reveals that Orderic, William of Malmesbury and Henry of Huntingdon use the model of divine providence derived from Bede as an organizational pattern for their insular histories. For instance, Henry of Huntingdon's 'five plagues' of insular history furnishes the fullest expression of this expansive cycle. Calling the five historical invasions of Britain – by the Romans, the Scottish–Pictish alliance, the Anglo-Saxons, the Danes and, finally, the Normans – 'plagues' upon the island, he suggests that these historical events are divine interventions inflicted upon faithful and faithless alike by 'ultio divina' (divine vengeance).[40] As Nancy Partner comments, 'Henry cast the divisions of his history, regarded equally as event or literature, into a series of moral events. He found in certain large segments of time and human history recognizable entities whose unity was neither artificial nor natural but truly divine – God's gesture.'[41] For Henry, therefore, divine providence becomes a unifying principle for his entire historical undertaking, linking the Saxon and Norman invasions as two movements in an ever-repeating cycle of providential affliction. Henry's 'five plagues' provide a pattern for his representation of insular history, concluding with a not-so-veiled warning that the Normans face a sixth plague: 'Patebit a modo quomodo et ipsos Normannos vindices quidem suos variis cladibus afficere inciperit' (It will also appear how He began to afflict the Normans themselves, the instruments of his will, with various calamities).[42] From his *exordium*, Henry's conception of insular history as a providentially ordained cycle of rises and falls becomes evident. Bede thus provided for these historians what translation theorists such as André Lefevre would term a *grid* for translating insular history, that dictated interpretation of historical texts and events.[43] By this I mean that the providential motif Bede applies to his narrative of the fall of the Britons provides Anglo-Norman historians with a way of translating narratives of other events in insular history, culminating in narratives of the Norman Conquest. By making accounts of the Norman Conquest look like Bede's narrative of the English military and ecclesiastical take-over in the sixth century, Anglo-Norman historiographic revision gives the impression that insular history is cyclic, and hence predictable, according to the providential model of rises and falls.

It is in this respect that Anglo-Norman historians differ from Bede. What for Bede was the one culture-shaping instance of a providential shift in *verus Israel* status became a full-blown cyclical vision of insular history, wherein successive cultural groups seize power through divine favour, only to lose it – and with it land and power – through their own sin and apostasy. Extending their accounts of English history beyond the period covered by Bede, where the only records were to be found in the *Anglo-Saxon Chronicle*, Anglo-Norman historians extrapolated Bedan providentialism into an elaborate model for explaining later events. Bede's single instance of a providentially ordained defeat thus provided the basis for twelfth-century Anglo-Norman historians' complex pattern for reading insular history. Following the Bedan model, Henry translates even the most perfunctory records of the *Chronicle* as visible manifest-ations of the divine will, embellishing accounts when necessary. For instance, he translates the terse *Chronicle* entry for AD 514 relating the victory by the Saxon chiefs' Stuf and Witgar over the Britons – 'Her cwomon Westseaxe in Bretene mid iii scypum in ðas stowem ðe is gecweden Cerdices ora, Stuf [and] Witgar, [and] fuhtun wið Bryttas [and] hie geflymdon' (In this year Stuf and Wulfgar came to Wessex in three ships to the place known as Cerdic's Shore and they fought with the Britons and routed them)[44] – into an illustration of the Britons' sinfulness and an exemplum of how divine judgement often contradicts human ingenuity and preparation:

Sexto namque anno post bellum prædictum, venerunt nepotes Certic, Stuf et Witgar, cum tribus navibus apud Certicesore. Primo autem mane duces Brittannnorum acies in eos secundum belli leges pulcherrime construxerunt; cumque pars eorum in montibus, pars eorum in valle progrederetur caute et excogitate, apparuit sol oriens, offenderuntque radi clipeis deauratis, et resplenduerent colles ab eis, aerque finitimus clarus refulsit, timueruntque Saxones timore magno et approp inquaverunt ad prœlium. Dum autem collinderentur exercitus fortissimi, fortitudo Brittanorum dissipitat est, quia Deus spreverat illos.[45]

[Among these, in the sixth year after the war, Stuf and Witgar, the nephews of Cerdic, came with three ships to *Cerdicesore*. At daybreak the leaders of the Britons arrayed their forces against the invaders with much military skill. They led one body along the ridges of the hills, and another in the valley with much silence and caution, until the rays of the rising sun glancing from their gilded shields, the hill tops and the very sky above them glistened with the bright array. The Saxons were struck with terror as they advanced into battle; but when the two strong armies came into collision, the courage of the Britons failed, because God despised them.]

Henry's embellishments bring to the foreground the role of divine providence in shaping British history and in reinforcing Bede's establishment of the Saxons as the *verus Israel*. According to Henry's historiography, when nations or races of people sin against God, they suffer communal punishment. Using a historiographic model extrapolated from Bede to give his text narrative as well as moral coherence, Henry makes the defeats that insular natives suffer, from the Roman to the Norman Conquest, punishments for their moral shortcomings.

Translations of the *Chronicle* narratives and intralinguistic historiographic extrapolations from Bede demanded revision of the transition from British to Saxon rule as a single culture-shaping event, rather than a slow process of migration; their narrative was then parallel to the Bedan account of the conversion and predictive of the Norman Conquest. For example, William of Malmesbury translates the rather sketchy *Chronicle* account of the exploits of the West Saxon leader Cerdic into an impressive *vita*, transforming his Viking-type inland raids into a narrative of conquest and resettlement that looks forward to William's victory at Hastings. The *Chronicle* tells us simply that Cerdic fought against the Britons at a place called Cerdic's Shore:

Her cuomon twegen aldormen on Bretene, Cerdic 7 Cynric his sunu, mid.v.
scipum in ðone stede ðe is gecueden Cerdicesora 7 ðy ilcan dæge gefuhtun
wið Walum. (entry for 495)

[In this year two *aldormen*, Cerdic and his son Cynric, came with five ships to
the place called Cerdic's Shore and on that same day fought with the Welsh]

The chronicler does not even attribute success to Cerdic and Cynric. In
William's translation, Cerdic does succeed and he does so because of his
own merits, and because of the lack of order in the British ranks:

uir veteris militiæ non difficulter arietantem multidudinem contudit et
fugere compulit. Quo successu et sibi profundam in reliquum securitatem,
et provincialibus quietem, peperit.[46]

[as a veteran fighter, he subdued the stumbling multitude and compelled
them to flee without difficulty. This success produced a future of deep
security for himself and peace for the inhabitants of the province.]

William's addition of causes and effects to his account of Cerdic's
victory, aided by the hypotactic structure of Latin prose, transforms the
Saxon leader from a coastal raider into a ruler and dynastic founder, an
appropriate forerunner of Alfred, the later ruler of Wessex, as well as of
William of Normandy, whose conquest also follows a signal military
victory. Unlike Henry, William attributes the military weakness to
the insular Britons that we see in Bede's and Gildas' accounts. Thus,
although William does not attribute Cerdic's successes directly to divine
providence, his translation makes the founding of Wessex a secular antetype for the founding of the Anglo-Norman kingdom, accomplished
through the efforts of a single ruler triumphing over a disordered, and –
one is invited to suspect – less 'civilized', opponent. Henry's *Brunanburh*
translation (*Chronicle* entry for 937) provides another instance of the
revision of early English history so that it reflects later accounts of the
Conquest. Henry's depiction of the *adventus Saxonum* as a single battle
by a single people serves as an encomium for the Normans' English
precursors and a parallel to the Norman Conquest itself.[46] The encapsu-
lated *adventus Saxonum* narrative that concludes the Anglo-Saxon original
becomes part of Henry's broader cyclical historiographic pattern, and
cannot but recall the Norman victory at Hastings. Henry, then, reminds
the Normans that, as masters of English territory and history, the
Normans are heirs to an illustrious and heroic tradition, but one now
part of an irrecoverable past. The narrative of a single battle involving

Angles and Saxons acting in concert against the Britons provides further precedence for Anglo-Norman depictions of the Conquest, which, as Stein observes, 'levels a diversity of peoples into a conqueror and a conquered, two *gentes* (peoples or nations or bloodlines) and two peoples only, each occupying the same space'.[47] Needless to say, the repeated narrative of maritime invasion may serve as a warning to the Normans as well, but, more importantly, it ties into Henry's conception of insular history as providentially directed and cyclical, with subsequent races of conquerors rising and falling according to divine approval.

However, the Anglo-Norman historiographic project involved more than simply assigning the events of the Conquest to divine providence. Faced with the difficulties presented by the Norman Conquest – not the least of which was the Christian-versus-Christian violence – Anglo-Norman historians applied the same discourse of apostasy (if not outright heresy) to the English that Bede earlier applied to the Britons. Following this model, the Norman-backed ecclesiastical officials were recast as redeemers of the apostate Anglo-Saxon church, just as the English church founded by Augustine had introduced orthodox Christianity into the island.[48] William of Malmesbury credits the Normans under Lanfranc with reviving the 'lifeless' religion of England.[49] Orderic states that the Church prospered under the 'good men' appointed by William.[50] This narration in part exonerates the Normans and forestalls their own punishment, and provides justification for (and perhaps explanation of) their continued dominion over English territory.

To some extent, historians' praise for an insular religious revival is justified. Certainly, the Normans engaged in a prodigious amount of church construction on their new territory, but this activity was done mainly over earlier Saxon edifices, and the Normans receive limited praise for the architectural innovation. Such distinctions, however, were of little importance to the Anglo-Norman historians, since, according to the providential model, the reality of English defeat was proof in and of itself of moral and religious degeneration. To support this view, William of Malmesbury characterizes the state of immediate pre-Conquest England as pervaded by sinfulness, ignorance and religious apostasy, significantly associated with a corresponding decline in literacy:

Veruntamen litterarum et religionis studia ætate procedente obsoleverunt, non paucis ante adventum Normannorum anni. Clerici literatura tumultuaria contenti, vix sacramentorum verba balbutiebant [. . .] Optimates, gulæ et veneri dediti ecclesiam more Christiano mane non adibant; sed in cubicula, et inter uxoros amplexus, matutinarum solemnia et missarum a festinante presbytero auribus tantum libabant.[51]

[Nevertheless, in process of time, the desire after literature and religion had decayed, for several years before the arrival of the Normans. The clergy, contented with a very slight degree of learning, could scarcely stammer out the words of the sacraments [. . .] The nobles, given up to luxury and wantonness, went not to church in the morning after the manner of Christians, but merely in a careless manner, heard matins and masses from a hurrying priest in their chambers, amid the blandishments of their wives.]

This depiction repeats William's adaptation of the Bedan-Gildan interpretation of spiritual affairs in the generation before the *adventus Saxonum*. The above admonition further bears a striking resemblance to Bede's depiction of religious affairs in Britain, especially of the moral laxity of the British clergy, immediately preceding the Saxon conquest. This narrative strategy enabled historians to explain the Conquest and its aftermath without the excessive lionization of William I characteristic of the previous generation of Norman historians, such as Guy. This representation of the English also conveys the implicit – and sometimes explicit – warning that a similar end awaits the Normans, should they suffer a lapse in piety. As a rhetorical device, English apostasy serves to justify the Norman conquerors' position of power, while warning them that rises and falls are an integral part of insular history. Further, the early eleventh-century testimony of Wulfstan the Elder – though his concern was with Danish rather than Norman invasion – provided supporting evidence for English moral turpitude. From this perspective alone, we can see how these historians found in Bedan providentialist discourse a precedent for their representation of the pre-Conquest English.

Beyond the language of religious apostasy, however, Anglo-Norman historians occasionally incorporate into their narratives of 1066 a discourse of 'barbarism' and exoticism borrowed from Bede and Gildas, though perhaps extending ultimately to Julius Caesar's account of the wars with the Britons. William of Malmesbury's strategically placed rhetoric of exotica inscribes the pre-conquest Saxons into a role similar to that of the Britons immediately before the Roman invasions and of the Irish at the time of the Anglo-Norman conquest: all are treated as inferior cultures, ripe for, and even benefiting from, outside conquest. More subtly and equivocally, William of Malmesbury refracts what he sees as the ecclesiastical deficiencies of the Anglo-Saxon people into his representation of their culture and habits. Unprecedented in any known source, William highlights the exotic, if not outright barbaric, appearance and practices of the pre-Conquest English:

> Ad summum, tunc erat Angli vestibus ad mediam genu expediti crines tonsi, barbis rasi, armillis aureis brachia onerati, picturatis stigmatibuscutem cum insigniti.[52]

> [In fine, the English at that time, wore short garments reaching to the mid-knee; they had their hair cropped; their beards shaven; their arms laden with golden bracelets; their skin adorned with punctured designs.]

William earlier depicts the Britons as 'half-savage' or 'given up to luxury', coming close in tone to the sort of discourse of barbarism applied to the sub-Roman Britons by historians beginning with Julius Caesar, and promulgated in the works of Gildas, Bede and Guy of Amiens.[53] The last overtly compares Duke William favourably to Julius Caesar – 'Iulius alter, enim cuius renouando triumpham / Effenem gentem cogis amare iugum' (Another Julius [Caesar], indeed, in renewing whose triumphs you force a headstrong race to love the yoke).[54] Later, William makes explicit his already implicit association of the Anglo-Saxons with the early Celts, as he compares the long hair and moustaches of the English (used to distinguish them from the Normans in the Bayeux Tapestry) to the facial hair of another 'uncultivated' Celtic race, the ancient Britons:

> Angli enim superius labium pilis incessanter fructicantibus in tonsum dimittant, quod etiam gentilium antiquis Britonibus fuisse Julius Caesar asseverant libro Bellici Gallici.

> [For the English leave the upper lip unshorn, suffering the hair continually to increase; which Julius Cæsar, in his treatise on the Gallic war, affirms to have been a national custom with the ancient inhabitants of Britain.][55]

I do not suggest that William's depiction of this period in English history is inaccurate; however, his placement of this description near the end of the English dynasty is curious. It seems to create a historiographic boundary that allows William to differentiate the present Anglo-Norman/English insular inhabitants from the pre-Conquest Saxons, rendered here as exotic or Other, separated by a temporal barrier both from their present-day descendants and from their heroic and divinely favoured ancestors. The discourse allows William to renegotiate and re-establish ethnic and national boundaries. He can identify himself with the English nation as an ideal, while separating himself and his contemporaries from the

debased or apostate English who inhabited the island in the decades
leading up to the Norman Conquest. Whether unconsciously or by
design, William's rhetorical strategy seems to involve the depiction of
the English nation as a barbaric entity upon which he could impose the
'civilizing' influence of the Normans, paralleling the ecclesiastical reforms
initiated by the conquerors. William's temporal boundary between Anglo-
Saxon and Anglo-Norman England, like Giraldus' geographic one between
England and the Celtic lands, effectually distances the subjects from
their new conquerors. The images William employs in his history (whether
accurate or not) suggest a cultural gap between the English and their
Norman overlords, enhanced by the religious gulf evident in the pious,
active Norman clergy who correct the apostate English church. It more
significantly separates the 'admirable' English who overcame the Britons
and embraced Roman Christianity from the pre-Conquest English,
devoid of both piety and courage. The English were thus removed as
active participants in the shaping of insular history, becoming a race
doomed, as Henry of Huntingdon claims, to 'perpetual slavery'. The Celtic
Britons, beyond both the geographic boundaries of 'England' and the
temporal boundaries of Anglo-Norman history, were entirely excluded
from the new historiographic scheme. As with the tradition established
by Gildas and perpetuated by Bede, the marginalization of the native
insular population followed both the providentialist model of the *verus
Israel* and the classical Roman model of the east-to-west spread of
'civilization'.

It is worth noting tangentially that this exoticization lexically links
the pre-Conquest English with the Irish of the twelfth century, whom
the Anglo-Normans were in the process of colonizing. The Angevin
historian Giraldus Cambrensis uses similar terms to describe the manners
of the Irish, regarding, especially, their unshorn hair:

> Gens igitur hæc gens barbara, et vere barbara. Quia non tantum barbaro
> vestium ritu, verum etiam comis et barbis luxuriantibus, juxta modernas
> novitiates, incultissima.[56]

> [This race is, therefore, a barbarous race, and truly barbarous. They are not
> only barbaric in their manner of dress, but indeed also in the extravagance
> of their neglected hair and beards, just as the modern novelty.]

Giraldus' pun on *barbara* (barbaric) and *barbis* (beards) not only establishes
a connection between a neglect of hair and a lack of cultivation, but also
implicitly links the Irish to the pre-conquest English and to the pre-

Roman Celts, all distinguished by their hirsute faces. Attention to these details separates both English and Irish from Anglo-Norman 'civilization' – one separate by geographic distance, the other by the temporal space of history.

Anglo-Norman historians extended the exoticization, or 'othering', of the English people into the realm of language. From its pre-conquest status as an official language of both State and Church, political circumstances reduced the English language to a level where William could deem it in need of 'civilizing' through 'Roman rhetorical art'. When English texts were translated with a degree of respect, as in the case of Henry of Huntingdon's Latin translation of the *Brunanburh*, the translations still underscore the foreignness of the English language. Henry's verbatim translation gives the impression of transferring text into a more prestigious (or at least more universal) language, as his reference to the problems translating the 'foreign' figures indicates:

De cuius prelii magnitudine Anglici scriptores quasi carminis modo proloquentes, et extraneis tam uerbis quam figures usi translatione fida donandi sunt.[57]

[The English writers describe the magnitude of these deeds in a sort of song, using foreign words and figures of speech, which must be translated faithfully.]

Like the *Weallas*, or Welsh, before them, the English have become, quite literally, foreigners in their own land. Henry thereby (perhaps inadvertently) duplicates in text the same sort of marginalization upon the English – in the very act of celebrating their achievements – that they had previously inflicted upon the insular Britons. For Henry's twelfth-century audience, the 'magnitude' of the English language is evident only through the Latin translation, which supplants the English version even as it extols the greatness of the original. Although he never dubs the English language 'barbaric', his explicit identification of the language – and presumably of the people who produced it – as alien inevitably asserts the absolute difference and implicit inferiority of the English to the Latin-Norman culture.[58] Inevitably lost in the process of translating history was the English language itself, which ceased to be regarded as a worthy medium for conveying insular history, in spite of the prestige it enjoyed under Alfred and his successors as an apt language for both poetry and history. As a later instance of the stigmatization of English, the Norman historical poet Wace, in his *Roman de Rou*, marks the Anglo-Saxons' loss of rightful rule by an ingenious bestialization of the English language, depicting it as 'barking': 'Norman dient qu'Engleis abaient' (the Normans say the English bark).[59] Emblematically depriving the English of speech, Wace anticipates their exclusion from the political, cultural and linguistic order.[60]

However, Anglo-Norman adaptations of Bede worked both ways: using Bedan providentialism as a means of translating insular history, but at the same time translating sections of Bede, in particular his narrative of the Fall of the Britons, so that they resembled contemporary accounts of the Conquest. In expanding Bede's providential historiography to represent the Saxon and Norman conquests as mirror images, the role of the leader took on increasing importance. A major part of this revisionist process applied back to Bede was a reconception of the role of Vortigern, the British king who invites the Anglo-Saxons into Britain, along the lines of contemporary representations of the Anglo-Saxon king Harold. Little more than a name in Bede, Vortigern serves in many Anglo-Norman histories as the catalyst for the Saxon invasion, in the same way that Harold was said to have single-handedly instigated the Norman Conquest. Henry stresses the British king's innate 'wickedness', which culminates in his marriage to the pagan Hengist's daughter and incest with his own daughter; Henry adds that Vortigern was excommunicated by St Germanus and that he refused to hear the latter's ministry. William of Malmesbury, however, gives us the first characterization of Vortigern as:

> Erat eo tempore rex Britanniæ Wortigernus nomine, nec manu promptus nec consilio bonus, imo ad illecebras carnis pronus, omniumque fere vitiorum mancipium.[61]
>
> [a man calculated neither for the field nor the council, but wholly given up to the lusts of the flesh, the slave to every vice.]

The amplification of Vortigern's character in these early twelfth-century historical works may have developed from historical accounts of the Norman Conquest. Although Harold was never referred to as a 'slave of all vice', historical authors impute to him the sins of falseness, excessive pride and cruelty. Orderic consistently refers to Harold as 'Anglicus tirannus', and refers to his rule as having been illegitimately seized (*inuaserat*), following, apparently, the convention of Harold as illegitimate ruler because of his alleged oath to William. Henry describes Harold and his brother Tostig in like terms:

Tante namque sævitiæ fratres illi erant, quod cum alicujus nitidam villam conspicerent, dominatorem de nocte interfici juberunt totamque progeniem illius, possessionemque defuncti obtinenerent.[62]

[[S]uch was the cruelty [sævitiæ] of the brothers that when they saw a well-ordered farm, they ordered the owner to be killed in the night with his whole family, and took possession of the property of the deceased.]

William cites Harold's 'unbridled rashness' (*effrænata temeritas*) and 'impudence' (*impudentia*) as part of the reason for the English disaster at Hastings (III.240), suggesting his earlier characterization of the British forces that opposed Cerdic. Orderic adds the suspended and hence illegitimate English archbishop Stigand, but stresses the coronation as Harold's own machination:

Tunc Heraldus ipso tumulationis die dum plebs in exequiis dilecti regis adhuc maderet fletibus a solo Stigando archiepiscopo quem Romanus papa suspenderat a diuinis officiis pro quibusdam criminibus, sine communi consens aliorum præsulum et comitum procerumque consecratus, furtim præripuit diadematis et purpuræ decus.[63]

[On the very day of the funeral, when the people were bathed in tears for the loss of their beloved king, Harold caused himself to be crowned by the Archbishop Stigand alone, though the pope had suspended him from his function for certain crimes, without the concurrence of any other bishops and the earls and baron, and nobles, and so by stealth stole the glory of the diadem and royal purple.]

In delegitimizing Harold's rule, Orderic separates him from the English people, who bear less culpability in the ensuing conquest, suffering on the principle by which divine vengeance falls on the innocent as well as on the guilty. Further, in presenting Harold as a usurper, even in the eyes of the English populace, Orderic reifies the central tenet of Anglo-Norman law and history (culminating in the Domesday Book) that stresses direct succession from the sainted Edward to William. On the use of the term *tyrannus*, William of Newburgh points out that, after Hastings, William the Conqueror sought legitimate coronation because he abhorred the name *tyrannus*.[64] Although the visual image of Harold crowning himself appears to be a later development, based perhaps on the Merovingian custom of figurehead kings and powerful Mayors of the Palace (cf. Einhard's *Vita Karoli Magni*, c.820), it has its origins in earlier depictions of Vortigern's coronation. Although these are admittedly not close parallels, they do establish a general resemblance between Vortigern and Harold as depraved rulers presiding over the destruction of their own people. The motives of individual historians may differ: for Orderic, vilification of Harold allows for the exoneration of the rest of the English population, who become victims of, rather than co-conspirators in, Harold's treachery, but nevertheless suffer providentially ordained punishment along with him. As Marjorie Chibnall notes, Orderic's account shows a developing and 'hardening' of the legend of Harold as usurper.[65] If so, then cross-germination of the Harold and Vortigern legends, the latter drawn from Bede and Gildas, seems likely. For William of Malmesbury, Harold's rise to power seems symptomatic of the broader pattern of English degeneration preceding the Conquest. Whatever the historian's individual motives, however, the Haroldian narrative provides divine sanction for William's seizure of English power; indeed, Orderic overtly states that Harold's perjury is likely to ruin the chances of English success. The sanctification of Edward the Confessor, combined with these depictions of Harold, vindicates Norman claims of direct descent from Edward to William I. By heightening the resemblance of the Saxon to the Norman Conquest, these extrapolations from Bede reinforce the belief that history is both providential and cyclical: both the Saxon and Norman invasions are precipitated by a self-proclaimed ruler of dubious legitimacy; associations with the Vortigern legend provide a model for undermining the legitimacy of Harold. This rhetorical manoeuvre provides further legitimacy for the Normans by reconstituting the Conquest as an internal struggle between the legitimate and illegitimate rulers of the island. For the English, the tradition transfers at least some of the sins of the people into the body of a single ruler.

In the latter respect, we can see how the providentialist historiography of Bede provided a rhetorical linkage between the Saxon and Norman conquests. The differences between the narrative of the Saxon Conquest and of the Norman Conquest, however, argued against efforts that draw them as parallels. For one thing, it was impossible to see the long-Christianized Normans as the *tabulae rasa* for conversion, as were the Saxons before them. Nor could the English, with their longstanding literary and religious traditions, be easily tagged as 'barbarians'. Ethnographically, many of the second-generation Anglo-Norman historians, including Orderic Vitalis and Henry of Huntingdon, had mixed Norman and English heritage; therefore, the traditional 'us/other' 'civilized/ 'barbarian' distinctions characteristic of colonialist narratives could hardly apply to the complex cultural and linguistic situation of the late eleventh and early twelfth centuries. The hybridity of the historians themselves and of the texts they created reflected, as they recorded, the paradoxical nature of Anglo-Norman colonization. Moreover, William I was at pains to present himself as King of England and, hence, as king of the English with sanguinary rights to the throne, not as a foreign conqueror. Still, there was the undeniable fact of a ruling class of non-insular origin speaking a language not understood by most of the native population. The result in the histories is a much more complex reaction to outside invasion and occupation than is to be found in either Gildas or Bede. Thus, Henry can see the Normans as the fifth plague of Britain, but at the same time credit them for the revitalization of insular religious life. The aims of these historians were similarly complex: in grafting Anglo-Norman history onto English history, these writers served both sides: preserving the history of the Anglo-Saxons, while legitimizing the Norman ascendancy as the continuation of this historical tradition.

Anglo-Norman providential interpretations of insular history did not, however, overlook the reality of Norman oppression. Unlike Bede's depiction of the Angles, Anglo-Norman historians never accorded the conquerors the unambiguous status of *verus Israel*. They were, without a doubt, the instruments of divine justice, but were also themselves prone to oppression and corruption. Hanning and Stein both stress a dual view in William of Malmesbury's reading of 'the Normans as God's new Israel while seeing them simultaneously and unavoidably as imperial repressors of native English liberty'.[66] This ambiguity in William's reading of recent events underscores the uneasiness that existed between the actions of the conquerors and the way in which providential historiography expected them to be read. What was agreed upon, however, was that the pre-Conquest English had somehow brought their oppression upon themselves, either through apostasy or through their (perhaps coerced) obedience to an illegitimate ruler. This view of history provided divine legitimization for otherwise condemnable acts of conquest, as the Normans, like Attila or the idol-worshipping Babylonians under Nebuchadnezzar, became the divine 'scourges' for the apostate English and were given an opportunity to reconstruct their Church.

Variant historiographies: Geoffrey of Monmouth, Wace and Angevin historiography

Geoffrey of Monmouth's *Historia Regum Brittaniae* (*c.*1130) offers a serious challenge to the accepted genre of Anglo-Norman history. Translated, its author claims, from an unidentified (and probably fictional) source text in British (Welsh), its expressed subject is the Celtic Britons and their secular history. Coming sixty years after the Norman Conquest, Geoffrey's interest was not in the English people or in the justification of their downfall; as the title indicates, his concern was with *British* history, specifically, British secular history.[67] His use of Latin prose gives a sheen of historical legitimacy to his text, as does his occasional use of recognized historical authorities, such as Bede and Gildas. His motives remain somewhat unclear; he obviously wished to fill what he perceived as a gap in the historical record. He may also have wished to extend the history of the British Isles to remind the current Anglo-Norman dynasty that the land they occupied had a rich and venerable history. He may have even intended the text as a satire on the pretensions of monastic providential historians such as William, Henry and Orderic. Whatever his purpose, he redeemed the reputation of the Britons in the milieu of Anglo-Norman history. At the same time, however, he consigned the English to the margins of insular history in the process of bridging the gap between British and Norman history.

Generically, the *HRB* was presented, and apparently received, as history.[68] Clearly, the work resembles history in its use of Latin prose, and was considered as such, at least until the seventeenth century. However, it is equally clear that his work does not correspond to the prevailing historiographic trends of the period. In his own dedication, Geoffrey identifies his task as that of recording history, to fill in the vacuum left by Gildas and Bede:

> [. . .] quam de eis [G]ildas and [B]eda luculento tractatu fecerant nichil de regibus qui ante incarnationem [C]hristi auereant nichil etiam de Arturo ceterisque compluribus qui post incarnationem succerunt reperissem

> [among these Gildas and Bede made no mention of the kings who ruled before the incarnation of Christ in their brilliant treatises, nor anything of Arthur or of the many who succeeded him after the incarnation.][69]

In this regard, Geoffrey's approach to the gaps in the historical record does not differ dramatically from William of Malmesbury's, even though most historians see them as polar opposites.[70] Both writers sought to fill in sections of history where they felt a record was lacking, and both operated under a 'poetics' of history. It is important to note that William engages in the same sort of embellishment – including the addition of incidents and speeches – as Geoffrey does in his *HRB*. In this sense, Geoffrey's work is no more (or less) 'history' than that of his contemporaries. Whether Geoffrey's self-presentation as historian was ironic or not, his work was certainly *received* as a work of history.

Geoffrey's main difference from William is in his willingness to challenge indirectly Bede's authority in historical matters, and, more significantly, in his reduction of the notion of providence to one of many possible modes of interpretation. It is precisely in his seemingly poetic or fictional embellishments that Geoffrey poses his most serious challenge to the hitherto accepted Bedan historical conception of the downfall of the Britons as an act of divine retribution. Francis Ingledew comments on the secularization of the *Historia*: '[t]he Text [. . .] not of a non-Christian history, but of history constructed from another social starting point, that of the institutions of principality and aristocracy'.[71] Accordingly, Geoffrey's text drew considerable criticism from historical authors rooted in the Bedan Christian tradition, with the anti-Galfridian sentiment culminating in William of Newburgh's (in)famous condemnation of Geoffrey as a 'fabulator' and Giraldus Cambrensis' anecdote concerning demons alighting on Geoffrey's 'false' text.[72] Giraldus' anecdote concerns a Welshman named Meilyr, who could see demons alighting on the tongues of liars and on the pages of false texts, with many lighting on the *HRB*.[73] As recent criticism has noted, Geoffrey's *HRB* indeed proved to be the most controversial historical text of the period.

Although they represent a minority opinion among medieval English historians, these verbal attacks indicate the controversy stirred up by Geoffrey. Indeed, the *HRB* was innovative in a number of ways. First, it documented an entirely new segment of insular history – that of the British kingdom, from its semi-mythical foundations to the last British king, Cadwallader. It gave its twelfth-century audience an entirely new collection of characters, including King Arthur, and events to consider. Second, it pushed the date of the Fall of Britain into the end of the seventh century, radically destabilizing the periodization of insular history documented by Bede and accepted by Anglo-Norman historians, including William, Henry and Orderic. Third, and perhaps most profoundly, it offered an alternative to providential historiography in ways of reading historical events.

In the first respect, the new material Geoffrey offers forces a re-conception of who the early Britons were and what they contributed to insular history. He depicts them as neither spiritually nor militarily weak, as had Gildas and Bede. Instead, he presents them as a valiant race who establish a lengthy dominion over the island and who embrace Christianity early. Drawing on Welsh Latin annals, such as the *Hystoria Britonum* by 'Nennius',[74] Geoffrey provides the Britons with a foundational narrative linked to the legendary past of Troy through the figure of Brutus. He gives them a 'golden age' in the persona of King Arthur, and extends their struggle against the Saxon invaders for several generations there-after. He documents their fall, but includes with it a prophecy of their eventual return. Compared to other Anglo-Norman historians, Geoffrey had a demonstrable interest in the greatness of the Britons.[75] Geoffrey's purpose in this depiction is not certain, but he seems to see the ancient Britons as models for the current Anglo-Norman dynasty. In reconsidering the mytho-historical origins of the British nation from a British perspective, Geoffrey positioned himself as Aesop's lion, painting the picture of the duel between the lion and the gladiator.[76]

Geoffrey's second innovation regards the traditional periodization scheme of insular history. In developing an extensive dynastic history of the Britons, Geoffrey moved the conventional date for their fall from the early sixth to the late seventh century (corresponding, incidentally, with the life of the historical Bede). Obviously, this periodization would pose a problem for histories following the Bede-English tradition, in which the fall of the Britons is dated deliberately to correspond to the conversion of the English and to their assumption of the *verus Israel* mantle. The additional three hundred years of British history, which includes some conspicuous high moments, was to disrupt conventional twelfth-century understandings of the different phases of insular history. William Leckie observes that Geoffrey provided a viable alternative to the historical narrative that had placed the removal of the Britons from insular history at the turn of the seventh century:

> With the appearance of the *Historia*, writers in the twelfth century were brought face to face with a startling and very disquieting reality. The conventional periodization did not rest on a secure foundation. So long as only the pre-Galfridian data were available, Anglo-Saxon tradition seemed unshakable. Geoffrey's challenge, however, revealed hitherto unsuspected gaps and weaknesses.[77]

What Geoffrey provides, in other words, is an alternative to the fairly early removal of the Britons from insular history that occurs in Bede and in his Anglo-Norman redactors. This disruption of the conventional time-line prompted rethinking of the entire nature of insular history. In questioning the date of the transition of power, Geoffrey's *HRB* also calls into question the providential mode of interpreting history; after all, if the British loss of divine mandate no longer coincided with the conversion of their adversaries, was the concept of such a mandate reliable? An overview of the *HRB* reveals a vision of history where cultures and kingdoms rise and fall for reasons other than their sin or virtue. In the place of providence, Geoffrey offers the less comforting prospect of human control over history, as Hanning observes. Hanning situates Geoffrey in a milieu of the re-examination of divine providence in the twelfth century: 'It is readily apparent that a major change has taken place in the historical imagination of a writer who deliberately removes national history from its traditional context, the history of salvation.'[78] It is true that the Anglo-Norman historians re-examined the Christian providential model inherited from Bede, but Geoffrey is the first to challenge the entire notion of history as the unfolding of the divine will. In the *HRB*, for instance, the Roman, Pictish and Saxon invasions (three of Henry's five 'plagues') come about, not because of providential punishment for communal sin, but because of individual mistakes. The Romans under Caesar succeed because of Androgeus' internal feud with Cassivellaunus, and the Saxons gain a foothold in Britain because of Vortigern's ill-conceived political manoeuvring. In neither event does Geoffrey suggest that the Britons suffer divine punishment. In fact, both invasions in Geoffrey constitute only temporary setbacks from which the Britons quickly recover. Even when Geoffrey does evoke divine providence, as he does when the Scots, Picts and Scandinavians ravage Britain – 'O divinam ob præterita scelera ultionem' (Oh, the vengeance of God for past sins!) – he shifts the historiographic locus from the sins of the nation to the actions of an individual:

O tot bellicosorum militum per vesaniam Maximiani absentiam! Qui, si in tanta calimitate adessent, non supervenisset populus quem non in fugum pellerent![79]

[O that so many warlike soldiers were absent through the madness of Maximianus, who, were they here in such a calamity, no people could have assaulted them whom they would not have driven away in flight!]

This passage, along with Geoffrey's repeated reference to the British victims as the *plebs* (commoners), manifests his conviction that their defeat is not a punishment for their collective sinfulness, but the result of having the wrong societal stratum engaged in fighting. In other words, as Hanning suggests, the Britons suffer a military rather than a moral decline. This depiction, it almost goes without saying, challenges orthodox historiographic representations of the insular Britons as militarily and morally weak.[80]

Elsewhere, the providential model of Gildas and Bede appears, but as one interpretative voice among many, leaving open the meaning assigned to historical events. The exiled British king Cadwallo echoes traditional historiography in his indictment of the Britons as having brought divine judgement upon themselves, evoking the name of Gildas as a source, along with some of Gildas' accusations:

> [The Britons] exulterunt se ultra quam dignitas expectesat, et, ob affluentiam divitiarum affluentiam superbi, coeperunt tali et tantae fornicationi indulgere, qualis nec inter gentes audita est, ut Gildas historicus testatur, non solum hoc vitium, sed omnia quae humanae accidere solent, et perpetrarunt.[81]

> [They [the Britons] were made proud by the very vastness of their wealth. They began to indulge in sexual excesses such as had never been heard of among other peoples. As the historian Gildas tells us, they not only indulged in this vice but in all others which are the lot of human nature.]

Although such a reference appears to signal acceptance of providence as the guiding force in history, it is a speech by a single character (and one under psychological strain at that), so there is no reason to assume that the speaker reflects Geoffrey's thinking; if anything, the evocation of Gildas establishes rhetorical distance between speaker and author. In fact, these lines constitute only one of the myriad ways in which the fact of British exile may be interpreted. A few scenes earlier, Cadwallo's thane, Brian, had delivered a speech blaming the Saxons for British calamity; Geoffrey does not offer rhetorical preference for either interpretation of British history. Rather than supplying unqualified support for Gildan-Bedan providentialism, then, Brian's and Cadwallo's speeches subtly dramatize the imposition of variant historiographic systems on human events – in this instance, the fact of British defeat and exile. In supplanting the essentially ecclesiastical model of insular history inherited from Bede with a 'heroic' model (or aristocratic, to use Ingledew's term), Geoffrey implies that the individual is both agent and interpreter of history. Human error replaces divine providence as the controlling factor in history, and political unity becomes his dominant concern; Geoffrey ultimately suggests that people are responsible for their own history. As a means of legitimacy, history itself becomes absorbed into the power-plays of rulers and their conquests. It is in the process of systematization that Geoffrey offers perhaps his most profound challenge to the authority of Gildas and Bede; for if the recording of history is ultimately an act of human interpretation, and one subject to political or personal bias at that, then neither Gildas' nor Bede's, nor any other historiography, including his own, has any claim to absolute authenticity. Geoffrey thus implicitly questions not only the dominant historiographic mode of emplotment of his period, but the very idea that an abstract model can reliably explain human history.

Implicit in Geoffrey's conception of history – but explicit in Laȝamon's – is the prospect of history as translation, as a construct generated in the mind of the interpreter. As such, the *HRB* undercuts the a priori status of the providential model. Valerie Flint sees the text as a repudiation of the increasing self-assurance and self-importance of monastic historians. Flint, who characterizes Geoffrey as an expert littérateur, historiographer and parodist, summarizes what she sees as his purposes:

> If he displayed 'the literary gift of the historian', if, as we believe, he exaggerated certain trends in historical writing, it was to mock that literature and confound its authors. He meant to make telling points about the quality of the literature and to diminish the authority on which its exponents spoke. He meant, ultimately, to call into question the position held and hoped for in twelfth-century Anglo-Norman society by literate and celibate regular canons and monks.[82]

In other words, Geoffrey's methods, including his unique and probably fictional source text, ridicules the methodology of orthodox monastic historians.[83] Beyond ridicule or satire, however, lies a serious undermining of the entire concept of providential history.

For example, as part of his overall revision of providential historiography, Geoffrey presents the Roman occupation, which constitutes for Henry the first of the 'five plagues', as a site of resistance to colonialist aggression. Although Geoffrey does not deny the historical reality of Roman domination, he presents it as accomplished only through British treachery and maintained, sporadically, only with British cooperation – a revision of all traditional accounts. Geoffrey further breaks from the dominant line of historical narrative by setting rival historiographic traditions in dialogue with one another; as Flint and others have noted, Geoffrey includes a variety of historical accounts throughout his text and different means of interpreting them. The conflict between Roman and British visions of history is played out on the verbal plane before it occurs on the battlefield. Thus, in the section relating the Roman invasions, Geoffrey sets the traditional (Caesar–Gildas–Bede) depiction of the early Britons as militarily weak, not as the author's commentary, but as part of a speech by Geoffrey's Caesar:

> Sed, nisi fallor, valde a nobis degenerati sunt, nec quid militia noverunt [. . .] extra orbem commaneant. Leviter cogendi erunt nobis tributum nobis dare et obsequium Romanae dignitati prestare.[84]

> [But, unless I am mistaken, they have become very degenerate when compared with us, and they can know nothing about warfare [. . .] on the extremes of the globe. It would be a simple matter to force them to pay tribute and to swear obedience to the majesty of Rome.]

As the words of a single character, however, this speech carries no inherent claims to truth, and is in fact contradicted both by rhetorical response and by the events that follow; an equally plausible counter-response is forthcoming from the British king Cassivellaunus. The British ruler evokes a central trope of the British or 'Nennian' version of insular history – the common ancestry of both the British and Romans through Aeneas – and their reputation for patriotic defence of their homeland in his rebuke to Caesar:

> Opprobrium itaque tibi petiuisti cesar cum communis nobilitatis uena britonibus & romanis ab enea defluat & eiusdem cognationis una & eadem catena prefulgeat qua in firma amicitia coniungi deberent. Illa a nobis petenda esset non seruitus quia eam potius largiri didicimus quam seruitatis iugum deferre. Libertatem namque in tantum consueuimus habere quod prorsus ignoramus quid sit seruituti obedire. Quam si ipse dii conarentur nobis eripere elaboraremus utique omni nisu resistere ut eam retineremus. Liqueat igitur disposicioni tue cesar nos pro illa & pro regno nostro pugnaturos si ut comminatus es infra insulam brittiae superuenire inceperis.[85]

> [What you have sought from us, Caesar, is an insult to yourself, for a common inheritance of noble blood comes down from the Trojans to Briton and to Roman alike, and our two races should be joined in close amity by this link of glorious kinship. It is friendship which you should have asked of us, not

slavery. For our part we are more used to making allies than to enduring the yoke of bondage. We have become so accustomed to the concept of liberty that we are completely ignorant of what is meant by submitting to slavery. If the gods themselves try to take our freedom from us, we shall still do our utmost to resist them with all our strength in our effort to preserve that freedom. If you start attacking the island of Britain, as you have threatened, you must clearly understand, Caesar, that we shall fight for our liberty and for our kingdom.]

The British king's bold reply and consequent resolute resistance to the Romans directly refute not only Caesar's conception of the Britons, but also Gildas' assessment of them as 'nec in bello fortes sint nec in pace fideles' (neither brave in war nor faithful in peace).[86] Furthermore, Geoffrey directly cites classical sources in support of his characterization of the Britons. Lucan's notable line, 'Territa quesitis ostendit terga Britannis' (He [Julius Caesar] ran away in terror from the Britons he had sought) and Juvenal's 'Regem aliquem capies, aut de themone Britanno decidet Arviragus' (either you will capture a certain king, or Arviragus will tumble from his British chariot), are summarized in Geoffrey's *Historia* as part of his counter-discourse of British military competency.[87] Geoffrey's employment of these references at significant moments within the narrative not only establishes his personal erudition, but, more importantly, supports his variant historiography with recognized classical authority. In thus adhering to accepted standards of historical authority, Geoffrey poses what is perhaps his strongest challenge to the historiographic tradition of Gildas, Bede and the Anglo-Norman historians.

Geoffrey's historical revisions of British–Roman dealings, projected into subsequent passages, provide justification for later military action in his extended Arthuriad. His depiction of the British king Belinus' conquest of Rome – and his translation of the Gaulish warrior chieftain into a British king – serves to provide the legendary King Arthur with a warrant for resisting the Roman emperor's demand for tribute:

Nam si ideo quia iulius cesar ceterique romani reges britanniam olim subiugauerunt uectigal nunc debere sibi ex illa reddi decernit similiter ego ceseo quod roma tibi tributum dare debet quia antecessores mei eam antiquitus optinuerunt Belli etenim serenissimus ille rex britonum auxilio fratris sui usus brenni uidelicet ducis allobrogum suspensis in medio foro xx ex nobilioribus romanis urbem cepit captamque multis temporibus possedit. Constantinus etiam helene filius nec non & maximianus uterque mihi cognatione propinquus alter post alterum diademate britannie insignitus thronum romani imperii adeptus est. Censetis ne ergo uectigal ex romanis peterendumð.[88]

[If the Roman decrees that tribute ought to be paid to him by Britain simply because Julius Caesar conquered this country years ago, then I decree in the same way that Rome ought to give me tribute, in that my ancestors once captured that city. Belinus, that most glorious of the Kings of the Britons, with the help of his brother Brennius, the Duke of the Allobroges, hanged twenty of the noblest Romans in their own forum and, when they occupied the city, they held it for a long time. Similarly, Constantine, the son of Helen, and Maximianus, too, both of them close relations of mine, wearing the crown of Britain one after the other, each gained the throne of imperial Rome. Do you not agree, then, that it is we who should demand the tribute of Rome?]

Geoffrey's revised anti-Bedan history not only legitimizes Arthur's demand for Roman tribute, but also gives it precedence over the emperor's claim. Juxtaposed with hegemonic accounts of Roman, and later Saxon, conquest and colonization, Geoffrey's history problematizes the entire idea of historical precedence. By interweaving these historiographic conflicts with military conflicts, Geoffrey establishes a parallel between territorial conquest and temporal conquest, accomplished by gaining control of historiographic narrative. As long as the Britons remain active producers of history, they succeed in maintaining their cultural and national identity.

Geoffrey further tropes the rhetorical battle between historiographic traditions as an actual battle; the pugilistic duel between Geoffrey's Nennius and Caesar serves as an inventive analogue to the textual struggle between the Romanocentric version of insular history, transmitted through Gildas and Bede, and the British (Nennian) tradition inherited from 'Nennius', the reputed author of the *Hystoria Brutonum*. The sword of Caesar wounds Nennius as fatally as the pen of Caesar had ruined the Britons' reputation, prior to Geoffrey's rehabilitative text. Like his opponent Caesar, Geoffrey's Nennius combines a historiographic role with his military function. He recommends maintaining the British capital's original name, 'Trinovantum' or 'New Troy', to preserve evidence of the Britons' Trojan ancestry, just as the ninth-century Nennius had textually 'recovered' the Britons' descent from the Trojan Brutus:

De nomine quoque suo iussit eam dici karlud id est ciuitas lud. Vnde postea maxima contentio orta est inter ipsum & nennium fratrem suum qui grauiter ferebat illum uelle nomen troie in patrie sua delere. Quam contentionem quia gildas hystoricus satis prolixe tractauit eam preterire prelegi ne id quod tantus scriba tanto stilo parauit uidear uilliori dictamine maculare.[89]

[He [Lud] ordered it to be called Kaerlud, or Lud's City, from his own name. As a result a great quarrel arose later on between him and his brother Nennius, who was annoyed that he should want to do away with the name of Troy in his own country. Because Gildas the historian has recounted at great length this contention, I choose to omit it.]

The alteration of place-names signals a motif important to the *Historia* and to its French and English redactions, the association of land and people. Lud's egocentric renaming of the city effaces the association of the capital with its people, the Trojans, threatening their historiographic links with the classical past and finalizing their transformation from Trojans to Britons. The transformation (translation) of place-names both signals and finalizes the transformation of people and places with text, as the dissociation of Britons from their Trojan past is one of the factors on which Caesar has based his decision to invade and try to colonize Britain. Geoffrey's significant – if inaccurate – insertion of Gildas in this section (Gildas makes no mention of any such quarrel) further grounds his narrative in acknowledged insular history. Geoffrey's association of a 'Nennius' with the name-changing dramatizes resistance to the translation of land and history associated with conquest and colonization. Geoffrey in effect translates Gildas 'the Historian' into a supporting source for his non-Gildan history.

Despite Geoffrey's discernible departure from twelfth-century providential historiography, the overall effect of the *HRB* is to support the Norman ascendancy, and, specifically, to provide a pattern of unified rule for a leader – Stephen or the Empress Maude – who can maintain it. The *HRB* in effect makes the current regime the heirs to a venerable British historical tradition. Manipulating the historical account by 'Nennius' to undermine the primacy of Bedan historiography, Geoffrey provides the Norman nobility with an alternative to the providential pattern of inevitable national collapse. Geoffrey implicitly promises the mantle of Arthur to the Anglo-Norman ruler who can successfully reunite the kingdom, and not so implicitly warns of the dire consequences of national disunity. In both events, the issue is political rather than moral or religious. As with the Britons, Norman success is tied to their ability to assert unity over the island. Further, human control of the political sphere mirrors the human *authority* over the historical text. Hanning observes Geoffrey's emphasis on personal behaviour as a controlling factor in Geoffrey's vision of history.[90]

Lost in Geoffrey's historiography were the English and their role in insular history; Geoffrey makes them the villains of his narrative and reduces their dominion over the isle to two or three hundred years. He in fact questions the valour that Anglo-Norman historical texts assign to the early Saxons (and subsequently deny to their eleventh-century descendants). Rather than conquering the island, Geoffrey's Saxons gain control of it through subterfuge. In the post-Arthurian section of the *Historia*, Brian, nephew of Cadwallo, recites the history of Saxon misdeeds in Britain – many of these events verified by both Gildas and Bede – as sufficient reason for Cadwallo to nullify a treaty with the English king Edwin:

> Consueverunt namque proditionem semper facere, nec ulli fidem firmam tenere; unde a nobis opprimendos esse, non exaltandos censerem. Cum ipsos primo rex Vortegernus retinuit, sub umbra pacis remanserunt, quasi pro patria pugnaturi; sed cum nequitiam suam manifestare quiverunt, malum pro bono reddentes, prodiderunt eum populumque regni saeva clade affecerunt. Prodiderunt deinde Aurelium Ambrosium: cui post horribilia sacramenta, una cum eo convivantes, venenum potare dederunt. Prodiderunt quoque Arturum, quando cum Modredo nepote suo, postposito jure quo obligare fuerant, contra illum dimicaverunt.[91]

> [Trickery has always been second nature to them [the Saxons] and they have never kept faith with anyone. In my opinion, we should keep them under, instead of doing them honor. When King Vortigern first took them into his service, they made a show of remaining at peace with us, pretending that they would fight for our country. The moment they were in a position to reveal their wickedness and return evil for good, they betrayed him and the people of this kingdom with great savagery. After that they betrayed Aurelius Ambrosius, giving him poison to drink as he sat eating with them, and this after the most awe-inspiring oaths of fealty. Next, they betrayed Arthur, for they conveniently forgot the oath by which they were bound to him, and fought against him on the side of his nephew Modred.]

Because Edwin's ancestors had gained power through murder and treachery, Brian maintains, neither he nor any of the Anglo-Saxon race has any legitimate claim to insular rulership. Saxon poisoning and oath-breaking may well be intended to reflect the worst in Norman behaviour; their own historians document their tendency toward treachery and internal dispute.[92] In deploying the Saxons as a mirror of recognizably Norman vice, however, Geoffrey apparently provides rhetorical poles for Anglo-Norman rulers – Arthur versus the perfidious Saxons – and coincidentally discredits the English and their contributions to insular culture and history; Geoffrey effaces five hundred years of English dominion by establishing continuity between Britons and Normans. If, as Warren has argued, Geoffrey's use of Latin 'breaks down the discursive barriers between the Britons' past and present', we must note that the breaking of these 'barriers' involves the reduction of four hundred years of English rule.[93]

A subtext of Geoffrey's revisionist history, then, is that the Normans, in fulfilment of Merlin's prophecy, had in fact delivered Britain from its 'illegitimate' Saxon overlords. In making this statement, I do not argue that Geoffrey consciously sought to discredit any Anglo-Saxon claim to the English throne – a moot point by the twelfth century; neither do I suggest that he offered his text as a deliberate insult to those of Anglo-Saxon descent. However, promoting the Britons comes inevitably at the expense of the Anglo-Saxons, who, under Geoffrey's historiographic paradigm, lack a divine mandate for their dominion; hence, the ethnic and national implications of William of Newburgh's outburst against the historian who treated the 'noble' Angles as 'ministers and vassals' of the Britons.[94] As Geoffrey pushes the temporal boundary of British rule further into the future and magnifies the accomplishments of the Britons, the English diminish in comparison.

Although Geoffrey's narrative concludes long before any Normans arrive in England, the *HRB* indirectly participates in the historiographic denigration of Harold, through its depiction of the British ruler Vortigern's rise to and fall from power. Like Harold Godwinson, Vortigern is not the rightful heir to the British throne, but only a *dux* (duke), a magnate who assumes power after the death of the lawful king. When Geoffrey depicts Vortigern crowning himself, he echoes traditions surrounding Harold's 'illegitimate' coronation. The image of Harold's usurpation appears as early as 1070 in William of Jumièges, who asserts that Harold 'Cujus [Edward's] regnum Heroldus continuo invasit, ex fidelitate perjeratus, quam juraverat duci' (undertook to continue his [Edward's] reign breaking the faith he had promised to the duke).[95] Harold's seizure of the realm bears some similarity to Geoffrey's image of Vortigern's self-coronation:

At Vortigernus cum neminem sibi parem in regno conspexisset, capiti suo diadema regni imposuit, et coprincipes suos supergressus est.[96]

[As soon as Vortigern realized that there was now no one at all in the realm
who was his equal, he set the kingly crown upon his own head and assumed
power over his fellow princes.]

Geoffrey's depiction of Vortigern may, in fact, have influenced later
depictions of Harold's coronation; an illustration in the thirteenth-
century Anglo-Norman *Life of Edward the Confessor* shows Harold
actually placing the crown on his own head.[97] Geoffrey's distancing of
Vortigern from the Britons absolves them from guilt for their ensuing ill
fortune, as did Orderic's vilification of Harold.

Overall, the effect of Geoffrey's *HRB* is to present a history of the
Britons for the Norman ascendancy. Geoffrey's Arthur provides a model
of unity for Geoffrey's courtly audience, whereas rulers such as Vortigern
provide negative exemplars of divisiveness and self-interest. Grounded in
a mythologized past and conveyed through British success, British unity
provides a model for Norman behaviour. The prophetic passages –
including the expansive *Prophitae Merlini* – serve to link Anglo-Norman
to British history, making the Norman victors (of either faction in the
twelfth-century civil wars, apparently) responsible for the fulfilment of
British history. Rather than standing as the next phase in a cycle of sin-
and-purgation, the Norman conquerors have taken control of a venerable
historical continuum that will persevere as long as they are able to
maintain unity among themselves. If we accept Tatlock's assertion that
the *HRB* offers a rhetorical model for Anglo-Norman rulers, in the
person of King Arthur, we can see how Geoffrey grafts Anglo-Norman
history on to British, rather than English, history.[98]

Similarly, the Anglo-Norman historical poet Wace, La3amon's immediate
predecessor, presents a British history for a primarily Anglo-Norman
court. The *Roman de Brut*, offered to Henry II's French queen Eleanor,
furthers Geoffrey's thematic linkage between the Celtic Britons and the
Normans, at the expense of the English.[99] Wace incorporates Geoffrey's
narrative into his Anglo-Norman metrical history, the *Roman de Brut*
(1155), which forms a companion piece to his historical account of the
foundation of Normandy and of the Conquest, the *Roman de Rou*
(*c.*1160).[100] Combined, the two *Romans* form Wace's master narrative of
insular history – with English history elided between the two. When the
English appear in Wace's works, they are characterized by inherent
tendencies for treachery, expressed even more strongly than in the *HRB*.
For example, the innate and habitual perfidy of the English provides
impetus for William the Conqueror, evidenced by the speech Wace

assigns to William denouncing the St Brice's Day massacre of the English
Danes (1002):

> jo ne vinc mie solement
> por prendre ço que jo demant
> ne por aveir mon covenant,
> mais por vengier les felonies,
> les traïsons, les feiz menties
> qu li home de cest païs
> ont fait a nostre gent toz dis;
> mult ont fait mal a mes parenz
> mult en ont fait altres genz,
> par traïson font quantque il font,
> ja altrement mal ne feront.[101]

[But I say very truly, I do not fight for myself alone, to take what I seek, nor to
have my due, but to avenge the felonies, the acts of treason, the many crimes
that the people of this land have done to our people on many occasions.
They have done much evil to my relations and have done much to other
peoples, for they do all the treason they can and do no other than evil.]

The slaughter itself is not Wace's invention. According to the Laud
Chronicle (E), the attack came on St Brice's Day (13 November) 1002,
because the king (Æðelred) had been told that they wished to slay him
and his counsellors and usurp his kingdom.[102] Henry of Huntingdon
omits justification for the English in his account, calling the massacre
'treacherous' (*clandestine*) and 'a terrible outrage' (*scelere*).[103] Neither text,
however, mentions the murders occurring during an actual feast. On the
bare statement that the massacre was perpetrated during the Feast Day
of St Brice, Wace elaborates, 'ensemble od els mangié aveient / e en
dormant les ocieient' (ll. 7419–20)(a feast where they had eaten and
were killed in their sleep). Wace's addition of the meal itself doubles the
heinousness of the treachery, for an Anglo-Saxon feast was expected to
be a celebration of fellowship.

The present need to avenge the past felonies of the Saxons resonates in
the earlier *Roman de Brut*, which describes Arthur's pledge to avenge the
oath-breaking and the injuries the Saxons have inflicted on his ancestors:
'Je vengerai les felunies / E vengerie les feimenties. / E vengerai mes
anceisurs / E lur peines e lur dolurs' (I will avenge the felonies and
avenge the infamies, and avenge my ancestors, and their pains and
sadness).[104] The *Roman de Brut* thus provides a precedent for the *Roman
de Rou*'s William the Conqueror – an 'authentically historical' figure –

to characterize the English as hereditarily untrustworthy: 'faus furent e
faus seront' (false they were and false they will be), even though Wace is
later critical of Norman abuses in England.[105] The parallel between
Vortigern's and Harold's usurpations, suggested by Geoffrey, becomes
textually explicit in Wace's two Anglo-Norman poetic histories, each of
which includes seizure of the crown: 'Vortigern out les fermetez / E lé
chastels e les citez; / Rei se fist, mult fu orguillus' (Vortigern seized the
fortresses, the castles and the cities; he made himself king through his
great pride);[106] and 'Des que li reis Ewart fu morz, / Heraut, qui ert mananz
e forz, / se fist ennointre e coroner' (When the King Edward was dead,
Harold, who was wealthy and strong, had himself crowned and anointed).[107]
Through the paralleled reflexive phrases, Wace makes Harold's seizure
of the kingdom resemble that of the tyrant Vortigern, underscoring the
English monarch's alleged lack of legal sanction. The two romances
thus mark both the Anglo-Saxon ascendancy and fall with illegitimate
coronations, undercutting the legitimacy of the entire dynasty. Nonetheless,
neither of Wace's *Romans* iterate the role of providence in the events that
follow. Human machinations mark the fall of the Britons and of the English.

By problematizing the role of divine providence in the course of insular
history and by introducing the possibility of multiple readings of events,
Geoffrey and Wace provide precedents for later revisionist historians, who
either reject the notion of divine providence or refract it through multiple
interpretations. Other historians – both Geoffrey's contemporaries and
writers of the next generation – posited alternative interpretations of the
calamities of 1066. For example, John of Worcester's attribution (*c*.1150)
of the events of 1066 to naturalistic causes offers a sharp challenge to
providentialist histories. Although more of a chronicler, one who records
events on a year-by-year basis, than an 'historian' in the strictest sense
of the term, John – or Florence – offered an important source for other
historians, including Henry of Huntingdon and William of Malmesbury,
thus participating fully in broader cultural conversations on history and
historiography. As a Latin history, John's chronicle was free of the label
of 'barbarism' William attached to the *Anglo-Saxon Chronicle*. In translating the Anglo-Saxon prose into Latin, and hence enhancing the sense
of cause and effect, the causes he assigns for the English defeat are
strictly naturalistic – Harold's insufficient forces and the militarily
disadvantageous space the English occupy.[108] Like the Anglo-Saxon
historians, John makes no mention of Harold's oath to William, or even
of his journey to Normandy; as a result, the Conquest comes across as
another foreign raid, with no more divine mandate than the previous

Danish invasions. Further, although John almost certainly follows the Worcester-based D text of the *Anglo-Saxon Chronicle*, he makes no reference to English sins as the reason for their downfall, omitting even the D text's passing reference to 'sins of the nation'. John follows English vernacular sources in stressing Harold's nomination by the dying King Edward and his election by the English *witod*; both details are in contradiction to early Norman accounts of the succession, as well as to the later Anglo-Norman narratives of Orderic, William of Malmesbury, and Henry of Huntingdon.[109] John adds that Harold was crowned by Ealdred, rather than by the discredited Stigand, giving Harold a more legitimate claim than William, who acquired the realm by force. In this respect, John keeps the question of William's legitimacy open and invites doubt about the reliability of the providential model as a whole.[110]

As a case in point, the late twelfth-century author of the *Vita Haroldi* inverts the entire reading of the Conquest, transforming it into a sign of the beatification, rather than the condemnation of its titular hero. Borrowing from hagiographic traditions, this hermeneutic tour de force reinterprets the symbols associated with Harold's downfall as an un-mistakable sign of his divine election. Presenting the variant possibilities of interpreting signs (*signis*), the *Vita* presents two ways of reading a cross and crucifix that bowed to King Harold en route to Hastings:

> Hoc quoque tante pietatis opus quam dulce et propicium tunc pretentibus visum est omen portendisse tam nulli pretendisse dixerunt. Triumphanto namque in brevi post hec cum suis rege eropum: subjectionem Anglorum lamentabilemque depressionem regni inclinacionem istam presignassi plurimi estimabant.[111]

> [Although this sweet work of piety seemed to have portended a propitious and auspicious omen, yet some said it portended an unlucky event. A short time thereafter the king being defeated, many thought the inclining of the image prefigured the loss of the kingdom and the lamentable subjugation of the English.]

This passage indicates two possible readings of divine signs, calling into question the efficacy of the interpreter. The anonymous author, however, adds a third meaning, the life of penitence and sainthood that Harold is to ascend to; the text reminds its readers that God often grants prayers in ways other than those expected by the supplicants.[112] The potentially negative sign, the impending defeat of Harold and the English, becomes a positive prefiguration of Harold's life of sainthood. The signification system of hagiography, wherein bodily deprivation is evidence of divine favour (rather than retribution), thus counters the sin-and-purgation paradigm of providential history. Applied to insular history, the *Vita* suggests that the interpretation of historical signs depends upon the perspective of the interpreter and how they are read. Providence operates, but not always in easily interpretable ways. Far from being an example of the 'quietist literature of a defeated nation', as Holt terms it, then, the *Vita Haroldi* is from this perspective a direct affront to traditional readings of the Conquest as the transfer of *verus Israel* status from the English to the Normans.[113] By denying the Normans the body of the king, the text further denies completion of their conquest, a denial that ultimately calls into question the divine mandate for the entire enterprise.[114] What texts such as the *Vita* reveal is a changing understanding of how providence works in history and how historiographic signs may be interpreted.

William of Newburgh's description of the blood oozing from the floor of Battle Abbey shows a similar case of the free play of historiographic signs that occurred near the end of the twelfth century. William questions conventional providential readings of the events of 1066 by placing the sacred and secular interpretations of the abbey of Martin of Battle at odds, stating that the site signifies 'et ad homines æternus foret Normannicæ victoriæ titulus, et ad Deum propitiatio pro effusione tanti sanguinis Christiani' (to men an eternal monument of the name of the Norman victory and to God as a reminder of the effusion of so much Christian blood).[115] Through this dual reading, William, converts – or translates – a monument to Norman triumphalism into an emblem condemning the Christian-versus-Christian violence that enables Norman imperialism. William adds, moreover, that, after a rain shower, the floor of the abbey exudes blood, presenting a literal subtext lying beneath the abbey's architectural stratum:

> quod adhuc vox tanti sanguinis Christiani claret ad Deum de terra, quæ aperuit os suum et suscepti eundem sanguinem de manibus fratrem, id est, Christianorum.[116]
>
> [as if the voice of so much Christian gore still cries to the Lord from the ground, which has opened her mouth and drunk in that blood at the hands of their brothers, that is, of Christians.]

His evocation of implied fratricidal bloodshed links the Conquest with Cain's primal sin.[117] The narrative translates a sign of Norman triumphalism into a reminder of William the Conqueror's morally and theologically reprehensible attack on fellow Christians. William's passage further foregrounds the role of interpretation and translation in determining history; the edifice acquires a deeper exegetical meaning that subverts its intended triumphalist meaning. In the same way, the historical text may acquire additional interpretative possibilities outside the control of the historian. Although William does not dismiss providentialism, the possibility of different and conflicting interpretations of divine providence calls any singular historiographic paradigm into question.

The presence of variant historiographic traditions, each with its own interpretative matrix, problematized not only providential historiography, in its various Anglo-Norman manifestations, but also the possibility of a stable historiographic master-narrative. Historians became increasingly aware of the possibility of multiple ways of interpreting historical events. This destabilization, although disturbing, left history open for alternate voices. As a product of a Latin-reading minority, however, these texts left the vernacular-speaking majority – the ethnic English – out of the community of readers of history. In translating history into the language of the educated, Geoffrey translates the people out of participation in history. Wace's French likewise removes insular history from the understanding of the common people.

Laȝamon and providential historiography

In contrast, Laȝamon, a self-consciously English historian-translator-poet, does more than simply undermine the providential model. His choice of English restores history to the vernacular audience. Laȝamon's 'radical vernacularity' (using Otter's term) allows a history which the majority of the population could understand, and hence one in which they could participate.[118] In the first post-Conquest historical text in English, Laȝamon follows Geoffrey, Wace and other variant historians of the twelfth century in presenting a vision of history controlled by (often subtle) human machinations in the place of providential dictates. Although Geoffrey's master narrative would appear to denigrate the English people – to the point where some readers have accused Laȝamon of ethnic treachery – the paradigm's challenge to providential historiography seems to have served Laȝamon as a way to expose the workings of providential historiography.[119] Lesley Johnson has observed, 'Laȝamon does not present a narrative history in which the rise and demise of a political community are necessarily to be understood as the result of a divine judgement on the sins of a people'.[120] As a priest, La3amon would in no way question the idea that God controls worldly affairs. However, as a poet, he offers a strong challenge to Anglo-Norman providential historiography.

La3amon often seems to set up his readers deliberately for providential narrative, only to thwart these expectations, confronting providence more directly than does either Geoffrey or Wace. Thus, La3amon's positive assessment – not found in Wace – of the British ruler Cadwalader, 'hi leoden hine luueden / he wes swiðe god cniht and swiðe sturne inne fiht' (ll. 15868–9) (beloved of his people; a good knight, very stern in fight) is followed, not by the successful reign a reader might expect, given the foregoing description, but by devastating famines and a plague, presaging the Britons' loss of sovereignty over the island. By inserting praise for Cadwalader, La3amon enhances the tensions between the British expectations of a successful and prosperous reign (as the providential model would dictate) and the undeniable actuality of their impending fall. Conversely, the bellicose knights of an early king, Ebrauc, are said to earn God's anger for their love of war:

> Cnihtes he hæfde gode, stronge and wode,
> heo wilneden after wore for heom wes heora drihten wroð
> þe king hit wel iwurðe ah his hit suggen ne durste. (ll. 1313–15)

[He had good knights, strong and wild; they lusted after war, for that was their lord angry. The king knew this well although he dared not mention it.][121]

The element of divine displeasure, La3amon's invention, invites expectations of a providentially ordained punishment, yet none is forthcoming. A more expansive challenge to providence occurs in La3amon's narrative when Arthur's nephew and immediate successor, Constantine, twice violates holy sanctuary by killing the sons of Modred (one in a monastery and one in a church), defiling an altar with blood in an act unmistakably reflective of the murder of Thomas à Becket for informed members of La3amon's audience (though obviously not for that of Geoffrey or Wace). Originating in Gildas' *De Excidio*, in a section known commonly as the 'Complaint to the Five Tyrants' – in which a 'Constantine' is condemned for slaying two 'royal youths' ('regiorum tenerrima puerrorum') before an altar – the scene is expanded by Geoffrey, who invents the victims' affiliation with Modred, as well as Constantine's with Arthur. Even Geoffrey, critical though he is of providential historiography, attributes Constantine's death to divine judgement, probably because of the severity of violating holy sanctuary: 'Ex in quarto anno sentencia dei percussus iuxta utherpendragon infra lapidum structuram sepultus fuit' (Four years afterwards, struck by the judgement of God, he was buried beneath the stone structure [Stonehenge] next to Uther Pendragon).[122] Geoffrey's additions to the Gildan narrative complicate the morality of the scene, making it a case of a ruler doing the right thing in the wrong way. Wace is somewhat sceptical about the immorality of the action, but still raises the question of Constantine's sinfulness to his readers, asking them to 'Gardez s'il fist pechié e mal' (l. 13320) (Consider if this was sinful and evil). Wace then notes, without comment, that Constantine was killed after reigning for three years.[123] Laȝamon, however, omits all reference to sin or to divine judgement, even as he more sharply dramatizes the violation of holy sanctuary:

> Constantin braid ut his sweorde and þat hafde him ofswipte
> þat seint Anfibales weofd iwrað þerof a blode. (ll. 13246–7)

[Constantin drew out his sword and struck off his [Meleu's] head, so that Saint Anfibal's altar was covered in blood.]

Laȝamon intensifies the tension between providential expectations and the events that follow; the defilement of the altar is his addition. Nonetheless, rather than the expected providential judgement, Laȝamon presents a prolonged narrative of Constantine's rule, giving the ruler a successful, if brief, reign (not in Wace or Geoffrey), worthy of a nephew of Arthur:

> ðeo wes Constantin king here of þessere kinerice;
> þa begunnen blissen in Brutene to wunien.
> Her wæs grið, her was frið, and freoȝ laȝen mid folke,
> And ful wel heolden þa ilke laȝen þat stoden on Arðures daȝen.
>
> (ll. 14349–51)

[Then Constantin was king here in this kingdom; then bliss began to dwell in Britain. Here was peace and prosperity and free laws among the people, and they held well the laws that stood in Arthur's day.]

When Constantine is killed, it is by a decidedly earthly *feond* (l. 14354), his treacherous nephew Conan, rather than by divine judgement. Laȝamon's moralizing on the event is directed against the regicide, rather than against the ruler; the consequences to the land itself outweigh abstract theological concerns, such as divine sanctuary. One might conclude that the king's death was the result of divine judgement, but it would be the reader's and not La3amon's interpretation. By setting up and subsequently thwarting expectations of providential judgement, La3amon implies that human history works by means often beyond human understanding. He also implies that the literal presence, or *sign*, of divine sanctuary has no legitimacy when sought for immoral political purposes.

La3amon's apparently deliberate subversion of providential expectations finally invites the question as to whether the Britons – and, by extrapolation, the English – have lost sovereignty as a result of divine judgement for their sins. Of course, it may be objected that they are indeed divinely punished with loss of sovereignty, just as Cadwaladur's virtue is ultimately rewarded with a sort of sainthood. To reach such a conclusion, however, would demand that the reader of or listener to La3amon supply an interpretative matrix of sin-and-purgation not forthcoming in the text. Indeed, according to Elizabeth Bryan, glossators of the Otho manuscript did just that:

> As manuscript schematics that might cue the reader not just to store the names in memory but also to start the recollective process of intertextual sorting, the genealogies of La3-*Brut*-Otho could indeed invoke the 'meditational' process of analogizing 'our people' (or 'those British people') to 'the Chosen People' – the basic mechanism of the eschatological patterning of providential history.[124]

If providential historiography can be applied to the *Brut*, the model would have to be considerably more complex than the interpretative patterns provided by the bulk of Anglo-Latin historical texts, as the need for interlinear glossings seems to affirm. Such comments would not be needed to make the histories by Bede, William of Malmesbury or Henry of Huntingdon conform to the paradigm of providential history. Therefore, although La3amon maintains the general idea of divine guidance of worldly affairs, he presents the ways in which this guidance functions in the *Brut*'s historiography as being indeterminate. In so doing, La3amon can be seen to reject the popular motif of divinely inspired rise-and-fall cycles in favour of a more Augustinian view, that the working of divine providence in human history is inscrutable, unpredictable and ultimately unrepresentable in historical writings: 'And if you should ask why this permission was granted, indeed it is a deep *providence* of the Creator and Governor of this world; and unsearchable are His judgements, and His ways past finding out.'[125]

In his own challenge to Anglo-Norman providentialism, Laȝamon further questions whether the cultural eradication imposed by this model was either complete or irreversible. In contrast, Wace dismisses the Britons from the scene of insular history entirely:

> Unc puis ne furent del poeir
> Qu'il peüssent Logres aveir;
> Tuit sunt mué e tuit changié,
> Tuit sunt divers e forslingié
> De noblesce, d'onor, de murs
> E de la vie as anceisurs. (ll. 14849–54)

[They have never regained their power, those who once ruled Logres; all has moved and all has changed, all is different and altered of the nobility, the honour, the customs and the lives of their ancestors.]

Henry of Huntingdon similarly – and erroneously – affirms that the Saxons 'completely subjugated and occupied the country'.[126] He assigns a like fate to the post-Conquest Saxons:

> Declaratem quidem constat, quomodo Dominus salutem et horem genti Anglorum pro meritis absulerit, et jam populum non esse jusserit.[127]

[It has already been made clear how the Lord deservedly took from the English race their safety and honour, so they no longer exist as a people.]

Unlike earlier texts that dominate the landscape of early Anglo-Latin history, however, Laȝamon questions the historian's confidence in the supposed extinction of the Britons by citing evidence of their perdurable survival. From the onset, Laȝamon's depiction of the Britons or Welsh does appear to join contemporary historical authors in dismissing them from continuing participation in history: 'þat neofer seoðöen heo ne arisen: ne her ræden funden' (l. 993) (never afterward could they rise up, nor find counsel). Wace offers no parallel for this statement. Near the text's conclusion, however, British/Welsh perseverance intrudes to modify, if not flatly contradict, these conclusions:

> Þes Bruttes on ælc ende: foren to Walisce londe. / and heore laȝen leofeden: and heore leodene þæuwen. / and ȝet wunie[ð] þære: swa heo doð auere mære. (ll. 16088–90)

[These Britons, from either end [of the isle] went to Wales-land and lived according to their laws and the customs of their people, and yet live there, as they [shall] do for evermore.]

La3amon's Britons are brought 'lower' (*neoðer*, l. 932), with the comparative indicating not the complete and irreversible destruction reported in
Wace and Henry, but, rather, reduction to a lower position in a changeable
hierarchical structure – '[v]nder fote', according to Otho, again suggesting
political reduction, not eradication. It is worth noting further that the
Britons' permanent occupancy of Wales that La3amon describes does not
necessarily mean confinement to Wales. Thus, although he conserves the
account of the Britons' defeat and their exile into Wales, La3amon, unlike
his textual predecessors, acknowledges the British remnant preserved in
the historio-political reality of Welsh sovereignty. Anglo-Latin historians
frequently overlooked this detail, except when Welsh military success compelled them to acknowledge it. Ethnic purgation, (or renewal – *neïee*, l. 1169),
with its implications of providential agency operating in either outcome,
becomes in the English *Brut* more a matter of temporal political control
than of complete erasure. La3amon thus resists imposing closure on ethnic
or national groups and their participation in history, as other historians
had attempted to do. In this regard, we have the suggestion that the
suppression of the English need not be a permanent state of affairs.

Furthermore, the possibility of such complete closure in the *Brut* is
internally contradicted by the prospect that, at some point in the future,
the Britons may regain their sovereignty when the prophecies of Merlin
have been fulfilled: 'þenne sculle Bruttes anan balde iwurðen: / al þat
heo beginne to done iwurðeð after heore wille' (ll. 16026–7) (then shall
Britons soon grow bold; all that they begin will be accomplished as they
desire). Stein argues that this passage imposes closure on British sovereignty
by postponing their return to a remote, and hence unattainable, future:

> But the time of the British resurgence is a finality out of history, 'Never-
> more', doubly reiterated, is unconditional; the time to come is not like any
> other: golden age motifs cluster (fruits, fine weather, abundance, and the
> satisfaction of desire), and the body of Cadwathlader is translated from
> Rome into a redeemed 'Brutlonde', that he himself redeems. Its effect is
> paradoxically to leave history for the English.[128]

Although the return of the Britons is postponed indefinitely, it is
important to note that it remains in the offing, and in this respect,
La3amon in fact resists imposing closure on British history. One could
also object that the second 'nevermore' Stein identifies – 'næuere seoððen
mære' (l. 16093) – is more accurately translated as 'never since', meaning
only that they have not *yet* regained their sovereignty, not that they never

will. There is another way of looking at the Britons' exclusion from history: while history has here undoubtedly passed to the English, as Stein argues, the Britons' position outside of history places them beyond the reach of its interpretative framework; their survival can be neither explained nor ignored by providentialist historiography. Further, they continue to harass the 'inheritors' of the island and of its history through raids and irruptions Laȝamon may well have witnessed.[127] The bodies of Cadwalader, kept out of English hands in Rome, and of Arthur, kept even from confirmable death, become emblems for the lack of completion and finality to the English takeover: Welsh customs and, more importantly, their language, survive. By implication, Laȝamon suggests that the English, although deprived of effective geographic control, may remain intact as a people. This survival may well provide a model of English resistance – cultural and linguistic, if not military – for Laȝamon, a move in which his English *Brut* can participate.

Thus, while the Britons have obviously suffered a military defeat, their absolute and divinely appointed extinction is a construed master-narrative of their conquerors. The Welsh, the twelfth-century descendants of the ancient Britons, by no means remained silent on this point, as their prolific Arthurian narratives indicate. Curiously, the Welsh language stands as the only one of the four extant in England at the time of Laȝamon's writing of the *Brut* to remain unrepresented in the work's prologue, and, indeed, the Welsh and their linguistic idiom may well have been a source of anxiety for Laȝamon, as the one local language he never mastered. The British language and customs, however, provide a model of cultural and linguistic resistance for Laȝamon. The attempted processes of cultural eradication need not succeed, if the English, like the Britons, take care to preserve their own cultural heritage. Since the more recent English defeat has not necessarily been dictated by divine providence, it may be resisted. By thus problematizing the utter annihilation imposed on cultures by the providential model of historiography, Laȝamon keeps open the possibility that the English might reassert control over their own history, while issuing a warning of the consequences of neglecting their historical tradition.

Notes

1   The historian Robert W. Hanning has traced the development of providential history from its Roman origins through the twelfth century. Hanning finds that the Roman Empire became the recipient of this covenant as the new Christian *verus Israel*, following the conversion of the Emperor Constantine in the third century AD. Eusebius' fourth-century *Ecclesiastical History* fixes the Roman Empire as the locus for the divine mantle. Although Augustine of Hippo refuted the Eusebian formula for providence by situating the divine covenant strictly within the *civitate dei* and outside any secular institution his pupil Orosius wrote a later history of Rome to refute pagan accusations that abandonment of traditional religious rites had brought destruction upon the Empire. In Orosius' historical vision, as Hanning states, 'the role of Rome in the divine scheme is that of a chosen nation progressing toward Christ, and finally enjoying triumphant union with the Church' (Hanning, *The Vision of History in Early Britain* (New York, 1966), p. 38). Hanning further observes: 'the Roman Empire of which Constantine is head becomes the definitive force of providence in history' (ibid., pp. 29–30). 'Everyone', Orosius informs his readers in the first book, 'who sees mankind reflected through himself and in himself perceives that this world has been disciplined since the creation of man by alternating periods of good and bad times' (*History Against the Pagans*, p. 33, I. 1). In this way, a modified Old Testament conception of divine providence became ensconced in early Christian historiography. Historians throughout Europe thus had a model for interpreting recent events and records of the remote past.

2   A Boethian view of history differed essentially in the existence of random Fortune, who rewards and afflicts individuals and communities regardless of their merit (*Consolotio de Philosophie*, Book II). See Alaistair Minnis, *Chaucer's Boece and the Medieval Tradition of Boethius* (Cambridge, 1993); and Seth Lerer, *Boethius and Dialogue: Literary Method in* The Consolation of Philosophy (Princeton, 1985).

3   Spiegel, *Romancing the Past*, p. 2.

4   See Partner, *Serious Entertainments*, ch. 4.

5   White, *Metahistory*, pp. 7–11. Joachim Knape argues further that 'In historiography we are dealing with the semiotical representation of the past. All that has passed is only palpable as a sign. We reconstruct complex structures of the past firstly by drawing conclusions from reduced traces, and secondly by creating new texts that generate a virtual reality in our minds' ('Historiography as rhetoric', in Erik Kooper (ed.), *The Medieval Chronicle II* (Amsterdam, 2002), pp. 117–29 (p. 118).

6   '[T]he historian', according to Morse, 'would try to understand what events had encouraged poets to create a symbol. It is a process akin to translation' (*Truth and Convention*, p. 102).

7   Colgrave and Mynors note that 'So deeply are we indebted to Bede for our knowledge of the history of England before the eighth century that it comes

as something of a shock to us to realize that if Bede had not written, the names of Chad and Cedd, Hild and Æthelfryþ, Edwin and Oswald, Cædmon and Benedict Biscop would either be completely unknown or names known only to scholars, around which to spin cobwebs of conjecture; and our knowledge of the greatest of his themes, St. Augustine's mission and the conversion of the English, would be fragmentary'; 'Preface' to *Historia Ecclesiastica*, p. xviii.

[8] Hanning attributes Bede's historiography to Gildas, arguing that Bede inherits from his British precursor not merely details about the Britons, but 'an historical system of specifically Christian character' (*Vision of History*, p. 70). Hanning further observes, 'By accepting Gildas's testimony on the sinfulness of the Britons he [Bede] made possible a depiction of the Saxons not simply as virtuous heathens [. . .] but, from his eighth-century vantage point, as the new Israel, chosen by God to replace the sin-stained Britons in the promised land of Britain' (ibid., p. 70). Hanning does not always observe Bede's use of amplification and how it transforms the basic providential model of Gildas. Nicholas Howe notes that Gildas' use of the phrase 'endows his narrative with biblical authority' (*Migration and Mythmaking in Anglo-Saxon England* (Notre Dame, 1989), p. 45).

[9] Bede, *Historia Ecclesiastica*, p. 14; Gildas, *De Excidio*, 21. 3, p. 96.

[10] Gildas, *De Excidio*, 20. 3, p. 95.

[11] Bede, *Historia*, 1. 14., pp. 54–5.

[12] Gildas, *De Excidio*, 24. 2, p. 97.

[13] Hanning, *Vision of History*, p. 72.

[14] 'In turning to Gildas for information on the history of Britain before and during the Saxon conquest, Bede obtained not simply an historical account, but, as we have seen, an historical system of specifically Christian character' (Hanning, *Vision of History*, p. 70).

[15] Bede, *Historia*, 1. 15, pp. 56–7.

[16] Gildas, *De Excidio*, 23. 2, p. 96.

[17] Ibid, 30. 3, p. 100.

[18] I quote from *the Old English Version of Bede's* Ecclesiastical History of the English People, ed. Thomas Miller (London, 1890, 1898).

[19] '[N]eque suscipere dogma perversum gratiam Christi blasphemando ullatenus vellent, neque versutiam nefariae persuasionis reutare verbis certando' (neither willing to receive the perverse doctrine by blaspheming the grace of Christ, nor able to refute resolutely their evil persuasions) (Bede, *Historia*, I. 17, pp. 54–5).

[20] Howe, *Migration and Mythmaking*, p. 120

[21] Hanning notes the significance of the Augustine episode to providential historiography and to Bede's narrative of the transition from British to English dominion: 'The fulfillment of Augustine's prophecy proves that God acts in history, and the British disaster at Chester prefigures the disaster of the wicked soul in passing to its final, eternal desert' (*Vision of History*, p. 81).

[22] As Hanning observes, 'It is clear, therefore, that Germanus, a missionary from beyond the sea, is helping the Britons in a way superior to the efforts of the military hero Ambrosius, himself a Roman. Bede puts Germanus' deeds

last in order of events, since his mission to the Britons makes the sharpest possible contrast to the refusal of the Britons to evangelize the Saxons' (*Vision of History*, p. 78).

23 'Interea Brittania cessatum quidem est parumper ab externis, sed non a civilibus bellis. Manebant exterminia civitatum ab hoste dirutatum ac desertarum, pugnabant contra invicem qui ostem eveaserant cives' (In the meantime foreign wars ceased in Britain, but not civil wars. The ruins of the cities that the enemies had destroyed remained deserted and the citizens who had escaped the enemies fought among themselves) (Bede, *Historia*, I. 27, p. 98).

24 Ibid., I. 27, p. 100 (italics mine).

25 Gildas, *De Excidio*, p. 98, 26. 1.

26 Indeed, Bede was apparently so convincing that Hanning concludes that 'Gildas would surely have decided that this *praesens Israel*, which worked in close cooperation with the bishop of Rome and received from Rome many excellent prelates, indeed loved God' (*Vision of History*, pp. 63–4). Given the ethnic themes underlying both Gildas and Bede, one has to wonder if Hanning's conclusion is overly optimistic.

27 According to Biddick, this sort of performance occurs at points of contact in the *Historia* between Latin and Old English – she cites the Caedmon narrative and the text of Caedmon's Hymn – in which a trace of Bede's Englishness emerges in the Latin narrative. In seeing the 'angel' that visits Caedmon as a surrogate for Bede, Biddick calls attention to Bede's personal dilemma in the role of Latinate clergyman and native Englishman ('Bede's blush', p. 32). Biddick further sees that the Caedmon narrative, from its marginal position and in its role as restructuring Old English reality, 'figures uncannily in the conditions of the contemporary cultural construct of the Middle Ages, which we have repeated and reinscribed in textual editions' (ibid., p. 32).

28 I quote from Dorothy Whitelock's edition of the *Sermo Lupi ad Anglos* (London, 1963), p. 41.

29 Howe, *Migration and mythmaking*, p. 12. Howe further observes: 'The infusion of history into this [Wulfstan's] deeply eschatological work has provoked remarkably little discussion [. . .]. The parallel throws his eschatology into doubt, for if the crisis of 1014 has a precedent in the history of the island, then one cannot be certain it truly portends the coming of the Antichrist' (ibid., p. 9).

30 Wulfstan, *Sermo*, ll. 150–3.

31 See C. Warren Hollister, *The Impact of the Norman Conquest* (New York, 1969).

32 Stein, 'Making history English', p. 97. Stein elaborates: 'In the writing of history in the twelfth century, the Norman conquest of the English marks a crisis of cultural identity, of the principles of legitimate sovereignty, and of historical explanation' (p. 97).

33 Hanning, *Vision of History*, p. 126.

34 Guy of Amiens, *Carmen de Hastingae*, ed. and trans. Catherine Morton and Hope Muntz (Oxford, 1996), p. 10; ll. 137–40.

35 Orderic Vitalis, *Ecclesiastical History*, ed. Marjorie Chibnall (Oxford, 1980), III. 144, p. 168; III. 150, 176.

36 'disponente Deo'; ibid., III. 156, p. 182.

37 Only the 'D' text makes this interpretation of the events of Hastings, and it is the only text of the *Chronicle* to read the misfortunes of the English as providentially ordained. Nonetheless, 'D', along with 'E', maintain Harold Godwinson's legitimacy, including in their panagyric to Edward the statement that Harold had been duly elected. None of the *Chronicle* texts mentions Harold's oath to William (The *Anglo-Saxon Chronicle*, D text, p. 336).

38 Biddick, 'Bede's blush', p. 31.

39 White refers to these rules as the 'formal, explicit, or discursive' argument of history: 'Such an argument provides an explanation of what happens in the story by invoking principles of combination which serve as putative laws of historical explanation' (*Metahistory*, p. 11).

40 Henry of Huntingdon, *Historia Anglorum*, I. 4, pp. 14–15.

41 Partner, *Serious Entertainments*, p. 120.

42 *Historia Anglorum*, 7. 1, p. 214.

43 André Lefevre, 'Composing the other', in Susan Bassnett and Harish Trivedi (eds), *Post-Colonial Translation: Theory and Practice* (New York, 1999), pp. 75–94).

44 *Anglo-Saxon Chronicle*, D text, p. 26. All versions of the *Chronicle* concur.

45 Henry of Huntingdon, *Historia Anglorum*, ii. 14, pp. 96–7 (cited in chapter 1).

46 William of Malmesbury, *Gesta*, l. 16.

47 Stein, 'Making history English', p. 98. Stein is accurate, but this reduction has its precedence in tenth-century Anglo-Saxon England, when a notion of the *English* as a single entity proved crucial to maintaining the West Saxon power-base of Alfred and his descendants.

48 'First of all, as Christians, they feel that the phenomenal rise to splendor of the Normans, and especially of William, is a clear indication of God's providence. In keeping with this judgement, they attempt to explain the Norman Conquest in terms reminiscent of those used by Gildas to interpret the ruin of Britain, i.e., as the work of God operating figurally in history to punish sinful men and nations' (Hanning, *Vision of History*, p. 128).

49 '[R]eligionis Normam, usquequaque in Angliæ emortuam, advenit suo suscitarunt' (William of Malmesbury, *Gesta Regum Anglorum*, III, p. 246) (Under the Normans, religion, grown lifeless everywhere in England, began to revive).

50 '. . . religiosis viris bonisque rectoribus est' (Orderic, *Ecclesiastical History*, I. 24, p. 153) (under the direction of religious men and good rulers).

51 William of Malmesbury, *Gesta*, III, p. 245.

52 Ibid., III, p. 245.

53 Ibid., I.c, p. 6. Guy of Amiens's characterization of the English as *Nescia gens belli* (race ignorant of war), because of their preference for foot over mounted combat, echoes depictions of the early Britons. He reinforces this connection through references to the hair of the English – 'Est sibi milicies unctis depexa capillis, / Feminei iuuenes, Martis in arte pigri' (Guy of Amiens, *Carmen de Hastingae*, eds Catherine Morton and Hope Muntz (Oxford, 1972), p. 22, ll. 325–6) (He has champions with combed anointed hair, effeminate young men sluggish in the art of war).

[54] Ibid., p. 4, ll. 32–3.

[55] William of Malmesbury, *Historia Rex Anglorum*, III, p. 239.

[56] Giraldus Cambrensis, *Topographia Hibernica*, 10. 3. Giraldus continues, '[E]t omnes eorum mores barbarissimi sunt. Sed cum a convictu mores formentur, quoniam a communi terrarum orbe in his extremitatibus, tanquam in orbe quodam altero, sunt tam remoti, et a modestis et morgeratis populis tam segregati, solam nimirum barbariem in qua et nati sunt et nutriti sapiunt et assuescunt, et tanquam alteram naturam amplectantur' (and all of their habits are most barbaric. But habits are formed from association, seeing that this nation is in the extremities of the globe, as if in another world, so remote, and so segregated from modest and cultivated nations, that they may truly learn and embrace only barbarism, to which they are born, nursed, and which they learn and embrace, and which is embraced as if it were another nature).

[57] Henry of Huntingdon, *Historia Anglorum*, p. 310, v. 19 (italics mine).

[58] As Bassnett and Trivedi observe, concerning English translation of Hindi, Sanskrit and Persian texts, 'but when we start to examine the premises upon which their translation practice was based, what emerges is that they clearly saw themselves as belonging to a superior cultural system. Translation was a means both of containing the artistic achievements of writers in other languages and of asserting the supremacy of the dominant, European culture' ('Introduction', *Postcolonial Theory and Practice*, p. 6).

[59] Wace, *Le Roman de Rou*, l. 8068.

[60] In the *Life of St Guðlac*, for instance, Guðlac, living beyond the confines of English law, hears 'devils' speaking Welsh.

[61] Henry of Huntingdon, *Historia Anglorum*, I. 4, p. 7.

[62] Ibid., 6. 25 (Stevenson, p. 207).

[63] Orderic, 3. 118.

[64] William of Newburgh, *Historia*, 11.

[65] Orderic, *Ecclesiastica History 3*, p. 138.

[66] Stein, 'Making history English', p. 98. Hanning adds that '[f]or one point of view, then, the Normans are God's chosen people – the latest heirs of Israel, and the successors in national-ecclesiastical history of Gregory's Franks, Paul's Langobards, and Bede's Saxons. But this is only one side of the story. From another point of view, one provided by classical liberty and rhetoric, the Normans are imperial repressors of English liberty. The juxtaposition of this theme to the first creates a tension within the historiography of the Anglo-Norman historians, and reflects the coexistence in the minds of the writers of two mutually distinct views of the past, the legacies of two different moral and rhetorical traditions' (*Vision of History*, pp. 128–9).

[67] Hanning notes Geoffrey's concern with secular 'greatness', ibid. (pp. 100 ff.).

[68] Geoffrey's *Historia Regum Brittaniae*, referred to hereafter as the *HRB*.

[69] *HRB*, x.i, p. 219. Julia C. Crick notes that the reception of Geoffrey of Monmouth's *Historia* was as a work of history. Among other things, it 'provided ammunition for Edward I's claims to lordship of Scotland' (*The Historia Regum Britanniae of Geoffrey of Monmouth, IV Dissemination and Reception in the Later Middle Ages* (London, 1991), p. 17).

[70] E.g. Leckie, Hanning, the latter differentiating between the 'monastic' William and the 'secular' Geoffrey (*Vision of History*, pp. 121 ff.)

[71] Ingledew, 'The Book of Troy', *Speculum*, 79 (1994), p. 680.

[72] *Historia Rerum Anglicarum*, Hans Claude Hamilton (London, 1856); Joseph Stephenson (trans.), *Church Historians of England*, vol. IV, Ii (London, 1856): 'A writer in our times has started up and invented the most ridiculous fictions concerning them [the Britons], and with unblushing effrontery, extols them far above the Macedonians and Romans. He is called Geoffrey, surnamed Arthur, from having given, in a Latin version, the fabulous exploits of Arthur (drawn from the traditional fictions of the Britons, with additions of his own), and endeavoured to dignify them with the name of authentic history' (p. 398).

[73] The demons allegedly fled from the Gospel, but 'Quo sublato postmodum, et Historia Brutonum a Galfridio Arthuro tracata experiende causa, loco ejusdem subrogata, non solum corpori ipsius toti, sed etiam libro superposito, longe solito crebrius et tædiosius' (Giraldus Cambrensis, *Opera*, J. S. Brewer (Nendeln, 1966), (line 5) (If it [the Gospel] were afterwards removed and the History of the Britons by Geoffrey Arthurus were put there in its place, just to see what would happen, the demons would alight all over his [Meilyr's] body and on the book, too, staying there longer than usual and being even more demanding).

[74] The text has traditionally been ascribed to 'Nennius', even though only a minority of texts bear the name 'Nennius' (or 'Ninnius', or even 'Nemnivus'). See David Dumville, 'Nennius and the *Historia Brittonum*', *Studia Celtica*, 10 (1976); 78–95, and David Howlett, 'The literary context of Geoffrey of Monmouth', *Arthuriana*, 5. 3 (1995), 25–69.

[75] Hanning observes of Geoffrey's 'Brutus' narrative that 'The aim of this [the first] origin story is clearly to attach the Britons to the ancient world and make them the heirs of Roman greatness' (*Vision of History*, p. 104).

[76] See Chaucer, *Wife of Bath's Prologue and Tale*, l. 692.

[77] R. William Leckie, *The Passage of Dominion* (Toronto, 1981), p. 29.

[78] Hanning, *Vision of History*, p. 123.

[79] Geoffrey, *HRB*, 6. 3.

[80] Hanning, *Vision of History*, p. 110. Leckie adds that 'Although the need for reconquest [of Arthur's territories] presupposes an earlier loss of control, clearly the military might of the Britons has not suffered in consequence of their rulers' degeneracy' (*Passage of Dominion*, p. 64).

[81] Geoffrey, *HRB*, 12. 6.

[82] Valerie I. J. Flint, 'The *Historia Regum Britanniae* of Geoffrey of Monmouth: parody and its purpose. a suggestion', *Speculum*, 54, 3 (1979), 447–68 (449).

[83] Michelle Warren sees the *Historia* as vacillating between 'admiration and condemnation of the history of conquest' ('Making contact: postcolonial perspectives through Geoffrey of Monmouth's *Historia regum Britanniae*', *Arthuriana*, 8, 4 (1998), 115–32 (116)).

[84] Geoffrey, *HRB*, 4. 1, p. 306.

[85] Ibid., IV. 2, pp. 307–8.

[86] Gildas, *De Excidio*, 6. 2.

[87] Geoffrey, *HRB*, 4. 9, 4. 16.

[88] Ibid., 9. 16, pp. 462–3.

[89] Ibid., I.17, p. 252.

[90] 'In the *Historia*, the regulation of history by repetitive patterns of personal behavior and national progress has replaced the Christian system of movement toward a final happiness or reward. Geoffrey's story of the fall of Britain lacks, in short, the moral dimension provided in the versions of Gildas and Bede by the theology of history' (Hanning, *Vision of History*, p. 171).

[91] Geoffrey, *HRB*, 12. 2.

[92] Albu notes that '[t]he Norman hero appears as trickster as often as warrior', *The Normans and their Histories* (Suffolk, 2001), p. 4).

[93] Warren, *History on the Edge*, p. 13.

[94] '[. . .] faciensque eorum subregulos et ministros, quos Beda fortissimos dicet fuisse reges Anglorum, universe Brittaniæ nobiliter imperiantes' (William of Newburgh, *Historia Res Anglorum*, 'Prologue', p. 18) (and makes sub-kings and vassals of the noble Angles whom Bede says ruled all of Britain).

[95] William of Jumièges, *Gesta Ducum Normanum*, p. 133.

[96] Geoffrey, *HRB*, 6. 9.

[97] Cambridge University Library MS Ee.3.59, fo. 30v.

[98] According to Tatlock, '[t]he geography of Arthur's campaigns is far more like a skeleton-outline of William's than like that in Nennius, and it is hard to doubt that Geoffrey had been reading Henry of Huntingdon, William of Malmesbury, and others. With this close resemblance in their doings in England, and with William's far-flung empire which makes Freeman call him "Duke, King, and more than King, who gave the law, not only at Rouen and at Winchester, but at Dumberline and at Le Mans", one must call William the Conqueror one of Geoffrey's chief precedents for both Arthur's career and British imperialism' (*Legendary History*, pp. 308–9).

[99] La3amon documents Wace's presentation of the *Roman de Brut* to Queen Eleanor, presumably seeking royal patronage: Boc he nom ðe ðridde; leide ðer amidden. / ða makede a Frenchis clerc; Wace wes ihoten; / ðe wel couðe written and he hoe gef ðare æðelen Ælienor / ðe wes Henries quene; ðes heyes kinges (He took a third book and laid it amidst the others, a French clerk had made it, he was called Wace, who could write well, and he gave it to the noble Eleanor, who was Henry the high king's queen) (La3amon, *Brut*, ll. 19–23). Although there is no corroborating evidence for this exchange, most historians regard it as authentic.

[100] Matthew Bennett argues for the importance of the *Roman de Rou* as a source for interpretations of the Norman Conquest ('Poetry as history', *Anglo-Norman Studies*, 5 (1982), 21–39 (38)). It was not pro-Norman enough, evidently, given that he lost his position as court historian to Benoit Sainte-Mare, evidently for showing insufficient respect to Henry II's ancestors.

[101] *Le Roman de Rou de Wace*, ed. A. J. Holden (Paris, 1970), ll. 7403–14.

[102] 'On ðam geare se cyng het oflsean ealle ða Deniscan men ðe on Angelcynne wæron. Ðis wæs gedon on Britius massedæig forðam ðam cyninge wæs gecyd

ða hi woldon hine besyrwam æt his lif and siððan ealle his witan and habban siððan his rice' (In this year the king had all the Danish in England slain. This was done on Saint Brice's Day because the king had heard that they wished to kill him and his counselors and afterwards have his kingdom) (*Anglo-Saxon Chronicle*, 252, D; C and E concur).

[103] Wace, *Roman de Rou*, l. 174.

[104] Wace, *Roman de Brut*, ll. 9327–30.

[105] Ibid., l. 7466.

[106] Ibid., ll. 1687–9.

[107] Wace, *Roman de Rou*, ll. 5836–8.

[108] An English rendition of John's entry for 1066 reads: 'Thereat, the king, at once, and in great haste, marched his army towards London; and though he well knew that some of the bravest Englishmen had fallen in his two battles, and that one half of his army had not yet arrived, he did not hesitate to advance with all speed into South Saxony against his enemies; and on Saturday the eleventh of the calends of September [22 October], before a third of his army was in order for fighting, he joined battle with them nine miles from Hastings, where they had fortified a castle. But inasmuch as the English were drawn up in a narrow place, many retired from the ranks, and very few remained true to him; nevertheless from the third hour of the day until dusk he bravely withstood the enemy, and fought so valiantly and stubbornly in his own defence, that the enemy's forces could hardly make any impression. At last, after great slaughter on both sides, about twilight the king, alas, fell'; *Chronicle of John of Worcester* (Oxford, 1995), pp. 604–5.

[109] The A, B and C texts of the *Chronicle* state that Harold 'feng to rice', literally 'seized the kingdom'; however, since this phrase is repeatedly used in reference to legitimate succession, nothing need be read into it.

[110] Neither are such implicit (and even explicit) critiques of the Conquest unique. Even an apparently triumphalist artefact like the Bayeux Tapestry may embed subtexts that undermine its surface narrative. These biblical motifs and templates identified by David J. Bernstein form a biblically informed subtext, making the Tapestry a complex text that 'cannot be read simply as a naïve tale of the Norman Conquest as seen from a Norman point of view' (Bernstein, *Mystery of the Bayeux Tapestry* (Chicago, 1987), p. 166). His argument is that the Tapestry subtly intertwines the Babylonian Captivity with its apparent theme of Norman triumphalism, and thus criticizes William the Conqueror by associating him with the Old Testament tyrant, Nebuchadnezzar. Accepting Bernstein's argument, it would appear that the Tapestry designers turned the methods of providentialist historians against them.

[111] *Vita Haroldi* (London, 1895), p. 12.

[112] God is 'supplices suos supra quam petunt et intelligunt exaudire jugiter consuevit' ('wont to listen to those who pray to Him beyond what they ask and understand') (*Vita Haroldi* (London, 1895), p. 12).

[113] Holt, *Colonial England*, p. 4.

[114] For a discussion of the importance of the king's body in Anglo-Saxon society, see William A. Chaney, *The Cult of Kingship in Anglo-Saxon England* (Berkeley, 1970).

[115] William of Newburgh, *Historia Rerum Anglicarum*, 1.4.

[116] Ibid., l. 7.

[117] 'And the Lord said, "What have you done? Listen; your brother's blood is crying out to me from the ground! And now you are cursed from the ground, which has opened its mouth to receive your brother's blood from your hand"', Genesis 4: 10–11.

[118] Otter, *Inventiones*, p. 101.

[119] Readers of the *Brut* have often wondered why La3amon would choose to translate the anti-Saxon Geoffrey-Wace narrative; his decision has led early readers, such as Borges, to designate La3amon a 'traitor' to his race. Later critics, such as I. J. Kirby, have postulated a demarcation between treacherous Saxons and virtuous, or at least morally acceptable, Angles; Daniel Donoghue finds an answer in La3amon's 'ambivalence'. Others argue that the ethnographic struggle is ultimately subordinated to the struggle between Christianity and paganism. Although I do not claim to have a definitive answer to this rather complicated issue in La3amon studies, I do suggest that the variant historiography offered by Geoffrey and Wace in opposition to Bede provided La3amon with a way to dramatize the fabrication of historiographic paradigms.

[120] Johnson, 'Reading the past in La3amon's *Brut*', p. 146.

[121] The *drihten* has been variously interpreted as 'their god' (Barron and Weinberg); 'their Lord' (Allen); and 'God' (Madden). In the context of l. 1314, the term obviously refers to a divine rather than a secular ruler.

[122] Geoffrey, *HRB*, xi. 4.

[123] 'Treis anz regna, puis fud ocis, / Ço fud grant does a ses amis' (ll. 13327–8).

[124] Bryan, *Collaborative Meaning*, p. 127.

[125] From the *City of God*, trans. Dods, p. 33, 1.28, wherein Augustine explains why the bodies of faithful Christians have been violated by invading Goths. This passage derives from part of St Paul's Letter to the Romans: 'O the depth of the riches and knowledge of God! How unsearchable are his judgements and how inscrutable his ways! For who has known the mind of the Lord? Or who has been His counsellor? Or who has given a gift to Him, to receive a gift in return?' (Romans 11: 33–5).

[126] Henry of Huntingdon, *Historia Anglorum*, p. 4.

[127] Ibid., 7. 1, p. 214.

[128] Stein, 'Making history English', p. 114.

[129] Allen suggests that the Welsh leader Prince Llewellyn, who did homage to King Henry III in 1218 in return for confirmation of land he had retaken from the Anglo-Normans, may have served as a model for King Arthur ('Introduction' to *Lawman's Brut*, p. xix).

2

Translating the text: the historian-translator and the body of the book

In writing the history of the foundation of a new dynasty, historians typically refer to the historical texts of the precursor culture for information. Beyond sources of information, historians based their claims to authority on the possession of precursor texts and the ability to graft them onto new historiographic models. This authority often materializes in the prologues to their histories, which outline their reasons for writing history and for adapting the historical material in the source texts. For instance, when William of Malmesbury and Henry of Huntingdon explain in their prologues how they graft the textual matter of Bede's *Historia* and Anglo-Saxon historical texts on to their own histories, they establish themselves as their generation's authorities on insular history. Geoffrey of Monmouth claimed, in his prologue, exclusive authority to write about the sub-Roman Britons, based on possession of his (unidentified) 'ancient book', written in the language of the Britons. Wace would later assert the right to assess the truth or falseness of Geoffrey's text in his own prologue.

In this light, Laȝamon does not appear to differ radically from his precursors and contemporaries in his evoking of authority over his sources. Like the others, Laȝamon presents a prologue outlining his process of acquiring and translating source texts (MS Caligula ll. 1–35). He cites three sources: Bede's *Historia Ecclesiastica*, Wace's *Roman de Brut* and an unnamed, and possibly fictional, work by Augustine and 'Albin'. (In MS Otho, Wace is omitted, and Augustine and Albin are given credit for separate texts.) Reference to the *Historia* – the single most admired and emulated work of medieval English history – places Laȝamon squarely in the context of 'orthodox' twelfth-century historiography. Citing two other sources for greater credibility also corresponds to conventions of the time. The process he describes confirms his identity as historian-translator. La3amon's description of himself as acquiring and compiling his three sources, along with his pledge to extract from them the 'truer' (*soðere*) word (MS Caligula, l.27), enhances his own authority over his sources. At first glance, then, La3amon presents himself as a member of the community of historians, claiming to offer an authoritative account of insular history.

Upon further examination, however, we find that La3amon differs from other historian-translators in his conceptualization of the process of compiling and translating sources, a process he links to conquest and colonization. Reworking of these sources enacts a translation through which the historian alters previous material for his own historiographic vision. An element of domination similar to conquest pervades this notion of translation. By depicting the translator of historical texts as a conqueror, La3amon exposes the seizure and manipulation of source texts enacted in the prologues of other historians. La3amon also draws attention to the implicit gendered nature of historical translation, by expressing the relationship between the translator and the text as one between the masculine translator and the feminized book. Such translation is not only a translation of language; it inevitably involves literally taking the body of a book and appropriating its contents. As an act of conquest, seizure of the text heightens the masculinity of the medieval historian-translator by grafting it onto and transforming it into his vision of history. In La3amon's England, it also enabled Anglo-Norman/ Angevin historians to claim fellowship in a community of historians, in their possession of and mastery over sources. In this regard, translation of texts can be seen as analogous to the colonization of the 'feminized' landscape by 'masculine' conquerors. La3amon exposes the power dynamic that lies beneath the surface of other historiographic methodologies. At the same time, he problematizes the absolute authority claimed by historian-translators over their source texts, by using the tropes of seduction and romance. This chapter, therefore, examines La3amon's self-described translation project in his prologue as an act of the seizure of texts. It then discusses various tropes for translation throughout the *Brut*, illustrating how La3amon calls into question the historian's claim to authority by reconfiguring the relationship between translator and text as one of 'romance', wherein the source text exerts some authority over the translator. Going outside the prologue proper, the chapter concludes with La3amon's dramatization of the nuanced relationship between translator-conqueror and source in a colonial context, through examining his depiction of King Alfred's translation of the Mercian Laws.

Medieval masculinity and the translation of history

The assertion of the historian's authority over the source text(s) occurs in the prologue to the historical text; this prologue constitutes part of the broader generic category of medieval academic prologues, discussed by Minnis. According to Minnis, the neo-Aristotelian prologue that developed in the late twelfth and early thirteenth centuries employed four distinct causes:

> The 'Aristotelian prologue' was based on four major causes which, according to Aristotle, governed all activity and change in the universe. Hence, the *auctor* would be discussed as the 'efficient cause' or motivating agent of the text, his materials would be discussed as the 'material cause', his literary style and structure would be considered as twin aspects of the 'formal cause', while his ultimate end or objective in writing would be considered as the 'final cause'.[1]

Adherence to these conventions established the writer's authority. William of Malmesbury follows this pattern: outlining his efficient cause (himself); his material cause (the sources he employs, including Bede and the *Chronicle* for earlier history, and eyewitness accounts for later matters); his formal cause (the *res ordinatus*, 'order of things' or events); and the final cause (to fill the gap in English history between Bede and Æthelweard). Henry of Huntingdon's prologue likewise includes the four causes, albeit not in the orthodox order: the efficient cause (Bishop Alexander's request that he write); the material cause (Bede and the *Chronicle*); the formal cause (his description of past events, up to his own time); and the final cause (the multitude of virtues attached to reading history). Geoffrey offers as his final cause the elimination of lacunae concerning the history of the Britons, and his mysterious 'ancient book' as his material cause. William of Newburgh, writing a generation later, offers an even more formalized version of the neo-Aristotelian prologue: the younger William outlines the efficient cause (the request by his superiors to undertake an historical text);[2] material cause (eyewitness accounts); and his final cause ('ut a successore ejusdem Henrici Stephano [. . .] incipiam producere pleniorem') ('give a more copious narrative from Stephen, Henry's successor').[3] Even Wace, who writes in verse, embeds the elements of the academic prologue: his audience ('Ki vult oïr e vult saveir' [Whoever wishes to hear and know]) would serve as an efficient cause; his decision to relate the rulers of England sequentially, his formal cause; Geoffrey's *HRB*, the subject of his translation, would be his material cause; and the relation of its *truth* to the audience, his final cause. Laȝamon likewise presents a poeticized version of the academic prologue in his vernacular history. Rosamund Allen has noted that the Caligula version of the prologue constitutes 'an informal version of the Aristotelian Preface, with its four divisions of *causa efficiens* (i.e. the author (ll.1–13)); *causa materialis* (source materials (ll.15–23)); *causa formalis* (or *forma tractandi*, *forma tractatus*: procedural method and arrangement (ll.24–8)); *causa finalis* (aim of the writer and purpose of work (ll.29–35)'.[4] Indeed, Laȝamon gives as his *causa efficiens* his own name and the idea that occurs to his mod and mern-þonke. His *causa materialis* are the three source texts and the physical boc-felle on which he composes. The chronological history of the earliest inhabitants of Englene londe (l. 9) would serve as his *causa formalis*, while receiving prayers for his and his parents' souls constitutes his *causa finalis*. Collectively, the conventions of the academic prologue allow historian translators to establish themselves as *auctores* in their own rights. As a sub-genre of the academic prologue, then, the historian's prologue provides a means for the writer to establish his authority over the texts he translates. The paradigm established by historians further reveals a hierarchy, with God at the top moving the human *auctor*, who in turn moves the acted-upon text. However, the prologue to the historical text differs from academic prologues, in that the object of exegesis is secular history, which was for medieval historians a text from which to read God's word in worldly events. The commentators themselves then became the *auctores*, responsible for establishing the truth of history by assuming the capacity to interpret the word.

In asserting this authority, the historian-translator necessarily assumes a masculinist position over a feminized source text, appropriating it for his own ends, just as the conqueror-colonizer manipulates the conquered land and people. Annette Kolodny has written extensively on the impulse to feminize newly colonized territory, in reference to the colonialist narratives of the Americas, which leads to a gendered dynamic of male colonizers and a feminized landscape.[5] Traditionally, historical writers were men, writing for men, and, for the most part, about men.[6] For twelfth- and thirteenth-century historians, this evident masculinity in the historiographic paradigms is set forth in the prologues. As Bede relates in the prologue to the *Historia Ecclesiastica*, the genre was conceived of as an activity for the training and education of men, whether lay or ecclesiastical:

> Sive enim historia de bonis bona referat, ad imitandum bonum auditor sollicitus instigatur; seu mala commemoret de pravis, nihilominus religious ac pius auditor sive lector devitando quod noxium est ac perversum, ipse sollertius ad exsequenda ea quae bona ac Deo digna esse cognoverit, accenditur.[7]

> [For whether a history shall contain good things concerning good men, the careful hearer is thereby stirred up and provoked to follow after well doing: or whether it shall report evil things concerning forward men, the devout, well-disposed hearer or reader none the less, by flaying that is evil and noisome to his soul, is himself moved thereby more earnestly to follow after the things he knows to be good and acceptable to God.]

William of Malmesbury cites as his motivation behind historical writing the inspiration 'clarorum uirorum'[8] (of great men) and love for the fatherland: 'Vnde michi cum propter patriae caritatem, tum propter adhortantium auctoriatum uoluntati' (It was therefore my design, in part moved by love of my country [literally 'fatherland'] and in part encouraged by influential friends).[9] Henry of Huntingdon's panegyric to the study and knowledge of history serves as a further example of how historical prose relates to manhood, as a knowledge of history – including knowledge of one's fatherland – becomes a precondition to humanity:

> Habet quidem et preter hec illustres transactorum noticia dotes, quod ipsa maxime distinguat a brutis rationabiles Bruti – namque homines et animalia unde sint nesciunt, genus suum nesciunt, patrie sue casus et gesta nesciunt, immo nec scire uolunt.[10]

> [The knowledge of past events has further virtues, especially in that it distinguishes rational creatures from brutes, for brutes, whether men or beasts, do not know – nor, indeed, do they wish to know – about their origins, their race, and the events and happenings in their fatherlands.]

William of Newburgh expresses the gender implications of this conception of history in his condemnation of Geoffrey, which he voices in unmistakably phallic terms: 'scilicet, ut minimus digitus hujus Britonis grossor videatur lumbis magni Caesaris' (Apparently, the little finger of these Britons is seen as greater than the loins of the great Caesar).[11] For William, Geoffrey's promotion of the Britons at the expense of the Romans questions Caesar's masculinity and, hence, the manhood of orthodox historians.

Evident in these prologues, then, is a subtle link between possession and control of source texts and membership in a textual community of men reading and writing history.[12] This community constitutes what Eve Kosofsky Sedgwick terms a 'homosocial' bond of men promoting the interests of men, founded on the exchange of 'feminine' bodies.[13] Having established the writing of history as an undertaking for men to learn from men, Henry of Huntingdon presents his principal source text, Bede's *Historia Ecclesiastica*, as a property through which he is to establish his own authority as an historian.[14] Compiling Bede with 'aliis excerens auctoribus' and excerpts from other histories and chronicles, Henry endows his text with the same didactic weight he found in his source text:

> In quo scilicet opere sequenda et fugienda lector diligens dum inuenereit, ex eorum imitatione et evitatione Deo cooperante meliatorus, michi fructum afferet exotabilem. [15]

> [In this work the attentive reader will find what to imitate and what to reject, and if, by God's help, he becomes a better person for this emulation and avoidance, that will be for me the reward I most desire.]

Even the model of writing itself, viewed in terms of the author's application of the stylus to the 'flesh' of the manuscript page, has been recognized as a masculinist gesture, with what Carolyn Dinshaw calls 'the metaphorical identification between writing and male penetration of the female', citing Alan de Lille's twelfth-century *De Planctu Naturae*.[16] When the historiographer asserts an identifiably masculinist authority over his source texts, which come to be 'feminized' in the equation, he then works to regulate the language of these texts into a singular construct of authoritative history. The making of history thus constitutes an assertion of masculine authority by a member of a select community of literate men. However, in their relationship to the vernacular texts – the 'barbaric' works in the 'mother' tongue, as William of Malmesbury calls them – tension between the superiority of the (male) Latin rhetorician and the inescapable difference of the foreign text emerges. Working in Latin, Anglo-Norman historians made Anglo-Saxon history the property of an educated elite. Their skill at manipulating text is subtly challenged, however, by the unfamiliar words and phrases they confront, evident, for instance, in Henry's mistranslations of the Old English *Bruananburh*. The added element of mystery undermines the historians' confident authority in their ability to control source texts.[17]

The body of the book in Laȝamon's prologue

On the surface, both the Otho and Caligula prologues to the *Brut* seem to conform to the expectations of the historian's prologue. As cited above, the four neo-Aristotelian causes are to be found in Laȝamon's opening lines. In this brief but important passage, Laȝamon appears to set his material in a tradition of insular Christian historiography, evoking Noah and the Flood, and, more significantly, Augustine of Canterbury's mission to the English 'þe fulluhte broute hider' (he who brought baptism hither) (18). Considering Laȝamon's prologue in the context of the academic historical prologue, we can see Laȝamon presenting himself as an 'orthodox' historian, providing the sort of *exordium* to be expected of a historical text. It is also evident that he is not writing in any sort of intellectual or artistic backwater, but is fully engaged in the methods of historical writing of his century.[18] The *auctores* Laȝamon names – Bede, 'Austin and Albin' and Wace – provide respectable sources for a trad- itional historiographic project. As Johnson has observed, 'the rhetorical impact of the pedigree of the *Brut*, as it is described in the Caligula manu- script, is to suggest that in Laȝamon's work a prestigious historiographic tradition, principally concerned with the conversion of the English people, is to be interleaved with the more recent work of Wace'.[19] Thus, Laȝamon's evocation of his 'canonical' sources also betrays an apparent desire to be thought of as a 'historian', one of the elite community of men, living and dead, empowered to read, interpret and compose history. Bryan, in fact, argues that Laȝamon's prologue situates its authors, along with its readers and future scribes, in a community of text-producers. Warren identifies the readership as exclusively Christian and male.[20] The *Brut*'s prologue thus makes the case that the *Brut* is to be read and received in the same spirit as were the works of Henry of Huntingdon or Geoffrey of Monmouth – as authoritative history. At least until the nineteenth century, that was exactly how readers did receive it.[21]

In spite of Laȝamon's ostensible establishment of textual authority along similarly masculinist grounds, his prologue reveals a much more complex and problematic engagement with 'orthodox' historiography. His prologue represents the researching and writing of history as a dynamic of domination and threat of seduction, linked to the genre of romance. Through his dramatization of this process, La3amon exposes and undermines the authority asserted over source texts by historian-translators, even as he elevates his own *Brut* to the status of authoritative history. Although his narration of moving around the country and compiling sources seems to imitate the rhetorical pattern of other historical prologues, La3amon's assertion of the inherent masculinity of the historian exposes and critiques the domineering nature of compiling and translating history: 'La3amon gon liðen wide 3ond þas leode, and biwon þa æðela boc þa he to bisne nom' (ll. 14–15) [La3amon travelled widely throughout the land and took [literally 'seized' or 'conquered'] the noble books he took for models). Elsewhere in the *Brut*, the terms bi-won and nom denote military conquest': 'ða Grickes efden Troye mid teone bi-wonen' (l. 38) (The Greeks then seized Troy after a struggle).[22] The masculine posture implicit in Anglo-Norman histories becomes explicit in La3amon's description of his writing process. La3amon's treatment of his own translation furthers his gendered representation as historian-translator in possession of his sources. However, Elizabeth Bryan argues convincingly that the Caligula and Otho prologues to the *Brut* combine a number of medieval scribal traditions, leading to a textual experience that binds text, readers and writers:[23]

> That image of joining the fingers and feather and bookskin takes La3amon's act beyond compilation into collaboration. This word 'fiede' is an EME form of the verb Old English *fegan* [. . .] Its use here clearly draws on the history of Old English usage of *fegan* in contexts specific to language, rhetoric, and writing, but unlike those Old English uses it adds the idea of the writer himself joining the text.[24]

Such joining is undeniable; however, the idea of La3amon joining and continuing the text is countered by the assertive acts of seizing these texts: he 'biwon ða æþela boc' (l. 15), and he 'nom ða Englisca boc' (l. 16), another term denoting military conquest. My purpose here is not to refute the idea of 'joining' in this passage – indeed, the philological evidence is compelling – but I do suggest that the vision of historiographic translation set forth in the *Brut* may well include both aggressive appropriation and communal joining, in much the same way that colonized people may both desire and resent the culture of the colonizers. The fusion of desire and conquest – of peacefully 'joining' with a text and aggressively seizing it – reflects the complex view of the post-colonial translator, opposing the language and culture of the colonizers and simultaneously desiring union with the new culture.[25] Laȝamon's 'joining' of himself to the text may imply a desire to join the textual community of historians; membership in this community is, as I have observed, attendant upon control of source texts. Further, Bryan's observation underscores the physical, bodily reality of texts in Laȝamon's prologue. Books – both the ones he uses as sources and the one he composes himself – have bodies; they can be taken (*inomen*) or marked upon by the translator's quill. From this perspective, Laȝamon's application of the phallic pen to the 'flesh' of the text also suggests the stance of the warrior-hunter and his prey: 'Feþeren he nom mid fingren and fiede on boc-felle'(l. 26) (He took the quill with his fingers and joined them to the book skin). Not until Richard de Bury's fourteenth-century *Philobiblon* would English writing see another such overt linkage between the physical violence books suffer and the metaphoric violence inflicted by translators.[26]

The potential for abstract and material violence of translation inter-mingle in Laȝamon's *þrumming* of his source texts. In the *Brut*, source texts – Wace, Bede, and 'Austin' (Bede, Austin and Albin in Otho) – must literally be 'pushed' or 'trampled' into a single text: 'and þa þre boc þrumde to are' (l. 28). The term þrumde, a hapax legomenon whose only known Middle English usage is by Laȝamon, is glossed by Mossé as 'condense' or 'push together', and by Madden and Allen as 'set together or compress'.[27] Bryan suggests þrumde to mean 'threed', an original verb coined from Anglo-Saxon þrum, or 'three'.[28] Her reading thus points to the Early Middle English cultural model of textual 'joining' that she sees as informing the *Brut*. However, with its Germanic origins in the act of pushing, shoving or even drumming, the term also reveals a counter-discourse of conquest and control that reflects the conqueror's attempt to dominate his source texts. Laȝamon's *þrumde* may well be read as an economical expression of the nuances inherent in the linguistically and sexually charged act of translating sources. Both meanings function together as an exposé of the mixture of violence and desire that runs throughout the text. In other words, historical composition is a metaphoric invasion, making its source texts the property of the textual 'conqueror' in the same way that a military conqueror seizes a land and its inhabitants. Otter, in her discussion of the *Brut*, identifies an implicit comparison between Laȝamon the historian-translator and the masculine conqueror:

In the [Laʒamon's] prologue, the priest-turned-historian is surveying his 'territory', with an unmistakable, almost sensuous *affectus*. Like Geoffrey's Brutus, Denis's Edmund, or William the Conqueror in *Fouke*, he immediately proceeds to make this land his own by leaving his mark on it – in this case, with a quill.[29]

The paired tropes of joining and conquest also reflect Laʒamon's greater sensitivity to the book as physical object. As a resident of Worcestershire, within ten miles of the cathedral library, he had reasonably good access to texts. He may have been aware of John of Worcester's revisionist history, the *Worcester Fragment*'s lament for the decline of the English language, and the 'tremulous' glossator's attempts to recover Anglo-Saxon texts. In his emphasis on the book as body, Laʒamon implies a gendered relationship between author-translator and text. His possession of the texts signals the privileged position of the male authority over his feminized sources, which for Laʒamon exist as physical realities, tantamount to territory. The gendered dynamic seems to apply to Laʒamon's *boc* and to the *boc-felle*, both, like the *londe*, grammatically as well as metaphorically feminine.

The language Laʒamon uses to describe his own process of translating history conveys a similar blend of violence and sexual desire. Laʒamon's positioning of his source texts evokes images of sexual aggression: 'Laʒamon leide þeos boc and þa leaf wende' (l. 24). *Leide*, a strong, if not indecent, term, elsewhere in the *Brut* denotes rape. For instance, the rape and the breaking and disjointing of limbs suffered by the elderly victim of the Mont-Saint-Michel giant reflect the language of 'seizing' and 'laying' delineated in the prologue as part of the process of translating text:

þa hafeð þis idon, swa me soluen *inom*,
a uolden he me *laiden* and lai mid me seoluen.
Nu hafeð he mine ban alle ladlice abrokene,
mine leomen al toledeð; me lif me is ilaðed! (ll. 12938–41; italics mine)

[When he had done this, he seized me, and laid me on the earth and lay with me. Now has he horribly broken all my bones and disjointed my limbs; my life is hateful!]

Writing on the above scene, Finke and Shichtman comment on the link between dominance of territory and dominance of women: 'Control of the land as an economic resource [. . .] also depended on control of women as economic resources.'[30] For Laȝamon, territorial domination based on control of women also serves as a trope for the temporal control that depends upon appropriation and control of texts. If the former assures smooth succession and legitimate inheritance, through forced intermarriage between conquering men and conquered women, the latter assures the smooth and legitimate continuation of historical pedigree, through the forced appropriation of precursor histories into new historiographic paradigms. Laȝamon refracts this depiction of the historian's authority through a series of female bodies as texts that become internal tropes for historical texts, linked by textual formulae to acts of abduction directed at women throughout the *Brut*. The victim here thus becomes, at least on one level, a trope for the 'seized' text, voicing the textual violence inflicted upon it by the giant, who becomes a monstrous image – 'scaðe' – of the translator-conqueror.

The violence endured by text and by the female body – herself a metaphor for the text – reflects the language of Anglo-Saxon depictions of text-making; it is important to remember that the making of a manuscript was an explicitly violent affair. The Old English Exeter Riddle 26, the answer to which is a biblical codex, refers to the physical process the text undergoes in the transition from pelt to page, while it simultaneously admits the life-affirming possibility of the biblical text that results:

> Mec feonda sum feore besnyðede,
> woruldstrenga binom, wætte siððan,
> dyde on wætre; dyde eft ðonan,
> sette on sunnan, ðær ic swiþe beleas
> herum ðam ðe ic hæde. Heard mec siððan
> snaþe seaxses ecg, sindrum begrunden.[31]

[An enemy deprived me of life, seized my world-strength, and then wetted me, soaked me in water. They took me out again, and set me in the sun, where I lost all the hairs that I had. Afterwards they cut me fiercely with the edge of a knife, ground away the dross.]

In its reference to cutting and force, the anonymous riddler almost predicts the terms of seizure in the *Brut*'s prologue. The riddle further illustrates that, as early as the Anglo-Saxon period, the breaking of 'limbs' and cutting with knives would be understood as a trope for textual production. It is not difficult to see how this image could be extrapolated into a metaphor for the process of reading and compiling that Laȝamon himself claims to undertake. The seizure of the body of the animal to be used reflects the seizure – both material and abstract – of the text, the literal translation of the hide (or skin) into text and the process of drawing truth or meaning, as La3amon claims to do: 'ðe soðere word sette togadere' (l. 27) (he set together the truer words). Therefore, by combining these terms with the blatantly masculine image of La3amon applying the pen to the 'virgin' skin of the manuscript page a more complex image of the *Brut*'s prologue starts to emerge, as a dramatization of translating history that exposes its own masculinist underpinnings, even as its author participates in the process. La3amon's reinforcing of the pattern of seizure and abduction is even more striking in the context of the 'speaking book' (or 'books') to which he alludes in the first two lines of the *Brut* proper; it is as if they are being compelled by violence to speak. At the same time, in spite of the riddle's violent action, the process is ultimately redemptive: the murdered 'book skin' yields a biblical text, whose physical body is adorned with gold, assuring its fame. Its 'binding' by the smith for future readers seems predictive of the textual bonding process Bryan describes for La3amon's text. This life-affirming transform-ation of animal to 'living' book translates the riddle itself into a metaphor for the Crucifixion, reminiscent of the more famous transformation of the *Dream of the Rood*. The mingling of violence and beauty indeed seems also to characterize the complexity of La3amon's own prologue, which appropriates source texts but also gives them a voice as 'speaking books'.

La3amon, however, does not present such translations as a one-sided exercise of the translator's power over the source text. The historical text's claim to authority and stability remains problematic. In the prologue, it is challenged by several factors. First, early in the text, the intrusion of the *mern-þonke*, and the mysterious inspiration the term implies, disrupts the expectations of an identifiable *causus efficiens*. For the conventional male authority who commands or commissions the writing, La3amon substitutes uncanny and unpredictable inspiration. La3amon's split syntactic structure in this line, *hit*, postponing the antecedent until the following line, leaves suspended the motivating factor, as well as the primary cause. Indeed, the sudden visitation of inspiration seems predi-cated upon the 'love at first sight' trope of romance literature, as in the poet's inspiration for composing the *Roman de la Rose*.[32] This departure from the generic traits of the historian's prologue (or perhaps this poeticiz-ation of it) seems also to reflect the mysterious inspiration topos of the medieval dream vision, which runs parallel to the idea of love at first sight, also a factor in La3amon's revisionist historiographic prologue.

Laȝamon's exordium bears some resemblance to Chaucer's opening of
The Book of the Duchess:

> Thus sodynely, *I nyste not how,*
> Such a lust anoon me took
> To slepe that nyght upon my book
> Y fil aslepe, and therwith even
> Me mette so ynly swete a sweven. (ll. 272–6)

Although this text appears almost two hundred years after Laȝamon, in
it Chaucer, like Laȝamon, reveals the mysterious origin of inspiration,
as well as his concern for the material body of the book: Michael
Camille comments on medieval students sleeping with their books as
part of a materialist understanding of text.[33] What makes Laȝamon's
prologue unique among historical prologues is that this 'romance' inspiration occurs in a text typically received as history, as the inscription of
the Caligula MS clearly indicates. Thus, although the *Brut* purports to
be a historical text, the position of the author in the prologue suggests a
writer of romance or dream vision receiving inspiration. Coming un-
looked for and beyond the conscious control and understanding of the
author, this inspiration constitutes a counter-narrative of desire that undercuts the historian's authority from the outset. In this sense, Laȝamon's own
masculine authority is rendered tentative, open to outside and emotional
forces beyond his own conscious control.

Further, Laȝamon presents these source texts not as under the historian's
immediate control, but, rather, as items that must be sought out, and
that may resist discovery and translation. The *liðe–londe* formula used
to characterize this continual search for knowledge compromises the
self-assured authority of the historian by underscoring the difficulty in
finding his object. This formulaic expression, used to designate a search
for information, is almost invariably associated with rulers seeking
answers: 'ða sende Asscanius: ðe wes lauerd and dux / after heom yend
ðat lond: ðe cuðen dweomerlakes song' (ll. 136–7) (Then Asscanius, who
was lord and duke, sent throughout the land for those who knew magic
song). However, as the above example illustrates, when this formula is
applied to a quest for knowledge, the degree of control becomes problematic, with the answers to the seeker's question remaining beyond the
control of the historian or of historiographic discourse. Uther Pendragon's
'quest' for Merlin, for instance, leads into what Rider terms the 'fictional
margins' of history, and control over the transfer of information rests with
Merlin, not with the rulers who seek him.[34] Neither is there any guarantee

that either Asscanius or Uther will gain the information he seeks. Thus, in the act of obtaining the physical body of the book, the process of appropriating historical information becomes uncertain. Kolodny observes that the feminization of the landscape constitutes, in some sense, a psychological defence against the unknown, uncontrollable and potentially destabilizing elements within it: 'the total female matrix of attraction and satisfaction offers not only protection and nurture, but also arouses sexuality and the desire for exclusive possession'.[35] In this regard, the *affectus* felt by Laȝamon the historian-translator for his text and the conqueror for his territory bears a striking affinity to that of the lover, whose control over the body of the beloved is tentative at best.

'Leofliche biheold': historical authority and the masculine gaze

Laȝamon's reconceptualization of the dynamic between translator and translated text further informs his conception of gazing, or 'beholding', the source text. Like his contemporaries, Laȝamon peruses his acquired source texts, but the phrase used for the action – 'leofliche biheolden' – offers something beyond simple reading. Laȝamon's desire-laden 'beholding' could, of course, signify domination over source texts, as in other historical texts where to see is to confirm, and hence to control. Thus, William of Malmesbury stresses seeing events as a means of establishing authority over them: 'Quicquid uero de recentioribus aetigus apposui, uel opse uidi uel a uiris fide dignis audiui' (But whatever I have added out of recent history, I have either seen myself or heard from men who can be trusted).[36] Henry of Huntingdon uses similar language in the prologue to the seventh (and final) book of the *Historia Anglorum*: 'Nunc autem de his, que uel ab his uiderant audiuimus, pertractandum est' (Now, however, the matters to be studied are those that I have either seen myself or heard about from those who did see).[37] The gaze would also appear to function as a means of controlling in the *Brut*, especially given that *biheold*, from Old English *behealdan*, denotes the senses both of holding, that is, grasping or possessing, and seeing. Hence, it seems to establish Laȝamon's status as historical authority, making the expected rhetorical shift from the body of the text to historiographic discourse itself. The 'beholding' of the texts described by Laȝamon could also convey love for the text, and it is easy to imagine his tender regard for the books he has acquired, apparently with no small degree of effort.

In the context of such gazing and reflection, however, Laȝamon's more problematic relationship between beholder and beheld expressly subverts the authority of the gaze. Such gazing or 'beholding' is not without its attendant risks to the autonomy of the beholder. In the text of the *Brut*, desire-laden gazing upon the body of a significantly foreign woman presages the loss of authority, with the act of gazing itself signalling the transition from effective leader to object. For example, after defeating an army of invading Huns, King Locrin, son of Brutus, the eponymous founder of the British kingdom, seizes and gazes upon a captive foreign princess: 'Locrin iseh Æstrild and he heo *leofliche biheold*, and he heo mid armen *inom*'[38] (Locrin saw Æstrild and he lovingly beheld her, and he seized her with his arms). The formulaic *leofliche biheolden* and the verb *inomen* directly echo the language of Laȝamon's seizure and adoration of the French and Latin histories, all united by the concept of the loving gaze. Similarly, when the late British ruler Vortigern 'yeorne biheold' the Saxon maiden Rouwenne (l. 7166) (eagerly beheld Rouwenne), his gaze is followed by physical action: 'Ofte he heo custe, ofte he heo clupte' (l. 7167) (Often he kissed and caressed her). The gazes of Vortigern and Locrin reverse the typical trajectory of colonization: they are indigenous rulers who aim their gaze at the female body of an invader or outside settler. The resulting disruption of the typical power-dynamic, especially as it regards the exchange of women, threatens the authority of the insular rulers. Locrin's shift in identity from warrior to lover is, predictably, accompanied by a commensurate loss of masculinity, as it is understood in a warrior culture. When Locrin is confronted by Duke Corineus, father to the king's jilted fiancée, Laȝamon deliberately applies the epithet *ðe kempa* (warrior) (l. 1134) to Corineus, sharpening the contrast between the macho giant-slayer and the ruler who has risked effeminacy through his signal act of gazing.[39] This implicit questioning of Locrin's masculinity complements Corineus' challenge to the king's patrimony and to his very identity: 'þerfore þu shalt beon feie; for nes he [Brutus] neuer þi fader' (l. 1146) (therefore you shall be fated, for he was never your father). Locrin's manhood is thus compared unfavourably to Corineus' and to his own father's. Like Locrin, Vortigern suffers an inversion of masculinity and authority. After his significant act of 'beholding' Rouwenne, he consistently appears as acted upon and dominated by a man – Hengest – whom Laȝamon pointedly reminds us is the king's *dring* (l. 7175), or thane. Further, Rouwenne has been consciously decorated and presented, like a text, as Laȝamon adds the details of Hengest's deliberate decoration of his daughter:[40]

Hengest eode into þan inne þer wunede Rouwenne;
he heo lette scruden mid vnimete prude.
Al þat scrud þe heo hafde on he weorene swiðe wel ibon;
heo weoren mid þan beszte ibrusted mid golde. (ll. 71331–4)

[Hengest strode into the inn where Rouwenne was staying; he had her
dressed with matchless pride. All the clothing she had on was very well
made. She was ornamented with the best gold.]

The ornamentation of Rouwenne's body – original to Laȝamon –
transforms her into a crafted object, through which her father Hengest
can deliberately draw the king's passion and subvert his authority. Since
the outcome for both Locrin and Vortigern is loss of kingdom and life,
the implications for Laȝamon's persona as textual lover and conqueror
similarly obsessed with the object of his desire become serious. Vortigern's
gaze is especially pernicious because it opens Britain to colonization by
the Saxons, and thus marks the beginning of the end to their rule.

The two 'beholding' episodes are linked to the prologue via the
'leofliche biheolden' formula that Laȝamon applies to his own act of
gazing at his sources. As an English writer, Laȝamon's fixation on his
sources – especially on the *Roman de Brut*, which is associated with a
French-born queen – may constitute a threat to his sense of manhood
and to his sense of national identity; at the same time, however, his
obvious love for texts, especially for his sources, betrays a desire for the
foreign text and for the culture it represents. Post-colonial models of
translation, stressing complex interactions between languages of the
colonizer and colonized, provide a useful insight into what appears as a
mixture of aggression, earnest desire and anxiety. Colonized people may
seek the texts of the colonizers, but also resent the subsequent denigration
of their own. Accepting Otter's observation that 'Brutus looking at his
land sounds strikingly like Laȝamon looking at his books', it is equally
evident that Laȝamon's loving gaze at his 'books' – one associated with
the French-born Queen Eleanor – bears a striking and unsettling resemblance to the ineffectual rulers Locrin and Vortigern gazing at their
'illicit' love-objects.[41] It also calls into question the confidence displayed
by other historian-translators.

In both instances, what follows the signal act of gazing is a reversal of
events and, ultimately, the destruction of the king's authority and manhood. Locrin's and Vortigern's acts of gazing and seizing transform each
man from an effective ruler and warrior into the *derne*, or secret, lover of
the chivalric romance or even of fabliau; the lover was often stigmatized

with loss of masculinity, especially during the twelfth century, when conceptions of knighthood and chivalry were increasingly concerned with masculine identity.[42] This sort of sexual anxiety suggests uncertainty on Laȝamon's part concerning the authority of the gaze, especially when the object is that of an outsider. His gazing upon the bodies of his source texts could well reflect more of a carnal than an abstract or intellectual pleasure (which invites us to question whether the following half-line 'libetin beo Drihten!' [May the Lord be good to him!] is a plea for mercy or for divine help). For Laȝamon, to 'behold' something entails the risk of losing authority to the object beheld. His posture may thus betray an anxiety over losing linguistic authority over the text, as this act of beholding compromises the very authority it seeks to assert. The bibliophile's gaze – familiar to book-lovers such as the fourteenth-century de Bury – proves problematic in the *Brut*. As such, Laȝamon links it to the element of 'romance' that involves loss of self-control by the lover.

These episodes serve further to associate the language of Laȝamon's prologue with that of romantic love. Although a popular subject for romance writers in Laȝamon's century, the concept of 'romantic' love was often considered to be frivolous and irrational, if not absolutely idolatrous. Andreas Capellanus describes love as

passio quaedam innata procedens ex visione et immoderata cogitatione formae alterius sexus, ob quam aliquis super omnia cupit alterius potiri amplexibus et omnia de utriusque voluntate in ipsius amplexu amoris præcepta comeri.[43]

[an inborn suffering which results from the sight of, and uncontrolled thinking about, the beauty of the other sex. This feeling makes a man desire before all else the embraces of the other sex, and to achieve the utter fulfilment of the commands of love in the other's embrace by their common desire.]

Alan de Lille describes love as 'Pax odio, fraudique fides, spes juncta timori / Est amor, et mixtus cum ratione furor' ('peace joined to hate, loyalty to treachery, hope to fear and madness blended with reason').[44] The ambiguity connected with Andreas's and Alan's notions of *amore* also characterizes Laȝamon's prologue, and, by implication, other historical prologues, as involving the dynamic of desire and seduction, of conquest and surrender, characteristic of the romance. This apparently contradictory posture of love and hostility thus effectually undercuts the historian's assured masculine domination over the source texts, and expresses the author's own set of complex thoughts and emotions regarding foreign sources.

Elsewhere, La3amon uses formulaic 'beholding' to invert the conventional gender relationship of gazer and gazed-upon and to bring the concept of the gaze beyond the gazer's control. When the married Duchess of Cornwall Ygerne bestows her 'loving gaze' upon Uther Pendragon, La3amon comments on his own lack of knowledge: 'and heo hine leofliche biheold – ah inæt whær he hine luuede' (l. 9254) ('and she lovingly beheld him – but I do not know whether she loved him'). Here, La3amon not only shifts position from the male gazer to the object of the gaze by the female, but also omits judgement on his own part. Such problematic gazing has serious ramifications, given the parallel between La3amon's rulers and his own identity as historian-translator. With the relationship between the male ruler and female love-object linked verbally to the relationship between historian and text, this returned gaze suggests a fear of the text somehow returning the historian's commanding gaze and gaining control over him, as a manifestation of anxiety over loss of authority. The translator-compiler may thus become the one translated. It is important to remember, furthermore, that La3amon's Brutus is himself made the object of the controlling gaze of his patron deity, Diana: 'ða þuhte him [Brutus] on his swefne þar he on slepe læi / þat his lauedi Diana hine leofliche biheolde' (ll. 613–14) ('Then Brutus thought, in his dream where he lay asleep, that his lady Diana lovingly beheld him'). Set in the context of a sexually charged historiopoetics, the psychosexual implications of the formula 'leoflice biheolde' of the prologue become significant. As Maureen Fries has observed, women as the objects of male gazing in the *Brut* often become problematic: '[Guinevere] has served first as the shining face in the mirror the warrior uses to magnify his own reflection [. . .] and then as the looking glass's dull and dark side, whereby he loses the way she once seemed so splendidly to light.'[45] Similarly, the foreign text may have returned a double-sided reflection to its gazer-translator. With the potential for seduction rendering the historian as much a romancer as a conqueror, the trope of romance suggests how opening the source language to another language through translation brings about irreversible change. Le Saux has noted that La3amon shows 'some amount of discomfort [. . .] with male sexuality, which, in the form of passionate love, is repeatedly depicted as a destabilizing force'.[46] I find that this sexual discomfort extends to the act of research and writing history. This act may, I believe, be expressed aptly in terms of the romance, with its internal contradictions: it motivates the hero – or the historian-translator – to perform, but also raises the possibility of loss of control to a female love-object. By reconfiguring this relationship as the lover's 'beholding' – and being seduced by – the object of his desire, Laȝamon's prologue presents a 'romancing' of history that destabilizes the assertions of masculine identity and authority in historical prologues. Further, any translator will inevitably confront the inevitable word or phrase that defies translation, so in this regard, the absolute authority of the translator is qualified. Nor is Laȝamon himself immune to such effects of translation. In gazing upon and opening the French text, Laȝamon may acknowledge his own openness to the possibility of influence from the text that he translates, and that his language is itself open to change. For Laȝamon, then, the prologue represents the risk the translator undertakes when opening himself to other texts in other languages. However, this impending loss of control may also be a source of power for Laȝamon as a writer. As a member of a people whose language and historical traditions had become the object of translation, the possibility of the object asserting its own authority over the translator opens the possibility of resistance. From this perspective, the prologue of the *Brut* presents a challenge not only to Laȝamon's authority as historian, but also to the authority assumed by Anglo-Norman and Angevin historians who appropriated English historical traditions.

Further, with the assertion of historical truth based on the incontrovertible authority of texts and of eyewitness accounts rendered unstable, Laȝamon claims the rather oblique task of extracting the *sopere word* (l. 28) from the three source texts. Use of the comparative *sopere* (in both manuscripts), rather than an absolute (*sop*), opens the issue of historical 'truth' to debate: the reader/listener is tempted to ask if Laȝamon's words are truer than those of the source text, or if perhaps his rendition of history arrives at some sort of higher or more transcendent 'truth' than do those of his precursors. In either event, Laȝamon's usage implies scrutiny of his source texts and omission of the material he finds somehow less 'true'. He invites his readers/audience to undertake a similar hermeneutic task when he recommends that they read the text and 'leornia þeos runen'. *Runen*, etymologically linked to 'runes', suggests a demand for hermeneutic engagement on the part of the reader. In his exhortation to 'segge ætsomme' (together) Laȝamon imbues his text with a rhetorical function, to be shared by a wider – and possibly not fully literate – audience.[47] When Laȝamon tells us that the 'boc spekeð', however, his West Midlands dialect keeps the number ambivalent; hence, we cannot be certain whether the text states that the book (La3amon's) is speaking, as a vernacular text, or if La3amon's translation of the three books has made them speak, perhaps by putting them in the vernacular. In either event, the combined rhetorical and hermeneutic function of La3amon's composition is in keeping with the fusion of rhetorical and hermeneutic practices Copeland associates with medieval translation.

The ambivalent relationship between translator and source text dramatized in the prologue further illustrates the often complex relationship of the conquered (or colonized) translator to the texts of the dominant group. Translation theorists have long noted that translation runs parallel to – and is even a model for – colonialism.[48] For translators of conquered or colonized people, translating texts of the colonizers carried with it a risk, since these texts duplicated the ideologies and patterns of thought of the dominant class. At the same time, however, they offered revitalization of the underclass, by making new material available to them, and of the text, by giving it new vitality for a new vernacular audience. Translation also allows the translator to alter and subvert the patterns of representation of the conquerors. The mixture of resentment and resistance is counterbalanced both by a desire to identify with the dominant class – or at least to possess the power they possess – and by a desire to bring the material to an indigenous audience. Thus, in providing the first English account of Geoffrey of Monmouth's British history, La3amon makes a large section of accepted British history open to the English people. The trope of the 'speaking book' invites participation in insular history by a group heretofore excluded from active participation.[49] That the prologue to the *Brut* presents a picture of a man writing history need hardly be argued. However, the gendered relation expressed by the conflict between the author's obvious love for the source text and anxiety over being altered by it is played out in terms of sexual aggression and the threat of seduction. In this regard, La3amon's method of writing can be seen as a translation in the fullest and most complex sense of the term, embodying both an agonistic and a mutually supportive relationship between translator and source. What La3amon presents is a nuanced and often paradoxical view of both the masculine historian-translator and the text he translates. Simultaneously author and authored, working with a text that is both an object of desire and a threat to authority, La3amon dramatizes the sort of liminality and shifting identity characteristic of the translator in a post-colonial milieu.

Translation of text as translation of history within the Brut

Beyond the prologue and Laȝamon's expressed relationship with his source text, later sections of the *Brut* underscore the relation between translator and source text. In his unique prologue, Laȝamon dramatizes the rather complex relationship between masculine conqueror-translator and feminine text in the section dealing with the English king Alfred's translation of the Mercian Laws (ll. 3133–53). Beginning with Geoffrey, the tradition holds that the English Mercian Laws were in fact written by a literate queen, Marcie, and only translated by Alfred. The shifting orthography of the document from 'Marcie's Laws' to 'Mercian Laws' exemplifies the history of translation as a history of repeated conquest, from English, to Latin, to Anglo-Norman (and ultimately back into English). Using the same Latin sleight-of-hand he used to garner *Troy Nova* from *Trinovantum*, Geoffrey recasts the English Mercian Law as the Marcian Law:

> Erat ei nobile mulier Marchia nomine, omnibus artibus erudita, hæc inter multa et inaudita, quæ proprio ingenio repererat, invenit legem quam Britones Martianan appaverunt. Hanc etiam rex Aluredus inter cæteras transtulit, et Saxonica lingua la marchitie lage vocavit. (III. 13)

> [His [Guithelinus'] wife was a noble woman named Marcia, knowledgeable in all arts; among these many and unheard of things, which she devised through her unique talent, she invented the law that the Britons called 'Martianam'. This was among the other things Alfred translated, and in the Saxon language it is called the Mercian Law.]

Wace's verse follows Geoffrey's Latin prose fairly closely:

> Guincelinus fu de bone vie
> E sa mollier out num Marcie,
> Lettree fu e sage dame,
> De buen pris e de bone fame,
> Sun enging mist tut e sa cure
> A saveir lettre e escriture.
> Mult sout e mult estudia,
> Une lei escrit e trova,
> Marciene l'apela l'on
> Sulunc le language breton.
> Li reis Alvret, si cum l'en dist,
> Translata la lei e ecrist.
> Quant il l'out en engleis tornee,
> Marcenlega l'ad nomee. (ll. 3335–48)

[Guincilen led a good life, and his wife was named Marcie, a lettered and wise lady, of good praise and of good fame. Her ingenuity and her concern was all with knowing letters and writing. Much she knew and much she studied. She found and wrote the law that is called 'Marcian' in the language of Britain. King Alfred, as it is said, translated the law and rewrote it. When it was turned into English, it had the name 'Mercian law'.]

For Wace, working Latin prose into French courtly verse, the presence of a law-writing British queen might provide another means of pleasing his patroness, Queen Eleanor of Aquitaine – sometimes credited as authoring the 'law' of courtly love herself. La3amon's adaptation of this narrative seems to echo the apparently 'anti-English' sentiment of the Wace-Geoffrey narrative. However, La3amon differs from his immediate precursors by converting the scene into a depiction of the power of translation itself. La3amon's emendations, while amounting to only four additional lines of text in the account of Marcie's place in British history, make the scene a brief but poignant discourse on the sort of appropriation of a precursor culture's textual traditions that he identified in his prologue:

> Anne sune he hauede, aht mon Guencelin ihaten,
> he walde þis lond and þas du3eðe æfter his fader dæei.
> Þes wes þur3ut alle þing clæne mon and god king,
> he ledde swide feir lif and he hæfde a god wif,
> Marcie men heo clupede – þat is 3et widene cuð,
> nu and auere-mare is taken of here heare.
> Þeo quene leornede ane craft heo wes a boken wel itaht,
> heo leornede hire læere leofliche on heorten
> of hire wisdome sprong þat word wide,
> þat heo wes swiðe wis of wordliche dome.
> Þa makede heo ane læ3e and læide 3eon þat leode.
> [Þa] þeos la3e wes al iworhte
> Bruttes nemneden þa la3en æfter þare lafuedi
> to soðen wihuten wene, þe la3e Marchiane.
> Seoððen þer-after monie hundred winter
> com Alfred þe kinge Englelondes deorling
> and wrat þa la3en on Englisc ase heo wes ær on Bruttisc
> and whærfde hire nome on his dæ3e and cleopede heo Mærcene la3e.
> Ah þet I þe sugge þurh alle þing, ne makede heo noht ærst Ælured king.
> ah heo makede þa queen þe me Mærcie cleopede
> and Ælured heo seide on Englisc – þis is seoð ful iwis. (ll. 3133–53)

[A son he had, who was named Guencelin. He ruled this land and the people after his father's day. He was, throughout all things, a clean man and a good king. He led a very good life and he had a good wife. She was called Marcie, who was widely known; now and forevermore, here is a token [of remembrance] of her. The queen learned a craft, that she was well learned by the book. She learned her lore, lovingly in her heart. Word of her wisdom sprang widely; she was very wise in the judgement of words. She made a law and spread it among the people/land [literally 'laid it upon them']. When this law was all worked, the British named it after their lady, to the truth without second thought, the law was called 'Marcian'. Many hundred winters later came Alfred the king, England's darling, and rewrote the law in English, as it had earlier been in British; and he turned it in his day and called it 'Mercian Law'. But I tell, through all things, that Alfred the king did not make it first. But the queen named Marcie made it, and Alfred said it in English; this is indeed the truth.]

Laȝamon's extrapolative additions to this scene point to the cultural-political dimensions of the translator's role. From Wace's reference to the queen's 'good reputation' (l. 3338), Laȝamon stresses her fame as a product of her ability to create text (l. 3141); he thereby foregrounds the position of the book itself. The increased significance of the text is amplified as Laȝamon translates Wace's 'mult estudia' (very studious) into a more overtly linguistic – and covertly political – 'wordliche dome' (judgement of words).[50] Laȝamon's version shifts the emphasis from Geoffrey's and Wace's matter-of-fact praise for Marcie's erudition to the process of translation that underscores and informs the transformation of 'Marcian Law' into 'Mercian Law'. In so doing, Laȝamon brings to the level of conscious acknowledgement the potentially aggressive and appropriative nature of translation. As Laȝamon is at pains to note in the above-cited translation, Marcie's fame as lawmaker may invite appropriation through translation by rival cultures – in this instance, by the English king Alfred. By calling attention to Alfred's role as a translator, Laȝamon dramatizes the ways in which conquerors can, through translation, appropriate texts of precursor cultures for their own target audience, and thereby create the appearance of original authorship. Translating, or 'turning' (whærfde) Marcie's text, Alfred – 'Engelondes deorling' – has concealed his replacement of the British Marcie's laws with English Mercian Law, employing the same process later inflicted upon England and upon English historical material in the century following the Norman Conquest. Laȝamon uses a variant spelling of whðerfde to depict acts of conquest and translation of the land:

alle þa burhes þe Brutus iwrohte
and heora noma god þa on Brutus dæi stode.
beoð swiðe afelled þurh warf of þon folke.[51]

[all the cities that Brutus made, and their good names that stood in Brutus'
day, have all have fallen through change [or destruction] of the folk.]

The double-meaning of *warf*, as either 'turning' or 'destroying', serves
to link the work of the conqueror with the work of the translator.[52]
La3amon thus establishes an implicit parallel between Alfred the translator and Anglo-Norman historian-translators. The *Brut* implies that, in
the process of translation, especially where conquest and colonization of
one culture by another occurs, the conquered (Briton or Anglo-Saxon)
may face alienation from their textual traditions. These texts may be
translated, renamed, and 'pressed' (*þrumde*) into the service of the
conquerors' nascent literary traditions.

However, a trace of Marcie's efforts, her name, survives and apparently compromises Alfred's claim to sole authorship; thus, the translator's
attempted concealment of his act remains incomplete. It is important to
note that 'Marcie's' literary works do survive, in the trace of her name in
the title. Alfred's translation absorbs her text into a different culture, but
also assures its survival in changing cultural and linguistic milieus.
The Marcie passage may hold promise for La3amon and for the English
language; these ultimately untranslatable 'traces' of the language become
an important metaphor for the limited power of the conqueror-translator.
In this sense, the survival of the English language may lie in its translation of foreign texts and in its creation of text for the 'consumption' of
colonizers. Like the anonymous English author of the *Worcester Fragment*,
however, La3amon shows his awareness of the consequences of Anglo-
Norman colonization for the English language and for the English written
text. Either appropriated through translation (as was done by Henry of
Huntingdon and William of Malmesbury) or allowed to fade into obscurity through neglect, this effacement of the English language through
translation meant for the English a loss of a cohesive identity as a people
and, to an extent, a loss of collective manhood.

As historian-translator, La3amon brings to the surface the implicit
power and gender dynamics of the relationship of historian-translator
to source text. In the *Brut*, he portrays a distinctly 'masculine' historian
translating a source text that possesses both a gendered and a physical
body. As one engaged in the translation of history himself, then, his translation of French and Latin historical texts back into English marks a

reassertion of an English cultural and ethnic identity. Laȝamon seems to recognize that possession of a text and of its content involves the physical body of the book. As a body, it must be sensually admired but also physically seized and subdued. Gendered language reflects Laȝamon's conception of the translator's task throughout the *Brut*, as he describes the process of translating history, using the same terms and poetic formulae he elsewhere uses to depict male erotic pursuit of women. In Laȝamon's prologue, gendered terminology characterizes the translator's love of the text and the seizure and translation of source texts in the formulation of historical master-narratives. Laȝamon, however, depicts the process of historiographic translation as an exchange, rather than a one-sided assertion of power. The historian exercises a translator's authority over the text, but his emotional desire for the text compromises the authority implicit in this relationship. Laȝamon dramatizes a genuine concern that the text may change him and his language. He expresses this potential subversion through the tropes of romance and seduction, in which the persona of the translator resembles the 'courtly' lover of the comparatively new *fin amour* tradition as much as the 'heroic' conqueror-colonizer. Under this complex and ambivalent model, the significantly embodied (feminine) text questions the asserted authority of the (masculine) translator; the translator is to an extent translated, just as the conqueror is unavoidably altered by the colonized land and people. Hence, the Normans increasingly began to think of themselves as 'English', in spite of the cultural and linguistic gap separating them from the Anglo-Saxons. This relationship further reflects the mixture of aggression and desire characteristic of the colonizer's relationship to the colonized. Laȝamon's dramatization of this process thus provides a source of power to the translated text, as well as to the conquered people. With its similarity to, and striking difference from, the prologues of most 'orthodox' histories, Laȝamon's prologue occupies a unique space between 'historical' and 'romance' writing, and he exploits the liminal status of his text to question the claims of orthodox historiography.

Notes

[1] Alastair Minnis, *The Medieval Theory of Authorship: Scholastic Literary Attitudes in the Later Middle Ages* (Philadelphia, 1988), p. 5.
[2] 'sed tamen viri venerabiles quibus mos gerendes est, hoc ipsum meæ parvitati dignantur injungere ut et ego . . . saltem cum paupercula vidua aliquid de

tenuitate mea mittam in gazophylacium Domini'; William of Newburgh, *Historia Rerum Anglicarum*, pp. 18–19 ('some venerable characters, to whom I owe obedience, have deigned to enjoin such a labor, even to so insignificant a person as myself in order that I may yet be permitted, with the poor widow, to cast somewhat of my poverty into the treasury of the Lord') (*Church Historians of England*, trans. Joseph Stevenson, vol. VII, part ii).

3   *Historia Rerum Anglicarum*, p. 19; *Church Historians of* England, vol. VII, part ii, p. 402.

4   *Lawman's Brut*, trans. Allen, p. 411, n. 1.

5   Discussing the Americas, Kolodny describes a phenomenon she terms the 'American pastoral impulse': 'Obviously, such an impulse must at some very basic level stem from desires and tensions that arise when patterns from within the human mind confront an external reality of physical phenomena' (*Lay of the Land: Metaphor as Experience and History in American Life and Letters* (Chapel Hill, 1975), p. 8). Kolodny concedes, however, that the general concept is not necessarily unique to America: 'Let us remember, however, that gendering the land as feminine was nothing new in the sixteenth century; Indo-European languages, among others, have long maintained the habit of gendering the physical world and imbuing it with human capacities' (ibid., p. 8).

6   See Thelma Fenster, 'Preface: why men?', *Medieval Masculinities: Regarding Men in the Middle Ages*, Clare A. Lees (ed.) (Minnesota, 1994), pp. ix–xv.

7   Bede, *Historia Ecclesiastica*, 1.1, p. 2.

8   'Virtus clarorum uirorum illud uel maxime laudandum in se commendat, quod etiam longe positorum animos ad se diligendum inuitat; unde inferiores superiorum uirtutes fatiunt suas, dum earum adorant uestigia ad quarum aspirare non ualent exempla' (The excellence of great men has one laudable feature which perhaps more than any other recommends it; it inspires the affection even of those far off, so that men of lower degree adopt as their own virtues of those above them, reverencing the footprints of qualities they cannot hope to follow); William of Malmesbury, *Gesta Regum Anglorum*, pp. 10–11.

9   Ibid., pp. 14–15.

10 Henry of Huntingdon, *Historia Anglorum*, I. i, pp. 4–5.

11 William of Newburgh, *Historia Rerum Anglicarum*, p. 60

12 For a discussion of textual communities, see Brian Stock, *The Implications of Literacy* (Princeton, 1983), pp. 88–240.

13 Sedgwick cites the male 'desire to consolidate partnership with authoritative males in and through the bodies of females' (*Between Men: English Literature and Male Homosocial Desire* (New York, 1985), p. 38).

14 Henry of Huntingdon, *Historia Anglorum*, pp. 6–7.

15 Ibid., pp. 6–7.

16 Carolyn Dinshaw, *Chaucer's Sexual Poetics* (Madison, 1989), p. 7.

17 Henry mistranslates the common Anglo-Saxon formula *fæge feollan* (l. 13) – used in the English *Brunanburh* in reference to the defeated Scots and Danes

– as a reference to the invaders disembarking and attacking: 'et puppium habitores fatales corruerunt' (the fateful ship-dwellers descended) (*Historia Anglorum*, V.19, p. 313).

18 Tatlock, *Legendary History*, had so characterized Laȝamon.

19 Johnson, 'Reading the past', p. 149.

20 Bryan, *Collaborative Meaning*, pp. 45–6; Warren, *History on the Edge*, p. 87.

21 According to Bryan, 'LaȝBrut-Otho, regarded by the Elizabethan Society of Antiquaries as a record of the past, shows itself in these underlinings to be a still-living text that played a small role in the endgame of Elizabethan rule', *Collaborative Meaning*, p. 130.

22 Clark-Hall translates *winnan* as 'to labour, toil, trouble oneself: resist, oppose, contradict'; *A Concise Anglo-Saxon Dictionary*, p. 411.

23 Bryan, *Collaborative Meaning*, pp. 45–6.

24 Ibid., p. 44.

25 Post-colonial translation may be viewed as an exchange or dialogue that may even prove empowering to the colonized. Although Simon acknowledges the violence of colonial translation, she expresses the belief that this process may be more involved than the imposition of one culture upon another: 'Translation was part of the violence, then, through which the colonial subject was constructed. But this version of events does not tell the whole story of the processes through which the culture of the colonized and of the colonizers came to interact' (*Changing the Terms*, p. 11).

26 In this manifestation of textual violation, Laȝamon seems to predict the very physical elements of Richard de Bury's fourteenth-century *Philobiblon*, which links books explicitly to the body, and specifically – through the implications of rape and violation – to the female body, with the attendant masculinization of the compiler, translator or reader. Although separated from the *Brut* by over two hundred years, de Bury articulates a similar awareness of the book's body and of the potential for violence inherent in the translation process. Going beyond the image of the Exeter Riddle, de Bury combines the image of the abuse suffered by the physical body of the books with the metaphoric suffering inflicted upon the books' contents by the process of translation: his 'speaking books' lament their mishandling at the hands of interpreters and commentators: 'Interpretes barbaros sustimus multotiens et qui linguarum idiomata nesceunt nos de lingua ad linguam transferre praesumunt; sicque proprietate sermonis ablata fit sententia contra sensum auctoris turpiter mutiliata' (Oftentimes we have to endure barbarous interpreters, and those who are ignorant of foreign idioms presume to translate [transfer] us from one language to another; and thus all propriety of speech is lost and our sense is shamefully mutilated contrary to the meaning of the author!). As Michael Camille has noted, 'The book has lost much of its corporeal, communicative, and erotic associations with the speaking/sucking mouth, the gesturing/probing hand, or the opening/closing body' (Michael Camille, 'The book as flesh and fetish' in Dolores Warwick Frose and Katherine O'Brien O'Keeffe (eds), *The Book and the Body*, (Notre Dame, 1995), p. 40).

Camille further notes, 'Reading for the medieval literate was charged with these associations that made every turn of the page an act of intense interpenetration and one resonant with sensations, from the feel of the flesh and hair side of the parchment on one's fingertips to the lubricous labial mouthing of the words with one's throat and tongue. The way medieval books were bound with thongs between stamped leather or wooden boards, held shut with metal studs, encased in hide belts, and snapped shut with buckle like clasps made them mysterious' (ibid., p. 48).

27   The *Middle English Dictionary* defines the term as 'push together' and identifies it as a Middle English cognate of Dutch *drommen*, to push or shove. Another possibility, one perhaps more likely given Laȝamon's alleged Scandinavian heritage, is the Old Norse *þramma* ('trample'); both the Dutch and Scandinavian cognates denote violent action.

28   Bryan, *Collaborative Meaning* p. 44.

29   Otter, *Inventiones*, p. 90.

30   Laurie Finke and Martin Schichtman, 'The Mont-St-Michel giant: Sexual violence and imperialism in the chronicles of Wace and Layamon', in Anna Roberts (ed.), *Violence Against Women in Medieval Texts* (Gainesville, 1998), p. 61.

31   Exeter Riddle 26, ll. 1–6.

32   'In the twentieth year of my life, at the time when Love exacts his tribute from young people, I lay down one night, as usual, and slept very soundly. During my sleep I saw a very beautiful and pleasing dream; but in this dream was nothing that did not happen almost as the dream told it. Now I wish to tell this dream in rhyme, the more to make your hearts rejoice, since Love both begs and commands me to do so. And if anyone asks what I wish the romance to be called, which I begin here, it is the *Romance of the Rose*, in which the whole art of love is contained.' (*Romance of the Rose*, trans. Dahlberg, p. 8).

33   '[T]he medieval library was a site of performance, where people left their traces in their books without fear of censure. They marked them, doodled in them, defaced them, chewed them, tore them up, and even slept with them, as in fourteenth-century images showing books being used in bed, one of the few private spaces in medieval culture'; Camille, 'The book as flesh and fetish', p. 40.

34   'In Merlin's increased independence from royal power, in this increased tension between the historical, political centre and the visionary, fictional margin; in Laȝamon's movement away from historical discourse and toward fictional discourse, we see not only more effective romancing but also a reflection of the difference between Wace's and Laȝamon's circumstances'; Rider, 'The fictional margin the Merlin of the Brut', *Modern Philology*, 87, 1 (1989), 10.

35   Kolodny, *Lay of the Land*, p. 58.

36   William of Malmesbury, *Gesta Regum Anglorum*, 'Prologue', pp. 16–17.

37   Henry of Huntingdon, *Historia Anglorum*, 7. 1, p. 412.

38 Laȝamon, *Brut*, ll. 1116–17, italics mine.

39 Arthur Wayne Glowka discusses Locrin's 'being smitten in an unmanly way by love for a woman', 'Masculinity, male sexuality, and kingship', in Allen, Perry and Roberts (eds), *Laȝamon: Contexts, Language and Interpretation* (London, 2002), pp. 413–31, p. 420).

40 Wace states only that Ronwen came into the hall 'mult bele, e bien vestue' carrying a full cup of wine (ll. 6948–9).

41 Otter, *Inventiones*, p. 90.

42 Writing on the effects of 'romantic' love on traditional notions of masculinity, Jo Ann McNamara has argued that the social pressures of the Crusades had discredited such relationships, which came to be seen as a threat to the manhood of a knight: 'Freedom from women became the test of a true fighting man [. . .] the Crusade produced a new militia who would be so enthusiastically praised by Bernard of Clairvaux as a manly brotherhood, spurning the effeminate trappings of worldly knights and, of course, sworn as monks to forgo the company of women. The effeminate worldly knight in silks and curls was utterly disgraced by comparison with the Templars, who were celibate and bearded'; 'The *Herrenfrage*: the restructuring of the gender system, 1050–1150', in Clare A. Lees et al. (eds), *Medieval Masculinities: Regarding Men in the Middle Ages*, (Minneapolis, 1994), pp. 3–29, p. 17.

43 Andreas Capellanus, *On Love*, ed. and trans. P. G. Walsh, (London, 1982), pp. 32–33.

44 Alan de Lille, *De Planctu Naturae*, in Thomas Wright (ed.), *The Anglo-Latin Satirical Poets and Epigrammatists of the Twelfth Century*, vol. II (London, 1884; repr. Wiesbaden, 1964), p. 472; Alan of Lille, *The Plaint of Nature*, trans. James J. Sheridan (Toronto, 1980), p. 149.

45 Maureen Fries, 'Women, power and (the undermining of) order in Lawman's *Brut*', *Arthuriana*, 8, 3 (1998), 23–32 (25).

46 Francoise Le Saux, 'Paradigms of evil: gender and crime in *Laȝamon's Brut*', in *Text and Tradition*, 193–206 (p. 205).

47 Allen, in a detailed discussion of a possible audience for the *Brut*, suggests a family 'of some status' but not of the Norman rulers (*Lawman's Brut*, pp. xxi–iv).

48 According to Bassnett and Trivedi, opinions range from the view that colonialism and translation 'went hand in hand' to the view that translation 'both shapes and takes shape within the asymmetrical relations of power that operate under colonialism' ('Introduction', *Postcolonial Translation*, p. 3).

49 See Wickham-Crowley, *Writing the Future: Laȝamon's Prophetic History* (Cardiff, 2002), pp. 88–94.

50 Although translators, beginning with Madden, have emended the line to 'worldly', MS Caligula offers the unambiguous *wordlich*; admittedly inelegant, 'judgement of words' comes closer to the text of both manuscripts. Allen translates the line as 'the wisdom of the world' (82); Bzdyl as 'worldly judgement' (84); and Madden 'worldly dooms'. However, there is no evidence in either manuscript that Laȝamon intended *worldlich*; MS Otho offers

'wor(l)iche domes', with the (l) emended. It is further significant that Marcie literally 'lays down the law' on her people (3141), who in turn name the legal treatise for her (3143).

[51] *Brut*, ll. 1032–6.

[52] The 'felling' of names that comes about as a result of destruction of a people is especially pernicious because it obscures the ethnographic origins of the places themselves. In this respect, we may see how the supplanting of one language by another verbally reflects the struggle for control of territory. To conquer a land and a people is to translate both the land into a new political unit and the people from active participants in the creation of history into passive recipients of another culture's history.

3

Translating the land:
Laȝamon's historian-rulers

Laȝamon's conception of historiographic translation involves the translation of landscape, as the conquest of territory becomes a trope for the historian-translator's 'conquest' of text. New rulers establish new boundaries, build new structures to cement their power, and often commemorate their accomplishments by giving new names to their new acquisition. These changes to the physical landscape – new construction, including castles and churches, along with new boundary divisions – have the effect of permanently altering the landscape itself. Included in this process is the changing of place-names into terms familiar to the new conquerors. The transformation of *Britannia* (itself a construct of Roman imperial administration) into *Engelonde* is a dramatic example of the linking of place-names to both land and language. In the eleventh and twelfth centuries, topographic naming and renaming reinforced Norman control over England.[1] The overarching result of territorial conquest thus constitutes an act of translation, transforming the land into a new geopolitical entity. Such renaming activities give the appearance of a unified origin for the new dynasty. Origins, however, consist not of unity but of fragmentation and disparity, as Foucault points out.[2] Historical narratives of foundations provide fictions of unity as they cover the conflicts and contradictions upon which they are founded. Traces of these conflicts are only concealed, with new layers composed over subsequent ones.

In the works of Laȝamon's contemporaries and predecessors, foundational narratives enact this process of erasure and concealment. When successful, acts of translation of the landscape give the appearance of originality, or at least inevitability, concealing the violence wrought to the land in the process of seizing it and reorganizing it. For example,

Bede refers to the island's original name, 'Albion', its twenty-eight cities, and its five languages, all as part of the topography, omitting from this description the ethnic conflicts and ruptures that led to their existence.[3] Closer to La3amon's own century, Anglo-Norman historians document the establishment of new cathedrals and religious institutions without mentioning that the construction of such structures demanded the destruction of previous Anglo-Saxon buildings, the buildings concealing the very English foundations on which they depended.[4] La3amon's own parish church at Areley Kings was apparently constructed upon an Anglo-Saxon foundation, as were most churches and cathedrals during the Norman period. The 'archaeological' methods of La3amon's immediate precursors, Geoffrey and Wace, appear to counter the levelling and totalizing historiographic practices of the previous generation of historians, to expose, in Edward Said's words, the 'loss' that underlies the appearance of originality or repetition.[5] However, their efforts ultimately impose a master-narrative on insular history, one which substitutes for divine providence a British triumphalist discourse that rewrites the ancient Britons as prototypes for the Normans and that denigrates English contributions to insular history.

In contrast to his contemporaries' glossing-over of the conflicts that accompany changes in dominion, La3amon calls attention to the ruptures in historical narrative, through his depictions of the land and its fate. The *Brut* reveals how insular foundational history constitutes translation of the land itself. Ingledew documents a close connection between the possession of land and the possession of history in Anglo-Norman England: 'The possession of territory and power came to correlate distinctively with ownership of time; time came to constitute space – family and national land – as *home*, an inalienable and permanent private and public territory.'[6] Throughout the text, foundational figures – Brutus, Hengest (the leader of the first group of Saxon émigrés), Æthelstan (the first Anglo-Saxon ruler to control the entire island), Augustine of Canterbury (a foundational hero and possessor of land in his own right, in spite of his ostensible status as Christian missionary) and, proleptically, William the Conqueror – alter the landscape in the act of taking possession of it, renaming places and redrawing boundaries. In the process of asserting their authority over the land, they attempt to give it a sense of unity and contingency with the past, erasing traces of past cultures and institutions – hence the relationship between translating territory and translating history. The latter process, however, remains incomplete, giving the palimpsest appearance of the British land that mirrors the palimpsest of the insular historical text. In the following pages, I illustrate how Laȝamon's conception of conquest and translation brings to the surface the ruptures brought about in the various translations of the land. I examine the foundation of the British dynasty by Brutus as a translation of landscape that conceals the inevitable violence inflicted upon it and its inhabitants. I then discuss the subsequent translations of insular territory by the English leaders Hengest and Æthelstan, and by the Normans under William (not named, but a presence in the text nonetheless). Finally, I examine the missionary activities of Augustine of Canterbury as part of translating the land, and as an act that, ultimately, partakes of the same sort of violence associated with secular conquests; in this section, Laȝamon exposes the fissures in religious histories as a part of territorial conquest. Taken as a whole, his depictions of territorial conquest expose the metahistorical narrative through which historian translators represented conquest as part of a predictable and divinely directed cycle of conquest and reconquest.

Conquest, colonization and insular place-names

The conquest of the British Isles and the foundation of a new dynasty or new political entity constitutes, for Laȝamon, a translation of the land. Such translations occur four times in the *Brut*: when the Britons take control of the island and settle it; when the Saxons oust the Britons; when Augustine converts the Angles; and, proleptically, when the Normans achieve their conquest. Each act of conquest involves the division of the land and the establishment of borders, along with the linguistically significant act of changing topographical names. The first such insular translation occurs in Laȝamon's depiction of the foundation of *Britain* by the Trojan leader Brutus. The Trojans' colonization has the appearance of an original settlement, a pristine land divinely granted to its new possessors. However, this initial settlement depends upon the extermination of the aboriginal giants who inhabit it, and who are mytho-poetically linked to its prehistoric name, 'Albion'. For Geoffrey, the act of defeating the giants marks the accomplishment of the conquest and the beginning of his new dynasty; Otter observes that the details of the narrative remind the reader of the victims of the colonization process.[7] Brutus' translation of the land reconnects his people to the Roman–Trojan mythic cycle severed by his own act of patricidal violence. Geoffrey's narrative of the foundation of his capital, *troiam nouam* or *trinouantum*, follows with a display of linguistic sleight-of-hand on the name of the Trinovante tribe of south-eastern Britain.[8] In contrast to Geoffrey, Wace pays greater attention to the linkage between the founder Brutus' individual will and the new place-names. For Wace, constructing and mnemonically naming the island and the city become acts of rededication, undertaken to preserve cultural memory and to commemorate the Trojans' ethnic genealogy:

> La terre aveit nun Albion,
> Mais Brutus li chanja sun nun,
> De Bruto, sun nun, nun li mist,
> E Bretainne apeler la fist;
> Les Troïens, ses compainuns
> Apela, de Bruto, Bretuns.
> . . .
> Pensa sei que cité fereit
> E Troie renovereleit.
> Quant il out quis leu convenable
> E aisiez e delitable,
> Sa cité fist desur Tamise;
> Mult fud bien faite e bien asise
> Pur ses anceisors remembrer
> Le fist Troie Nove apeler. (ll. 1175–80, 1217–24)

[The country was called Albion, but Brutus changed its name, calling it after his own, and he had it called Britain. He named the Trojans, his companions, Britons . . . He [Brutus] considered where to build a city, and where to renew Troy. When he found a convenient, suitable and delightful place, he built his city beside the Thames. When the city had been well made and well placed, to remember his ancestors, he named it New Troy.]

In this passage, Wace verbalizes the practice of making the new land a copy – a translation – of the old land, in commemoration of Troy.

Laȝamon's amplification of the scene shifts the emphasis to the process of translating the land itself and to the alterations the conqueror-translator brings to it. Laȝamon expands upon the role of the conqueror, calling attention to the shaping activity that precedes the name-change. After securing the isle, Brutus' first act is to rename it after himself:

> Ðis lond was ihaten Albion þa Brutus cum her-on
> þa nolde Brutus na-mare þat hit swa ihaten weore.

ah scupte him nome æfter him-seluan.

He wes ihaten Brutus þis lond he clepede Brutaine. (ll. 975–8)

[This land was called Albion, when Brutus came here; he did not wish it to be so named any longer, but he shaped for it a new name, after himself. He was called Brutus; he called this land 'Britain'.]

As a shaper of names, Brutus is further linked to the scops or shapers of language, who spread historical material in the Anglo-Saxon period. The act of shaping emphasizes the kinship between historian and translator. Laȝamon also foregrounds the violence that accompanies such translation. He later duplicates the central events of the second episode, the naming of *Trinovant*, but with greater attention to the ruptures that underlie Trojan history:

al he iseih on leoden þar him leof was on heorten.

Þa bi-þohte he on Troyȝen þer his cun teone þoleden,

and he li[ð]de ȝeond þis lond and scæwede þea leoden.

He funde wunsum ane stude vppen ane watere.

þaer he gon aræren riche ane burhe;

mid bouren and mid hallen mid hæȝe stan walle.

Þa þe burh wes i-maked þa was he swiðe mare.

þa burh wes swiðe wel idon and he hire sette name on.

he ȝef hire to hire tirful name Troye þe Newe.

to munien his ikunde whone he icomen weore.

(ll. 1009–18)

[He saw all of this among the people (on the land/in the tongue) that was dear to his heart. Then he thought of Troy, where his kin had suffered such misery; and he travelled throughout the land, and saw the countries [people]. He found a fair place by a water where he began to raise a rich city, with rooms and with halls and with high stone walls. The city was well made, and very spacious. The city was very well done, so he gave it a name. He gave it a glorious name. Troy the New, to remember his kin and whence they came.]

Conspicuous in the Laȝamonic account is Brutus' memory of Trojan suffering, which informs Brutus' decisions regarding place-names.[9] It is important to note here that Laȝamon's Brutus seeks to commemorate not only his ancestral line, but also their tragic displacement from their homeland, the *teone* or 'horror' of cultural annihilation. In this way, the edifice becomes signifier not only of the cultural memory of its diaspora, but also of the violent ruptures that underlie the new dominion. Brutus, as the reference to the *teone* seems to remind us, caused the death of both of his parents, and the island itself could not be conquered or renamed until the impediment posed by the Albion giants had been overcome. Brutus here assumes the role of historian-translator, reinforced by La3amon's use of the *liðe–londe* formula used in the prologue in reference to his own process of acquiring historical texts. La3amon's unprecedented attention to the concrete details of the civic edifice reinforces his concern for the colonized. Further, his double assertion of the familiar term *leod* underscores the association of land, people and language. 'Albion', once the home of the non-literate (and non-history-producing) giants, is thus 'translated' into the property of the new ruler whose name it bears. Underneath Brutus' tacit decision to rename the land is the fact that the land possessed both a name and a community of inhabitants. Lacking language and the ability to record their own history – 'Heora nomen ne herde neuer tellen a leoda ne a spella' (l. 903) (I never heard their names either in story nor in tale) – the giants are subject to cultural erasure, with the eponymous 'Goemagog's Leap' ('Goemagog's Lupe') remaining as the single geographic trace of their existence.

The building of the capital and the renaming of the island are both acts of construction. 'Troy the New' commemorates cognate violent displacements: the exile of Brutus and the Trojans from the Mediterranean, the destruction of the insular natives, and the severance of the Britons from their own history. The cultural heritage of the Trojan exiles is, then, in Foucault's terms, 'an unstable assemblage of faults, fissures, and heterogeneous layers that threaten the fragile inheritor from within or from underneath'.[10] Narrative traditions of the divine grant of the land of original unity serve to conceal such faults, in the same way that the providential historiographic narrative attempted to smooth the ruptures and contradictions underlying the English and Norman conquests. In calling attention to the violence underlying insular history, the *Brut* questions the privileged status of insular historiographic master-narratives; it exposes such narratives as *translations* of violent acts inflicted upon the land and upon its people into cohesive – and hence predictable – narratives.

Accordingly, La3amon's translation of the narrative of the Trojan conquest exposes the struggle suppressed in his immediate source, Wace's *Roman de Brut*. Wace depicts this settlement as occurring over essentially blank territory, with Brutus establishing unqualified control over the landscape:

Brutus esguarda les montainnes
Vit les valees, vit les plainnes,
Vit les mores, vit les boscages,
vit les eues, vit les rivages,
vit les champs, vit les praeries,
vit les ports, vit les pescheries,
vit sun pople multepleier,
Vit les terres bien guaanier. (ll. 1209–16)

[Brutus regarded the mountains, he saw the valleys, he saw the plains, he saw the moors, he saw the forests, he saw the waters, he saw the shores, he saw the fields, he saw the grasslands, he saw the ports, he saw the fisheries, he saw his people multiply and take over the land.]

Wace's Brutus assumes the proportions of a biblical patriarch observing the settlement and growth of his people over the now pacified territory. At first glance, Laȝamon appears to have translated his source almost verbatim. Le Saux and others have noted the apparently close translation of the two accounts:[11]

Brutus hine bi-ðohte and þis folc bi-heold
bi-heold he þa muntes feire and muchele.
bi-heold he þa medewan þat weoren swiðe mære.
bi-heold he þa wateres and þa wilde deor.
bi-heold he þa fisches bi-heold he þa fuȝeles.
bi-heold he þa leswa and þene *leofliche* wode.
bi-heold he þene wode hu he bleou bi-heold he þat corn hu hit greu.
al he iseih on leoden þat him leof was on heorten.

(ll. 1001–8; italics mine).

[Brutus bethought himself and beheld this folk, beheld the mountains, fair and great, beheld the meadows that were so broad, beheld the waters and the wild beasts, beheld the fishes and beheld the birds, beheld the grass-lands and the lovely meadows; he beheld the meadows, how they flowered; he beheld the corn how it grew. All this he saw in the country among the people, that was beloved to his heart.]

However, Laȝamon's translation qualifies both the conqueror-translator's absolute authority and love for the land itself. Whereas Wace's repeated *vit* evokes possession and serves as a trope for the unqualified domin-ation of the land and of its productive capacities, Laȝamon's translation of *vit* as *bi-heold*, along with the paired term *leofliche*, must be read in

terms of the ambivalent scenes of 'lovingly beholding' in the prologue
and in the text that express love and desire for control, but also present
the possibility of change and alterations to the beholder. It embodies, in
other words, a more complex relation between colonizer and colonized
land than is to be found in Wace. In this respect, Laȝamon's choice of
word in this scene establishes and calls into question the historian-
translator's authority, and compromises it by evoking the idea of the
bibliophile's 'gaze'. Laȝamon follows this incremental repetition with a
specific detailing of the particulars of construction, emphasizing again
the consciously artificial aspects of his history, while featuring the novelty
of its name-change. Laȝamon's 'beholding' of the land emphasizes a more
reciprocal admiration and reverence between the conqueror-colonizer
and the land itself, a combination of aggression and desire that – as
chapter 2 demonstrates – the land (or text) returns. In the exchange between
colonizer and land, both are altered. *Albion* – after the destruction of its
aboriginal inhabitants – *Britain* (after Brutus), but at the same time,
Brutus becomes a *Briton*, rather than a Trojan. The exchange symbol-
ized by Laȝamon's reciprocal *beholding* thus provides a fitting metaphor
for the process through which both translator and translated territory
are changed. For Laȝamon, as a resident of a conquered land, this act
poses a threat to the territorial identity of England, but also offers the
prospect of resistance and survival through the reconstruction of conquerors as English and the revivification of the English language. It may
likewise belie a desire for at least something of the culture represented
by the Normans, evidenced by Laȝamon's own erotically charged desire
for the *French* book that Wace had composed for Queen Eleanor. In this
light, the beholding of the land is best understood in terms of the
colonist's mixture of contempt and desire for the colonized. It obviously
suggests Laȝamon's desire for his own source text, and also the later
searches in the text for figures such as Merlin, found only through the
'liðde ȝeond þis lond' process. As with the complex relationship between
Caliban, Ariel and Prospero in *The Tempest*, the questing and seeking
for the indigenous betrays both a desire to possess and appropriate, and
also a desire for the Other and the culture (s)he represents. The colonized,
in such relations, typically returns the attention of the colonizer with
desire for the (allegedly) superior culture the invader represents, but also
with a degree of resentment. Further, Brutus' status as one situated *on
leode* heightens his association with Laȝamon as translator-colonizer;
both terms associate this scene lexically with the prologue's explication
of the historian's task.

With the land under control of a literate and history-producing populace (the insular Britons), its seizure by the next group of invaders becomes more complex, and the concealment of the violence underpinning the process becomes more difficult. In his narrative of the first phase of the Saxon conquest, Laȝamon casts both attackers and defenders as translators of territory, placing the name-shaping potential of the Saxon leader, Hengest, and of his British opponents in conflict. In a scene originating with Geoffrey, Laȝamon's Hengest takes on the capacity of territorial translator when he makes what appears to be a modest request for as much land as he can cover with a bull's hide.[12] Wace expands on Geoffrey's rather brief account, emphasizing the act of construction that follows:

> Un quir de tor prist, sil fendi
> Ne cureie en estendi
> Dunt un grant terre avirona.
> Bons uvriers quist; chastel ferma
> Cest nun Wancastre li ad mis
> En language de sun païs. (ll. 6913–18)

[He [Hengest] sought out good workmen and constructed a castle, giving it the name of Thoncaster in his land's tongue.]

Although Hengest's geographic 'translation' circumscribes only a small portion of land, this act becomes, in Laȝamon's translation of Wace, an emblem for the translation of the entire island, which soon follows (historically, if not in terms of narrative). Hengest's activities leading up to the foundation of his landholding show the sleight-of-hand Laȝamon sees as characteristic of the translator:

> And þu ȝif me swa muchel lond to stonden a mire aȝere hond
> swa wule anes bules hude ælches weies ouer-spræden,
> feor from ælche castle amidden ane ualde.
> Þenne ne mai þe atwite þe hæne ne þe riche.
> þat þu æi hæhne burhȝe hæðene monne habbe bitæht.
>
> (ll. 7079–83)

[If you will give so much land, to hold in my two hands, as a bull's hide may spread either way, far from each castle, amidst a field. Then it may not be voiced, by your low men or high, that you gave any high burgh to a heathen man.]

Readers of Geoffrey (and possibly Wace's and some of Laȝamon's readers) would almost certainly recognize the scene as a Virgilian reference to Dido's founding of Carthage; Laȝamon's English readers/ audience, however, would also see in the scene a mytho-poetic origin for the Anglo-Saxon system of measurement of lands by 'hides'. Hengest loosely interprets Vortigern's modest land-grant, bending the king's words to convert a 'hide' of land – about 120 acres or half a square kilometre – into a lordly domain, at least twenty times as much land as Vortigern had in mind.[13] An act of translation and interpretation in its own right, Laȝamon expands on the material elements of his narrative. His amplification further underscores the fate of the land itself, literally wounded through Hengest's act of partitioning:

> He hæfden ænne wisne mon þe wel cuðe a craften.
> þe nom þas hude and a bord leide.
> and whætte his sæxes alse he shæren wolde.
> Of þere hude he kærf enne þwon swiðe s[m]al and swiðe long.
> nes þe þwon noht swiðe bræd buten swulc a twines þræd.
> Þa al islit wes þe þong he wes wunder ane long.
> abuten he bilæde muche del of londe.
> He bigon to deluen dic swiðe muchele.
> Þer-uppe stenene wal þe wes strong oueral.
> ane burh he arerde muchele and mare.
> Þa þe burh we[s] al ȝare þa *scop* þe he hire nome.
> he hæhte heo ful iwis Kær Carrai an Bruttisce.
> and Ænglisce cnihtes heo cleopeden þwong-chastre.
> (ll. 7102–4; italics mine)

[He had a wise man, who knew his crafts well. He took the hide and laid it on a table, and whetted his knives as if he were going to shear. From that hide he carved a thong, very thin and very long; that thong was not as broad as a thread of twine. When the thong was all slit, it was wondrously long, and with it he encircled a great deal of land. He began to delve a very great ditch, and thereupon erected a stone wall, very strong, overall. He built a great and strong burgh there. When the town was ready, he then *shaped* a name for it; he named it truly, 'Kær Carrai' in British, and the English knights called it 'Thongchester'.]

In Laȝamon's translation, the elaborate preparation of the thong for marking the land bears an unmistakable resemblance to the Exeter riddle's book (see pp. 107–8) being scraped and carved to receive the written word, including especially the fierce (*sindrum*) cutting with sharp *sæxes*. Laȝamon's poetic emphasis on the careful preparation of the material used to measure land suggests a further link between the 'hide' of the sacrificial bull and the boc-felle on which he composes his own poetic history: one circumscribes and establishes control over geographic space; the other, over temporal space. With this possible textual trope in mind, the marking of the confines of Hengest's fief is thus based fundamentally on an act of 'translation'. Hengest's skill in bending Vortigern's words to his own intentions – his subtle 'translation' – predicates his skill as a shaper of names; the 'shaping' of a name for his stronghold reflects the language of the *scop* applied to Brutus, who similarly *scupte* a name for his realm. Laȝamon's expansion of Hengest's 'translation' of a section of British land into English land thus marks the beginning of the lengthy and bloody process whereby the English overcome the land of the British and supplant British history. In this sense, although Laȝamon in no way condones Hengest's treachery, or swikedom, he does acknowledge Saxon contributions to insular history.

Later in the narrative, following Hengest's orchestrated massacre of the British nobles, he and his sæx-wielding 'Saxons' are inscribed onto the insular landscape in a paradoxical act of conquest and renaming that provides the orthographic root of the term 'Saxon'. Wace states:

> Pur remembrer la traïsun
> Des cultels orent issi nun;
> Sexes, ço dient li Engleis,
> Plusurs culteurs sunt en Franceis,
> Mais cil les nuns alques varient
> Ki ne sevent que senefient. (ll. 7297–302)

[To remember the treason of these knives, they now have the name 'Saxon', as it is said in English, 'Great Knives' it is said in French. But since then, some of these names have changed, so that we no longer know what they signify.]

Wace thus attaches a measure of political import to the act of translating names: 'Saxon' becomes a term of infamy, but loses its currency with the next group of conquerors (the Normans).[14] Laȝamon, in contrast, treats the ensuing linguistic history not as a passing term of usage, but as an act of shaping the land that effects a lasting change:

> ˈat iseȝen Bruttes þat balu wes on londe.
> and hu Sæxisce men isiȝen woeren to heom.

Bruttes *scupten* þan londe nome for Sæxisce monnen scome.
and for þan swike-dom þat heo idon hæfden.
for þan þe heo mid cnifen biræden heom at liue.
þa cleopeden heo þat lond al Æst-sæx and West-Sæx,
and þat þridde Middel-sæx. (ll. 7674–80; italics mine)

[When the Britons saw that bale [evil, destruction] was upon the land and
saw how the Saxon men had treated them, the Britons shaped names for the
land, to the Saxons' shame, and for the treachery that they had done to
them; because they had, with knives, deprived them of lives, they called the
land 'Essex,' 'Wessex', and the third, 'Middlesex'.]

Unlike Wace, Laȝamon depicts the English geographic names as still
being active as signifiers. Here, we see Laȝamon's heightened concern
for the effects of actions on the land. By renaming the provinces, the
Britons seek to effect resistance to Saxon domination, an act that may,
ironically, commemorate their enemies by applying their names to the
provinces they seize. In an act that constitutes a surprising reversal of
the relationship of colonized to colonizer, the colonized participate in
the process of translating their own land. The Britons' geographic 'translation' alienates them further from insular history. The consequences of
such a loss are evidenced in the admonition (cited in chapter 1, p. 73) given
by Geoffrey's Nennius to Lud about the memorial renaming his capital.
Nonetheless, the process initiated by the Britons effects the renaming of
the conquerors as well, who henceforth become identified with a weapon
that compromises their honour as warriors. Whatever the final outcome,
the English poet's account of the Ambresbury massacre's denouement
dramatizes the conviction that the ability to translate is the ability to
control history. Loss of this power, accordingly, reduces a race to a state
of passive receptivity to another culture's history. The overall outcome
of the Britons' translatory project following the slaughter remains indeterminate, as what follows is a long struggle for insular control.

Territorial translation and the passage of dominion

In the Galfridian tradition, British rule is not fully terminated until a
plague finally depopulates the isle – devastating, presumably, members of
both the British and Saxon populations – and a new wave of English settlers
arrives, establishing what proves to be the final translation of the land
from *Britain* to *England*. Laȝamon's narration of this final reoccupation

of the island is important to understanding the overall view of the translation of the land expressed in the *Brut*, because it concerns the colonization
of one insular culture (the Britons) by another (the English). His depiction of the English king Æthelstan's final assumption of place-names
differs from Geoffrey's and Wace's narratives of the renaming enterprise
in that, in the English *Brut*, the English ruler assumes agency for translating the land from *Britain* to *England*.[15] In a passage unprecedented
either in Wace or in Geoffrey, Æthelstan is identified specifically as a
translator by Laȝamon; after the king consolidates his power over the
Britons' former homeland, he begins changing the names: 'and þa nomen
of þan tunen: on Sexisce runen' (l. 15974) (and the names of the towns
in Saxon runes). The consequences of these changes, initiated this time
by the English conqueror, threaten alienation of the Britons not only
from their land but also from their history: new place-names, as we have
seen, obscure the participation of precursor cultures in foundational
acts, and hence give to the conquerors the illusion of self-authorship.

Comparing Laȝamon's redaction of this passage to Wace, a heightened
concern for the land becomes immediately evident. In these two hundred
and thirty lines of verse in the Caligula MS, the *Brut* features thirty-
three occurrences of the word *lond* (fire damage to this section of MS
Otho is too extensive to draw any conclusions, although the fifteen occurrences of *lond* in the surviving lines suggests a similar ratio).[16] Wace's
French equivalent, *terre*, occurs only fifteen times in two hundred and
nine lines. Accepting Le Saux's reading of a single line of Wace's verse
as a single line of Laȝamon's (rather than the one-for-two pattern usually
observed), Laȝamon still refers to *lond* once every seven lines, compared
to once every fifteen lines in Wace. If we add to this term the nine occurrences of *leod* – which combines the meanings of land, people and language
for which Wace's Anglo-Norman French has no equivalent (and which
does not occur in the surviving sections of MS Otho) – Laȝamon's total
references to the land in this section total forty-two, or approximately
once every five lines. However one tabulates lines, Laȝamon almost
trebles the frequency of references to the land found in Wace, displaying
a more consistent concern with what happens to the land itself during
periods of colonization and resettlement.

Further, Laȝamon's concentration of *lond* in the final sections of the
Brut is directly associated with the fate of the land, more so than in either
Wace or in Geoffrey, especially when he departs from his principal source.
Following Geoffrey, Wace documents the depopulation of the land
brought about by a devastating famine and flood:

Cil ki porent fuïr fuirent,
Lur fieus e lur meisuns guerpirent,
Tant put la grant chierté de blé,
Tant pur la grant mortalité. (ll. 14694–7)

[Those who could flee, fled, leaving their lands and their lands and their houses, as much for the great scarcity of corn as for the plague.]

La3amon, in contrast, adds the dimension of the calamity's effect upon the landscape:

And swa hit ilomp wide; 3eond Ænglene þeode.
þat folc ut of londe flah on ælche ænde.
monie hundred tunen; bi-læued weoren of monnen.
þat lut me uinde mihte; men uaren 3eond londe. (ll. 15896–9)

[And so it befell throughout the land of England that folk fled out of the land from both ends. Many hundred towns were left bereft of people, so that one would meet few people when traveling through the land.]

La3amon's double reference to *lond* in his translation subtly shifts emphasis from the refugees' decision to flee to the consequences of this flight to the land: depopulation leaves England open to colonization and, ultimately, to *translation* by continental Anglo-Saxons. Further, depopulation disrupts the concept of *leod*, which binds people, land and language. La3amon's later positioning of the last British king Cadwalader as *on londe* (l. 15900), echoing the Otho prologue's situation of La3amon himself (*leod* in Caligula), serves as an ironic contrast to the status of ruler as representing the three facets of the *leod*: people, land and language.

This concept takes on central importance in La3amon's depiction of the Saxon resettlement under Æthelstan (ll. 15910–78). For La3amon, as for Geoffrey and Wace, this section marks the final 'passage of dominion' from British to English rule of the island. Offering what appears to be grudging respect for the English conquerors, Geoffrey praises their unified government. He unfavourably compares the divided post-Arthurian Britons to the more organized Saxons, who appear as kingdom-founders and builders in their own rights:

At saxiones sapientes agentse, pacem et concordium inter se habentes agros colentes ciuitates and opida reedificantes and sic abiecto dominio britonum iam toti loegrie imperauerant sub duce adelstano qui primus inter eos diadema portauit. (12. 19, 535)

[The Saxons did more wisely [than the Britons] in maintaining harmony among themselves and in building castles and cities and beautiful buildings and thus throwing off the lordship of the Britons and thus they possessed all of Logres under the lordship of Æthelstan, the first among them to wear the diadem.]

For Geoffrey, the disunity of the Britons, in contrast to the superior government of the Saxons, explains the expulsion of the former from their lands, and presumably explains the later defeat of the English by the Normans. Literally and metaphorically *abiecti*, the Britons are driven to the margins of insular territory and insular history. As founders and as a united people, Geoffrey's united Saxon kingdom serves mainly as a model for the Anglo-Norman kingdom under William and his successors. In other words, the narration of the English conquest becomes a vessel for Anglo-Norman ideals of kingship and kingdom building.

In translating this passage, Wace shifts the emphasis from the unified rule of the Saxons to the translation of place-names themselves, as the geographic features of Britain and, finally, of the island itself are transformed. As with his depiction of Saxon renaming, Wace depicts the sequence as a matter of linguistic curiosity:

> Les custumes e les leis tindent
> Que lur anceisur ainz teneient
> En la terre dunt cil veneient.
> Les nuns, les lages, le language
> Voldrent tenir de lur lignange;
> Pur Kaer firent Cestre dire,
> E pur Suiz firent nomer Sire,
> E Tref firent apeler Tune;
> Map est gualeis, engleis est Shire
> En gualeis est Kaer cite,
> Map fiz, Trev vile, Suiz cunté.
> E alqunt dient que cuntree
> Swiz est en gualeis apelee
> E ço que dit Sire en engleis
> Ço puet ester Suiz en gualeis.
> [Entre Gualeis uncore dure
> De dreit bretanz la parleüre.]
> Les cuntrees, Les seignuries
> Tindrent issi e devisserent
> Cume Bretun les eumpasserent. (14736–56)

[They [the Saxons] maintained the customs and laws that their ancestors had held. They wished to keep the names, the laws, and the language of their people. For Kaer they said Cestre, and for Swydd, they named Shire, and Tref was called Town; Map is Welsh, in English it is Sune. In Welsh a city is Kaer, Map, son, Tref, town, Kaer city, and some say a county is called Swydd in Welsh, and what Shire means in English Swydd means in Welsh. Among the Welsh the correct way of speaking Briton is maintained. The counties and the baronies, the countries and the seigniories, were thus seized and devised as the Britons had previously taken them.]

By transposing their language and their laws (*leis*) – Wace never indicates which ones, however – onto a new landscape, the Saxons in effect translate Britain into England, a detail not included in Geoffrey. Wace here dramatizes efforts by the English to transform their new possessions into a copy of the original country, according to colonial models of translation. Rather than founding new cities and building new structures, however, Wace's Angles change the names and, hence, the cultural references of existing ones; they are not, in the *Roman de Brut*, necessarily better governors than were the Britons, but the circumstances of their dominion gives them the prerogative to rename the island. In this dramatization, Wace gives the impression that such conquests are the normal and accepted state of affairs. His deliberate paralleling of the Saxon to the earlier British conquest of the island – 'Tindrent issi e devisserent / Cume Bretun les eumpasserent' – reminds us that conquests have happened and continue to happen. Further, Wace participates in the acts of translation he documents; the Saxons mirror Wace's own role as translator, making Geoffrey's *Historia* a French text – 'Maistre Wace l'ad translaté' (l. 7). Wace affords his own French language privileged status in his abbreviated language lesson, standing above both Welsh and English terms as the 'real' names for the landscape features: 'cite, vile, cunte'. Wace's narrative of the English colonization thus reflects a palimpsest landscape, with subsequent layers of names (letters) glossed over previous ones.

La3amon's version of this passage offers neither the Galfridian reading of the Anglo-Saxons as builders nor Wace's depiction of them as intruders who add their bit to the linguistic irregularity of the island. Instead, La3amon's synopsis of the Anglo-Saxon conquest and resettlement conveys specific and distinctly English aspects of the transformation from *Brutlonde* to *Anglelond*, with his customary attention to the effect of such activities on the land itself. La3amon foregrounds the Anglo-Saxon *leis* – their laws and customs – that in Wace occur as a single word:

Þa tiden comen sone to Cadwalaðer kinge
into Brutaine þer þar he wunede
mid Alaine kinge þe wes of his cunne.
Me dude him to understonde of al þisse londe
Hu Aðelstan her com liðen ut of Sexlonden,
And hu he al Anglelond sette on his aȝere hond;
And hu he sette moting, and hu he sette husting,
And hu he sette sciren and makede frið of deoren,
And hu he sette holimot, and hu he sette hundred,
And þa nomen of þan tunen on Sexisce runen;
And ȝilden he gon rere mucle and swiðe mære,
And þa chirchen he gon dihten after Sexisce irihten,
And Sexis he gan kennen a nomen of an monnen;
And al me him talde þe tiden of þissen londe. (ll. 15965–78)

[The tidings came soon to King Cadwalader, into Brittany where he dwelled with King Alaine his kinsman. One made him understand concerning this land, how Æthelstan had come here from Saxony, and how he set all of England in his own hand; and how he established the *moot* and set the *husting*; and how he established shires and made enclosures for deer; and how he established holy-*moot*, and how he established the hundreds, and how he set the names of the towns in Saxon letters, and how he established many great gilds, and how he established Saxon rights in all of the churches and gave Saxon names to all of the people; and one told him [Cadwalader] such things concerning this land.]

It may seem curious that Laȝamon omits the various terms for place-names, since he is demonstrably concerned with language elsewhere in the *Brut*. In his narrative of the transition from Britain to England, however, Laȝamon seems to dramatize the establishment of an Anglo-Saxon England. Laȝamon credits his Anglo-Saxon ancestors with the foundation of English laws and customs; in so doing he transforms the sequence into English foundational narrative. Further, by inserting familiar Anglo-Saxon institutional and legal terms, such as *sciren*, *husting*, *holimot*, into his translation, Laȝamon, with his insider's knowledge of English history, rehabilitates the specifically English contributions to the insular landscape. James Noble has argued that Laȝamon carefully differentiates between the Saxon invasions and the second English conquest of Britain by depicting the second as a settlement of already vacated land, hence possessing more legitimacy than Hengest's attempted usurpation of British sovereignty.[17] Although there is, doubtless, an echo of William I and the Domesday Book in Æthelstan's methodical partitioning of the land, as Stein argues, there is also strong historical evidence for all of these institutions being of Anglo-Saxon origin.[18] Whether the institutions are historically English or not, it is evident that La3amon makes an effort to highlight English contributions to the insular landscape, crediting them with the foundation of institutions that remain in place in his own day. In contrast to Geoffrey's and Wace's narratives, in which the achievements of the Angles are ephemeral and subject to reversal-revision by Anglo-Norman conquerors, La3amon's translation of this passage renders his Saxons as Saxons, not as 'alien reality' but on their own terms, with their own laws and customs. He thus resists the closure of previous cultures demanded by orthodox historiography, and further exposes ways in which previous historians translated histories for their own ends.

In La3amon's amplification of this scene, the repeated use of the incremental *hu he* calls attention to the agency of the Anglo-Saxon leader Æthelstan in founding the new Anglo-Saxon kingdom; as a cultural founder, Æthelstan becomes yet another emblem of the historian-translator. His reorganization of the land, especially his establishment of the shire (hundreds) system, cements his possession of the land, and hence finalizes its transition from Britain to England. Wace and Geoffrey both ascribe the transfer of insular dominion to the English en masse, with the English king coming after the fact as the first Germanic ruler to govern the entire island. Although Leckie dismisses La3amon's presentation of the Saxon succession as 'confusion', what La3amon accomplishes through his loose translation of Wace is the elevation of Æthelstan to the status of foundational hero – parallel in stature to, yet distinct in method from Brutus. In representing the imposition of English law as the single act of a single ruler, La3amon transforms the entire passage into an assertion of collective English identity, with the king as symbol of the English *leod*.[19] Æthelstan's resettlement of the island, which significantly includes the imposition of Saxon names on the people, translates territory into England and the inhabitants into Saxons. It is no accident that the above passage contains only the fourth use of the term *Anglelond* (England) in the *Brut*: the first occurring in the prologue (l. 9), the next in reference to the English colonists who come in the wake of Gurmund's invasion, and the third during the account of Augustine of Canterbury's mission to the English.

Concerning the passage of dominion, the difference in philosophies between La3amon and his sources is small, but significant. In both Geoffrey and Wace, English control only coincides with the succession of Æthelstan; in Laȝamon, it is Æthelstan who initiates the unification of the kingdom and the final renaming of the landscape.[20] Indeed, examination of Laȝamon's resettlement episode reveals translation enacted upon the landscape and upon the people in a way that celebrates the English colonization project as the founding of a distinctive social order, unlike that of its precursor culture. Connecting the land to the historical text, which Laȝamon does overtly in his prologue, Æthelstan can be seen as analogous to the historian-translator, whose translation alters the source text while effacing traces of this act of territorial translation. Laȝamon's translation of Wace's French text thus reasserts the English *leod* in terms of language, land and people. The English *Brut*'s unprecedented reference to the imposition of Anglo-Saxon names on the human inhabitants reminds the reader that it is not uninhabited land that the English inherit. Rather, the renaming, or literal translation, of the remaining (presumably British) inhabitants gives the appearance of original settlement. This (apparently anthropologically accurate) line bears an unmistakable resemblance to the habit of post-Conquest Saxons of adopting French names. The latter process has been linked to the process of translation in post-colonial environments.[21] Thus, in this short but significant passage, we find the translation of two elements of the *leod* – people and land: the people from Britons to Angles, and the land itself from Britain to England.

Just as Laȝamon complicates his narrative of the inception of British dominion, he modifies and qualifies its conclusion. His precursor, Wace, proleptically documents the demise of British rule, presenting this fact as a complete erasure of the British people and of their history: 'Tuz les Bretuns si eissillierent / Que unches pis ne redrescenent' (They [the Saxons] drove out all the Britons, who never returned).[22] Wace, though not invested in the providential historiographic model, nonetheless consigns the insular Britons (Welsh) to oblivion as part of his Anglo-Norman historiographic agenda, as did Anglo-Norman providential historians. In contrast to Wace, Laȝamon cites the enduring trace of British (or Welsh) in the otherwise Anglicized landscape: 'and ȝed þe nome [Brutus] læsteð and a summe stude cleouieð faste' (l. 981) (And yet the name lasts and in some places cleaves fast). A first-hand witness to the reality of Welsh (British) survival and resistance, Laȝamon translates Wace's narrative of complete displacement as one of layering, reinforced by his choice of the comparative *neoðere* (lower) for Wace's totalizing presentation of all the Britons being driven out and never returning. British history thus continues underneath the successive layers of English and

Norman domination; it further exerts its influence on the historical traditions of both cultures through the introduction of Arthur and other figures.[23] Laȝamon's depiction of the insular Britons carries with it the implicit understanding that the English and their history need not suffer complete erasure from the geographic page of insular history.

Norman *nið-craften and the land in context*

The latest group of conquerors, the Normans, make no direct appearance in the *Brut*, but Laȝamon mentions them twice as future conquerors. Their central act is the translation of the capital city's name, from Lunden to Lundres; through this, they provide the last in a series of such translations that each mark a new conquest of the island: 'Seoððen comen Normans: mid heore nið-craften, / and nemneden heo Lundres' (ll. 3546–7) (Afterward came the Normans, with their evil craft, and named it [the capital city] 'Lundres'). The term *nið-craften* seems central to our understanding of the role the Normans play in translating England. Although readers agree that the term is unflattering, interpretations of it vary: 'evil crafts' (Madden), 'evil ways' (Barron and Weinberg), 'nasty malice' (Allen), among others. Of course, how strongly the negative connotations of *nið-craften* are read determines how Laȝamon's view of the Normans is to be understood. A possible interpretation of the term that has not been explored by critics derives from the Icelandic saga tradition of the *nið-visu*, or *nið*-poem.[24] The *nið* was a psychosexual insult directed at an enemy with the intent of reducing his manhood. Significant to the *Brut* is the explicit association between insular invasion, such as the Norman Conquest, and the use of the *nið*. Margaret Clunie Ross further observes a connection between 'incantations arousing the *landvættir* (land spirits) to defend the land and the sexually expressed idiom of humiliation, called *nið*, applied to their victims'.[25] Associated with narratives of insular invasion and conquest, especially in the Icelandic *landnaman* (literally 'land-taking') episodes, *nið* may directly refer to the Norman seizure and translation of English territory.[26] By Norman *nið-craft*, Laȝamon may well mean that the invaders have asserted control over the island by exercising a sort of ritual verbal humiliation upon the indigenous inhabitants. Whatever the etymology of this unique compound, it seems evident that, in Laȝamon's eyes, one of the most pernicious element of the Conquest has been the translation of place-names, through which the conquerors effect the translation of the land. This concern is evident in Laȝamon's only other direct reference to the Norman Conquest, in which he depicts the Normans as having changed the name of its capital *mid heore leodþeaw* (MS Caligula). A verbal parallel to the later line, *mid her nið-craften, leodþeaw* also carries linguistic implications. In the context of Laȝamon's expressed view of translation and its impact upon the land, the *nið-craften* Laȝamon accuses the Normans of practising would seem to refer overtly to their activities as territorial translators. Given the linguistic associations of the name-changes executed by the Normans, the reference becomes a complex wordplay on the Normans' ability to control English history through their imposition of new names and a new language on the land. I suggest that the renaming of the capital *is* the Normans' *nið-craften*: as translators of territory, the French name gives it the appearance of being a French city, in much the same way that Anglo-Norman and Angevin courts had the appearance of French courts. For Laȝamon, the translation of the capital city into French works as a metaphor for the process of translating English history into French and Latin: both give the impression of original possession and conceal the displacement of earlier cultures. Laȝamon's writing, in contrast, brings the previously suppressed elements to the surface.

Through the process of territorial translation, insular conquerors, from the Romans to the Normans, create the appearance of original creation and authorship. Albion becomes Briton, then England; the British become the Welsh; and New Troy becomes Lundene; then London, and finally, Lundres (Laȝamon might feel vindicated to learn that the city has recovered its English name, London). For Laȝamon, the possibility that a similar linguistic and cultural displacement may be inflicted upon the English – like the one that has already befallen their capital – is all too real. He accordingly deploys historical translation as a means of resistance to continental encroachment. At the same time, the *Brut* brings the English people and their language back into full participation in the construction of insular history, heretofore dominated by French and Latin.

Heresy and martyrdom: the missionary as conqueror-translator

In Laȝamon's history, the conversion of the English precedes the final conquest of the island, as it does in Geoffrey and Wace. Although conversion would seem to affect the populace more than the land itself, Laȝamon's unique treatment aligns Augustine's mission to the English with the foundational narratives of Brutus, Æthelstan and William. In contrast to scenes of military conquest, conversion seems salutary because the invader also assumes the role of a benevolent converting missionary, and the object of 'translation' includes land and people in the broader framework of universal (Catholic) Christianity. The establishment of a 'Christian' kingdom has important implications for the land. In this instance, however, the potential for unity is undercut, both by conflicts between the clerics over control of territory and by disparities in the historical accounts of the conversion itself. Indeed, conquest initially serves as a metaphor for conversion in the narrative, but only until territorial control becomes the central issue of Augustine's activities. Uniquely among twelfth-century accounts of the event, La3amon's presents both the beneficial and aggressive aspects of conversion. He ultimately treats the conversion of the insular English to Christianity, which precedes the final conquest and settlement of the island, as another instance of territorial translation. The narrative of Augustine's mission to the English reached La3amon through two varying avenues: from the English version of Bede's *Historia*, and from Wace's translation of Geoffrey's account, itself an intra-Latin translation of Bede. The direct conflict between the accounts of the conversion in two of La3amon's cited source texts leads La3amon to dramatize the conversion as another instance of the power of translation to establish history.[27]

Augustine makes his first appearance in Bede's *Historia Ecclesiastica*. Bede initially depicts Augustine as an apostolic exemplar, predictably deploying the language and conventions of hagiography:

> At ubi datam sibi mansionem intraverunt, coeperunt apostolicum prmitivæ ecclesiæ vitam imitari; orationibus videlicet assiduis, vigilis, ac ieiuniis serviendo, verbum vitæ quibus poterant prædicando, cuncta huiusmundi velut aliena spernendo, ea tantum quæ victui necessaria videbantur, ab eis quos docebant, accipiendo, secundum ea quæ docebant ipsi per omnia vivendo, et par Atum ad patiendum adversa quæque, vel etiam ad moriendum pro ea quam prædicabant veritate animum habendo. (I. 26)

> [But after they were now entered into their lodging, they began to follow the apostolic life of the primitive Church; that is to wit by submitting to continual prayer, watching and fasting, preaching the word of life to as many as they could, spurning all the things of this world as alien, taking of those they were teaching only so many goods as were necessary, accepting the same life they had instructed others to follow, having a spirit ready for patient endurance of adversity even to death to defend the truth of what they preached.][28]

In his intralinguistic translation of the scene, Geoffrey includes no such references, thereby omitting mention of Augustine's purity, stating only that Augustine and his company quickly converted many of the English. Laȝamon's two sources thus recount the same conversion, but, being composed for two different audiences in two different historical periods, they differ dramatically; Laȝamon, however, makes no attempt to smooth over these contradictions. Rather, as the historical traditions of Geoffrey (via Wace) and Bede come to a crux, Laȝamon transforms the passage into an exemplum of the protean role of translation in forming even religious history; his presentation of the translation of land dramatizes the slippage from the genre of hagiography to that of secular history, as the narrative of Augustine's activities becomes another foundational narrative.

As the missionary Augustine intends to convert the English linguistic details from the *Brut*'s lexicon of conquest/colonization narratives underscore Laȝamon's particular depiction of the effect of conversion upon the land. For instance, the 'land-in-hand' formula – which would have become familiar to Laȝamon's readers by this point in the text – marks the outcome of Augustine's extensive baptismal campaign in religious terms: 'Þa iwende seint Austin vorð: æst and west and suð and norð, / and seoððe þurh-ut Engelond, and turnde hit to Godes hond' (ll. 14740–1) (Then Saint Augustine went forth, east and west, south and north, and throughout England, he turned it to God's hand). Laȝamon employs the same formula to mark the successful completion of Augustine's campaign: Augustine 'sette an Godes honde: al þat was on londe' (l. 14822). Applied to missionary activities in this phase of the narrative, Laȝamon's use of this word-pair invites contrast between Augustine and the secular colonizers, such as Brutus and Æthelstan, each of whom sets the 'land' on his 'hand'. Such metaphoric use of conquest is hardly unique to Anglo-Saxon poetry: for instance, the anonymous author of the Old English *Andreas* uses it in reference to the apostles, and the *Dream of the Rood* refers to Christ as 'Hæleð' (hero).[29] Laȝamon's use of the language of conquest in this passage places the *Brut* in an established tradition of English religious poetry. His portrait of Augustine as *Saint militant* associates metaphorically the missionary's winning of the land for God with the conqueror's seizure of territory for his and his people's dominion.

The ecclesiastical and the secular modes of discourse here work in seeming harmony, converting the entire landscape from pagan or mixed to Christian territory. The unifying possibility of translation is further

emblematized in the construction of 'Cernel', a holy place located at the
site of Augustine's divine vision. The founding of Cernel, along with the
Latin-Hebrew orthography underlying the name, originates with Wace,
who offers a fairly lengthy discourse on the fusion of the words *cerno*
and *el*:

> Puis ad un bastun fichié dreit
> Illoc u Deu veü aveit;
> Unve veine d'ewe en sailli
> Ki tute la place cuvri.
> L'ewe surt e li ruissels crut,
> Sun canol fist, aval curut.
> N'esteit mie anceis la cuntree
> Herbergie ne cultivee
> Pur ço que funteine n'il surdeit.
> Saint Augustins Deu mercia
> E ses cumpaignuns cunforta;
> La lieu ad Cernel apelé
> U il aveit Deu esgardé;
> Cernel cest nun que jo ai dit
> En romans est: Deu veit u vit.
> Li clerc le poént bien savioer,
> Cerno, cernis, ço est veeir
> E Deu ad nun en ebreu El;
> De ces dous moz est fait Cernel.
> Cerno e El sun ajusté,
> Li uns dit Vei, l'autre dit Dé;
> Mais une lettre en est sevree,
> De la fin de Cerno ostee,
> Si est par une abscisiun
> Faite la compositiun;
> L'un est ebreu, l'autre latins. (ll. 13777–804)

[Then he [Augustine] sank a rod just in the spot where he had seen God. A
spring of water spurted out, covering the whole place; the water bubbled
out and the stream grew, formed a channel and ran down. The countryside
had not previously been inhabited or tilled, because there was not water or
spring there. Saint Augustine thanked God and comforted his companions.
He called the place 'Cernel' where he had seen God. Cernel is its name, as I
have said, in Romance it is thus: 'Where I have seen God'. The clerks who
have good wisdom, know it as 'cerno, cernis', that is, to see, and God has in
Hebrew, 'El'; of these two terms is 'Cernel' made. 'Cerno' and 'El' are thrust

together. For one we say 'See' the other 'El'; but one letter has been severed. From this omission was Cerno made, so that through an excision [the linguistic process of compounding] the composition was made. One is Hebrew, the other Latin.

The 'thrusting together' of the two elements in Wace's etymological account of this place-name would seem to be echoed in Laȝamon's stated methodology of compiling sources. For Laȝamon, however, the linguistic condensation becomes a poetically resonant medium for bringing the divine Word into the English language and on to the English landscape by the manual taking-up of an episcopal *staf*, which Laȝamon links lexically with the pen he assumes in his prologue. Emphasis again falls on the land:

> Þa he isaid hauede þa sæhen of ure Drihten
> his staf he nom an honde and wolde to his inne ȝeonge.
> Up he læc tene staf þat water þer-after leop.
> þe ueȝereste welles stræm þe irneð on uolden.
> Ær nes þat na tun no wunende na man.
> sone uolc gader[de] to Austin þan gode,
> and al his læuen þider gunned liðen.
> and bi-gunnen þer to bulden bi watere þa was hende.
> Moni mon þer uætte hele þene stude he cleopede Cernele.
> (cerno cernis þat is Latin ful i-wis.)
> cerno an Englisc leoden ich iseo swa his is iqueðen.
> el is Ebreowisc þat is godd ful iwis.
> þene tun he cleopede Cernel ich iseo Drihtne wil-del.
> to þissere weorlde longe þe nome þer scal stonde.
> alse his is iqueðen after Godes leoden.
> þene stude to iwurðien þer stod ure Drihten.
> and his engles mid him þa he spac wið Austin. (ll. 14809–17)

[There he struck his staff near where he knelt and his comrades said things he liked very well. Then he said that he had the word of our Lord. He took his staff on hand and would return to his inn. When he took up the staff, water leapt thereafter. The fairest well-stream ever seen on land. Before there was no town, there dwelt no kin. Soon folk gathered to Austin the good and all his followers came thither and began to build there, by the water that was so fair. Many men were there made whole and the place was called Cernel. Cerno cernis, that is, truly, in Latin. 'Cerno', in English speech, is 'I see'. 'El' is Hebrew, for God, indeed. The town is called 'Cernel', 'I see God'. This name shall stand to the world's end, as it is called in God's own language. At the place where God stood, and his angels with him, where he spoke to Austin.]

Gone from La3amon's translation is the reference to the loss of grammatical suffix and the Latinate etymology of 'Cerno'. In its place, La3amon adds an unprecedented reference to Hebrew as 'God's own [antediluvian] language' – the divine vernacular existing before the biblical post-Babel diaspora of language – and the author's opinion that the name is to 'stand to the world's end', in contrast to the transitory nature of previous place-names. Steiner comments on the belief that 'God's actual speech, the idiom of immediacy known to Adam and common to men until Babel, can still be decoded, partially at least, in the inner layers of Hebrew and, perhaps, in other languages of the original scattering'.[30] Here, La3amon establishes a direct conduit from English, through Latin, to the divine language of the Old Testament patriarchs, omitting French as an intrusive vernacular. He thereby brings the English audience into contact with the eternal Word, expressed through the trope of the well and made to extend from ancient Biblical history to the apocalyptic 'last days'. The healing power of the waters uncovered by Augustine's staff reflects the salvific power of the divine Word, even as the iconic episcopal gesture of thrusting the staff into the earth and drawing forth revivifying water allegorizes that aspect of La3amon's own textual translation methodology, whereby the author penetrates the ground of the prior tradition in order to extract the life-giving version he inscribes in the vernacular for the English. Given the well-established link between the land and the text – evident in such texts as Alain de Lille's *Le Planctu Naturae* – it is not difficult to see a connection between Augustine's application of his staff to the textualized landscape and La3amon's application of his pen and stylus to the blank *boc-felle*: both are foundational acts, archaeological discoveries that look beneath the layers of the palimpsest of English historiography; as such, they seem, at least temporarily, to reach beyond translation and, thus, beyond history. Through their reproductive potential, both offer restoration and revivification to the populace.[31] Augustine's act promises to deliver the 'truth' La3amon claims in the prologue to have culled from his source texts. Translation, in La3amon's 'envisionment', seems capable of transcending its own immanent violence and of uniting disparate languages into a single, divine community. This passage also suggests an alternative reproductive and life-affirming conception of historical translation when it involves restoration of the vernacular. Laȝamon thus appears to cast Augustine as a deified spiritual 'conqueror', whose activities seem to transcend the secular process of repeated conquest.

The moment, however, proves fleeting, for intrusion of the institutional Church and its politics disrupts the unity promised by the Augustinian mission. Again, the 'disparity' identified by Foucault as lying at the core of historical beginnings undermines the unity that the discovery of the linguistic origin uncovered in this section of the text. The shift from conversion to conquest is predicted fairly early in the narrative of Augustine's mission. Wace's Augustine displays a secular side, with human foibles that threaten to undermine his saintly status. Wace presents an especially ludicrous Augustine, easily discouraged, impatient and vindictive: he adds to the Galfridian narrative a 'miracle', the attachment of tails to the intransigent citizens of Dorchester who mock and humiliate Augustine:

> E il pria nostre Seignur
> Que de cele grant desenur
> E de cele orrible avilance
> Ait en els signe e remembrance:
> E il si orent veirement
> E avrunt perpetuelment,
> Kar tresturit cil cil ki l'escharnirent
> E ki les cues li pendirent
> furent cué cues orent
> E unkes puis perdre nes porent
> Tuit cil unt puis esté cué
> Ki vindrent de cel parenté,
> Cué furent e cué sunt,
> Cues unt detriés en la char
> En remembrance de l'eschar
> Que il fieent al Deu ami
> Ki des cues l'orent laidi. (ll. 13727–44)

[And he prayed to our Lord, of this great dishonour and this horrible humiliation, that there be a sign and remembrance; and they had them to see, and to be around them perpetually, for those who mocked him and hung tails on him, had tails and will have tails and may never lose them; all of the place is tailed and they get them from their parents, tailed they were and tailed they will be, tails they had and tails they will have, tails have been placed on their seats in remembrance of the mock that they had done to the friend of the Lord and of the tails they had burdened him with.]

La3amon heightens the emotional content of the passage as we read of an even more petulant Augustine, one who calls on the vengeance of God in a state of very human anger:

> Seint Austin heo weoren laŏ, and he iwraŏ swiŏe wraŏ.
> And he fif milen iwende from Dorchestre,
> And come to ane munte þe muchel wes and hende.
> þer he lai on cneowe ibede and cleopede auere touward Gode
> þat he hine awreke a þan awarriede uolke
> þa hine isend hafden mid heore scaŏe deden. (ll. 14756–61)

[They were hateful to Saint Augustine, and he grew very angry with them. And he went five miles from Dorchester, and came to a great and high mountain. There he knelt on one knee and called to God, asking that he would avenge him on those vicious people, they who had shamed him with their wicked deeds.]

Shortly afterward, Augustine and his followers decide to return to Rome to complain about their ill treatment: 'he cleopede to Drihtene: þe scop da3es lithe, / særimod and sorhfulle: heom sceomeded wel sære' (ll. 14773–6) (called to God who shaped daylight, sorrowful and down-hearted that they had been so sorely shamed). Augustine's human foibles of fearfulness and vindictiveness provide some comic moments in Bede's *Historia Ecclesiastica* as well, for example when he and his colleagues nearly give up the mission and must be exhorted by a letter from Pope Gregory to return.[32] Beyond the mild humour, however, the Dorchester narrative marks a turning point in Augustine's career; in La3amon, after this event, he and his followers become increasingly concerned with the control of territory, tangential to their concern for worldly reputation in the above-cited passage. It may be telling in La3amon that, following the Britons' rebuke, La3amon refers to him as *Saint* Augustine only once more, whereas Wace maintains the title throughout the narrative.[33]

A more serious instance of the conflation of secular and religious issues occurs when Augustine's unsuccessful synod with the British clergy leads to the slaughter of hundreds of British monks. In this section, the issue becomes not conversion to Christianity, but control over church property and over the dissemination of religious ideology. In matters of language and translation, further, the different ways of interpreting the slaughter in La3amon's source texts, Bede, Geoffrey and Wace, provide La3amon with a poignant reminder of the different interpretative possibilities posed by historical translation. La3amon's significant reintroduction of the insular ethnographic conflict in this scene reminds his readers of the political power concerns that inform both historiography and religion. In Bede's *Historia*, Augustine represents the authority of the Roman church, to which Bede was allied, and the insular Britons represent recalcitrant and almost heretical dissent. Bede's narrative can be summarized thus: Augustine of Canterbury, having made great headway in converting the Angles, summons the British clergy of the nearest province to a synod; greeting them in 'pace catholica', the missionary asks that the Britons follow Roman doctrine and that they aid in ministering to the Saxons and, hence, in creating a unified Christian kingdom. The Britons initially reject Augustine's requests, but after failing a significant 'miracle test', they agree to a second synod. The British clergy then consult a hermit, who tells them that they should follow Augustine's dictates only if he practises Christian humility by rising in their presence. Augustine remains seated at the second synod, so the British refuse all of his requests, including the most important, that they aid in proselytizing the Angles and Saxons. Augustine threatens the British church with war with the Saxons if they refuse unity with the Roman church:

Quibus vir Domini Augustinus fertur minitans prædixisse, quia si pacum cum fratribus accipere nollent, bellum ab hostibus forent accepturi.[34]

[To whom the man of God Augustine is said to have threateningly prophesied, if they did not wish peace with their brothers, they must accept war from their enemies.]

Augustine's prediction proves accurate, as the British are crushed some years later at Chester, with the Saxons deliberately targeting the monks, although, according to Bede, Augustine had 'iam multo ante tempore ad cælestia regna' (many years before this time [gone] to the celestial kingdom).[35]

Bede's rhetorical solution to the potential dilemma of Christian-versus-Christian violence involves subtle use of the language of heresy and apostasy to denigrate the British clergy. In both Bede's original Latin and the Old English translation, the Britons are condemned for preferring their own traditions over those of the Catholic Church 'quæ per orbem sibi in Christo concordant' (which throughout the world agreed together in Christ) (2. 2) and for refusing to participate in the proselytizing of the English, which would unite the island under the authority of Rome. They thus threaten schism. By defying Augustine's attempt at unification, the British bishops miss a chance for friendship with their erstwhile enemies. In contrast to the saintly humility of Bede's Augustine, the Britons express constant concern with their secular status. Hailing from a 'nobilissimo' (most noble) monastery and jealously protective of their customs, these clerics accentuate their worldly power: they resist submission to Augustine for fear of suffering loss of prestige: 'si modo nobis adsurgere noluit, quanto magis si ei subdi coeperimus, iam nos pro nihilo contemnet' (they spoke among themselves: if he will not rise for us, much more, if we are his underlings, will he then hold us for nothing).[36] Although Bede never directly ascribes 'heresy' to the British clerics, he implicitly accuses them of this crime through deploying narrative events and lexical terms similar to those used elsewhere to denounce such sects as the Pelagian heretics. Bede uses the term *perfidia* (unbelief or heresy, *treowðleas* in English) in reference to both.[37] In the earlier episode where Saint Germanus rebukes the Pelagian bishops, Bede deploys the 'healing of the blind' motif, wherein the Pelagians' inability to heal a blind person signifies their spiritual impotence.[38] Although the Britons encountered by Augustine more than one hundred and fifty years later have committed no overt acts of heresy, the English Bede deploys a parallel scene to exemplify the Britons' inability to imbue a significantly English blind man with spiritual 'vision':

> [Augustine] bæd God Fæder ælmihtigne, þæt he þam blindan men gesyhðe forgefe, þæt he þurh anes monnes licomlice inlihtnesse in monigra geleafsumra heortan þæs gastlican leohtes gife onbærnde.[39]

> [Augustine prayed to God the Father Almighty that he might give the blind man his sight, that he might, through the bodily light in one man, make the spiritual light burn in the hearts of many.]

Augustine succeeds where their British rivals fail, with the Britons' failure emblematizing their lack of spiritual 'sight'.[40]

After the narrative of the British monks, Bede excludes the Britons from insular history altogether. For Bede, writing in eighth-century Northumbria, such realignment is necessary to clear the landscape for the rise of the English church. Bede, whose interest in writing ecclesiastical history lies in promoting the legitimacy and authority of the new religious order, treats the ensuing destruction of the Britons as a providentially decreed punishment for their sin. However, the very presence of the 'synod' episode in the *Historia* signals a key problem for Bede's rhetorical attempt to justify the Saxon takeover: Christian-versus-Christian violence directly contradicts the notion of a universal faith, and only employment of the discourse of heresy (*perfidia*) offers closure to the situation. Augustine's failure to rise in the presence of his British colleagues does seem arrogant. According to Howe, the episode serves Bede as evidence of the Britons' reliance on style and appearance over substance, a characteristic flaw of their religion.[41] Bede, however, offers no explanation for Augustine's action, other than that 'it happened': 'Facumque est, ut veneiuntibus illis sederet Augustineus in sella' (And it so happened that when they [the Britons] arrived Augustine was there and sat in his seat).[42] His failure to rise in their presence does seem a legitimate concern; British culpability in the events that follow thus becomes a matter of interpretation.

Heresy, of course, poses a particular threat to institutional Christianity as something neither fully Christian nor fully Other (pagan). As a further example from Laȝamon's own century, the German 'Publican' or 'Weaver' heretics condemned at Oxford in 1166 cast themselves as martyrs, justifying their position before the Great Council by citing passages from the Gospel that seem to justify martyrdom.[43] Responding with force, the bishops' council branded them with the 'hæreticæ infamiæ characterem' ('mark of heretical ignominy'), flogged them, and expelled them from the city, where they died from exposure.[44] The condemnation of the heretics involves an act of inscription akin to the translation of texts; the wounded bodies and branded foreheads of the condemned become textual surfaces for the inscribing of the visible signs of heresy. Literally and metaphorically *abject* (to use Julia Kristeva's term), its presence threatens the Church's conception of a singular unified Christianity.[45] The expulsion and deaths of the *Publicans* serve to 'purify' the English landscape and populace and to restore the Church's sense of unity. In like manner, the branding of the British clergy as heretics by Bede and later historians stigmatizes them in a way that justifies the ensuing violence enacted against their physical bodies. Bede's narration translates the massacre itself into a visible sign of the English ecclesiastical establishment's hegemonic ascendancy over the rival Celtic church.

As Geoffrey and later historian–translators prove, however, such translation practices can work both ways. Although Bede asserts that Augustine had died long before the massacre occurred, the suspicion of complicity in the act brought about by the 'prophecy' is unavoidable, and would be fully exploited by Geoffrey. Further, the massacre of the monks carries the conventional trappings of martyrdom – Christians engaged in prayer slain by a pagan host. It would seem that traces of an earlier and ultimately untranslatable narrative threaten to subvert Bede's providentialist reading from the onset. Geoffrey preserves the same plot skeleton, but modifies the scene to transfer hagiographic designation – along with audience sympathy – to the British clerics. As in Bede, Geoffrey's Britons refuse to participate in the conversion of the Anglo-Saxons. However, he gives his Britons a voice and a legitimate reason for so doing; their bishop Dinoot (named for the first time) backs up their argument with 'diversis argumentationibus' (diverse arguments), so that the encounter becomes a clash of doctrines, rather than a one-sided condemnation of British spiritual arrogance.[46] Geoffrey omits the second synod, along with the famous 'sitting' scene; instead, immediately after Dinoot's snub, the recent convert Ethelbert, perhaps out of misplaced loyalty to Augustine or improper understanding of Christian doctrine, contacts his kinsman Ethelfrid, King of Northumbria ('Alfred' in Wace), to attack Dinoot and his monks.[47] The massacre of twelve hundred clergymen in Geoffrey thus reconfigures the attack on Bangor as a direct retaliation for the British clergy's defiance of Augustine. As a result, the slaughter becomes less a providential judgement and more an act of vengefulness and a power play, with Augustine at least subtly implicated. Geoffrey's most important alteration, however, concerns the issue of temporal power. Augustine desires not so much the cooperation of the British as their submission: 'Augustino petenti ab episcopis britonum subiectionem & suadenti ut secum genti Anglorum communem evangelizandi' (Augustine demanded submission from the British bishops and urged that they join together in the evangelizing of the English).[48] With the martyrdom he assigns to the Britons – 'et sic mill ducenti eorum in ipsa die martyrio decorati, regni cælestis adepti sunt sedem' (and twelve hundred on that same day were adorned with martyrdom, gaining a seat in Heaven) – Geoffrey reverses Bede's carefully crafted condemnation, while preserving the central plot of the narrative. In his depiction of the event, Geoffrey echoes the orthodox conviction that those who die for the sake of their faith gain instant salvation. The motives behind Geoffrey's intralingual translation are not difficult to discern. Working to present the Anglo-Norman dynasty as the political and spiritual heirs of the exalted ancient Britons, Geoffrey promotes the British church. Transforming heretics into martyrs achieves this purpose; four hundred years after Geoffrey's death, post-Reformation historiographers would repeat this rhetorical move in a much more elaborate fashion to transform the independence-minded Britons into prototypes for English Protestantism. The sixteenth-century Protestant antiquarian John Bale, for instance, cited the passage as historical precedence for an insular British church independent of Rome.[49]

Wace places even more emphasis than does Geoffrey on power issues. He omits entirely the demand for aid in converting the English, shifting the focus to Augustine's assertion of authority over England, with emphasis on the land:

> Saint Augustine demander fist
> Les set evesques, si lur dist
> Que il ert de Rome legat
> E d'Engleterre esteit primat,
> Si deveient beneïçun
> De lui receivre par raisun
> E estre en sa subjectiun. (ll. 13835–91)

[Saint Augustine sent to these seven bishops, demanding that, since he was legate of Rome and primate of England, they should, by reason, receive benediction from him and be under his subjection.]

Further, unlike Geoffrey, Wace adds that Augustine spoke of the matter to King Æelbthert (l. 13867), yet he inserts the sinfulness of the Britons: 'Seint Augustin unt refuse / Par hunte d'els e pur vilté' (ll. 13882–4) (They had rejected Saint Augustine through their sin and their villainy). Further complicating his own moral stance on the event, Wace laments the ensuing slaughter of the Britons through a series of *exclamatio*:

> Deus, quell dolur! Deus, quell pechié!
> N'en eurent pas greinur pitié
> Que lus fameillu de berbiz
> Mult en firent grant tueïz. (ll. 13917–20)

[God, what misery! God, what sin! They showed no more pity than starving men would to a sheep; they made a great slaughter.]

The *Roman de Brut* shifts opprobrium from the Britons to the pagan Saxons, depicted not as instruments of divine justice but as cold-blooded killers. In both Geoffrey and Wace, the same clerics deemed 'heretical' by Bede gain the status of martyrdom through actions stemming from their rejection of the orthodox Augustine himself. Like Geoffrey, Wace also honours the slaughtered Britons with the title 'martyr', albeit in a more circumspect way:

Dous milliers e dous cent en pristrent
Sis decolerent e ocistrent
N'en est moine ne clerc estuers,
Martirs firent des comfessors. (ll. 13921–4)

[Two thousand and two hundred were taken, decapitated and slain. There
were no monks or clerics slain who were not martyrs or confessors.]

With his customary scepticism, Wace reverses the process of martyrdom,
implying that the victims achieved the mantle only by virtue of their
suffering violent deaths.

Perusal of both the Geoffrey-Wace and Bedan accounts of the event,
such as Laȝamon may well have undertaken (he claims to have done so,
and nothing in the *Brut* precludes the possibility), would logically call
attention to the discrepancy between the two events and the power of
the translator to impose meaning on them. The pen can literally inscribe
the difference between a martyr and a heretic. For Laȝamon, the issue is
one of power. His account differs from those of Bede and Wace in his
declining to assign either martyrdom or heresy to the British clerics.
This omission has, perhaps, led critics of the *Brut* to cite the passage
either as marking the 'shift' of Laȝamon's sympathies from the Britons
to the English, or as promoting religion, rather than race, as the central
locus for conflict in the *Brut*. I. J. Kirby, for instance, argues, concerning
this scene, 'that Laȝamon has now for the first time moved away from
the Britons to devote his attention to the Angles. But not only his
attention: his sympathy, too, and this is shown in the next episode, where
Augustine comes in contact with the Britons';[50] in contrast, Wickham-
Crowley states that Laȝamon 'condemns the British bishops who refuse
their king's summons to meet Augustine because the Christianizing of the
Saxons makes the enemies of the British equals', but elsewhere argues for
an overall balanced treatment of the scene in the *Brut*.[51] Lesley Johnson
acknowledges that 'the opposition of the British clerics to the Christian
conversion of the English and their rejection of Augustine's authority
are presented in a more negative light in Laȝamon's work', but argues
that 'the subsequent death of these British clerics at the hands of the
heathen King Aelfric is not represented as a just, divine punishment, but
rather as a terrible act of slaughter'.[52] Indeed, if we compare Laȝamon to
his immediate source, Wace, and to Wace's source, Geoffrey, we find
that Laȝamon is more condemnatory toward the Britons, yet he never
reaches Bede's level of pejorative. Beyond the question of which 'side'
Laȝamon takes, however, is the intrusion of secular matters of territorial

control into the concerns of Christianity, signalled by Laȝamon's marked shift to language associated with conquest and resettlement. Laȝamon dramatizes a clash between ecclesiastical (hagiographic) and secular (heroic) historical narratives, and the ways in which the translator can manipulate both in representing competing narratives. It should come as no surprise, then, that Laȝamon should present the massacre of the British monks as a lamentable atrocity, rather than as punishment meted out by just providence, since the entire passage in the *Brut* serves to dramatize the intrusion of secular into ecclesiastical discourse. Further, there is a possibility that Laȝamon's variations may represent a rather subtle intrusion of Bedan discourse into the fabric of the Geoffrey-Wace narrative. In this case, the struggle between churches parallels the conflict between historical narratives.

As evidence of Laȝamon's enhanced concern for territorial issues, we may consider the concentration of land references in this passage: we find twenty-five *lond* and four *leod* references in the Augustine section (MS Caligula, ll. 14684–923), as opposed to six references to *terre* in Wace. Le Saux notes a twenty-line contraction on Laȝamon's part – from two-hundred and forty-seven lines in the *Roman* to two-hundred and twenty-seven lines in the English *Brut* – meaning that Laȝamon references the land four times as frequently as does Wace.[53] After baptizing both English and Saxons (Laȝamon inherits the distinction from Wace), Augustine encounters the British clergy in the portions of land still under the rule of the Britons. Laȝamon's concern for the land further manifests itself in the geographic detail that the Britons held territory in the north of England:

> Norð in Englelonde Bruttes hæfden an honde
> Muchel del of londe and castles swiðe stronge;
> ða Bruttes nalden þan Englisce buȝen. (ll. 14824–6)

[In the north of England the British had a great deal of land and very strong castles in hand; the Britons would not submit to the English.]

Once Augustine makes contact with the British clergy, his role shifts from that of a missionary, seeking to incorporate insular peoples into a universal Christian community, to that of a prelate, fighting for control of the institutional Church and the land. The claim he makes to authority over the entire island is based on his personal (and very secular) authority and leads to a violent encounter with the insular British clergy, culminating in the massacre.

The language La3amon applies to Augustine and to his British adversaries in the scene of the Bangor massacre derives from the heroic-military
lexicon associated with conquest of territory. However, unlike La3amon's
earlier use of conquest as a metaphor for Augustine's missionary activity,
which places the land in the hands of God, the language of conquest
here stresses the temporal power claimed by Augustine; the heroic idiom
jars with, rather than reinforces, Augustine's actions:

> Writen sende Austin to an seouen biscopen:
> and hehten heom comen sone and speken wið him-seolue.
> and don him hersumness and þurh him singen masse.
> for *he* haude an *honde* þa hehnesse of þissen *londe*.
>
> (ll. 14836–9; italics mine)

[Augustine sent letters to the seven bishops and commanded them to come
soon and speak with him and give him obedience, and sing mass through
him, for he had in his hand the sovereignty of this land.]

The formulaic *lond–hond* is a familiar one, associated throughout the
Brut with territorial conquest. However, here it is Augustine who claims to
hold temporal power directly in *his* – rather than God's – hand. Translators
of the *Brut* tend to overlook the implications of this statement, displacing
the agency of Augustine's power: Bzdyl translates the passage as 'he was
the highest authority of the land'; Allen prefers 'because he had been
put in possession of the highness of this land'. If the line is glossed
verbatim, however, Augustine's assumption of the role of territorial
conqueror becomes evident, as does the fact that this role compromises
his spiritual stature.

No longer serving as a trope for religious conversion, the language
of conquest and colonization signifies Augustine's involvement with
specifically historical religious disputes: his appeals are no longer to
God's but to his own secular authority. After his confrontation with the
British clergy, he turns, not to God for vindication, but to a local ruler:

> Þa wes he sari-mod: and sorh-ful an heorten.
> and fuse him gon sone: And ferde to þan king.
> and mænde to [Aðel]berte: þan kinge of Æst-Angle.
>
> (ll. 14868–70)

[then was he sorrowful and downhearted, and gathered himself soon and
complained to Ethelbert the king of East-Anglia.]

Repetition of *sari-mod* and *sorh-ful* links these two scenes, thereby presenting a rhetorical parallel that serves dramatically to underscore their dissimilarities, again highlighting Augustine's growing secularism and increasing concern for control of the land. Further, unlike Wace's Augustine, who mentions the event to Ethelbert, Laȝamon's less-than-saintly missionary goes to the king apparently with the express purpose of informing on the British clerics and exacting revenge. King Ethelbert, responding to Augustine's complaint, devises a predictably temporal revenge. The most significant shift in Laȝamon's translation of this scene, therefore, is not from British to English sympathy, but from the language of hagiography to that of heroic conflict. Laȝamon translates Augustine and his British opponents as heroic-minded resistance-fighters, in confrontation with an ambitious foreign conqueror. Laȝamon's clerics more closely resemble the holders of a feudal dominion than a monastic community: a 'high-born' abbot – 'Dinoot hæhte heore abbeod: he wes of heȝe monnen' (ll. 14832) (the abbot was named Dinoot; he was high-born) – commands a company of 'bold' monks:

> He hæfden on seuen hepen: sixtene hundred muneken.
> And ȝet þer-to: munekes swiðe balde
> And of Bruttisce streonen: stiðe imodede men. (ll. 14833–5)

[He had in seven companies, sixteen hundred monks, and yet more there, of very bold monks; and they were British-born, strong-hearted men.]

Laȝamon may be alluding obliquely to Bede's *nobilissimo* monks. In addition to foreshadowing realistically the Britons' strong defiance of Augustine, these epithets may also imply criticism of the British clergy, because of their seeming inappropriateness to monks. However, the language used to depict Laȝamon's 'high-born' and 'strong-hearted' clergy comes from the lexicon of heroic poetry used by Laȝamon himself, as well as by other authors of English poetry. For example, Laȝamon uses 'stiðmod' elsewhere in the text to characterize favourably secular luminaries such as Arthur, the 'stiðmoden king' (10592). *The Dream of the Rood*'s heroically tempered Christ bears the same epithet: 'Ongyrede hine þa geong hæleð – þæt wæs God ælmihtig! – / strang and stiðmod!' (39–40a) (Then the young warrior undressed himself – he was God almighty! – strong and strong-hearted). It is difficult, in this context, to read the 'strong-heartedness' of Dinoot and his followers strictly as condemnation. Rather, it seems to mark a determination to defend their status from outside domination, equal to Augustine's desire to obtain their submission. The Britons' masculine 'heroic' posture signifies their control of the land, tangential to their continued secular authority in parts of Britain. Nor should the significance of Augustine's status as *uncuðe* (foreign) be overlooked.[54] In a century when native English clergy were increasingly being replaced by Continental ministers, the issue of foreign priests and clerical officials would seem very urgent. We need look no further than the 'First Worcester Fragment' for the effects of having ministers who were not, as La3amon was, 'on þe leoden'. By recasting Augustine's mission in terms of colonization and conquest, therefore, La3amon underscores the dangers inherent in mixing ecclesiastical and political matters. Moreover, the tension between ecclesiastical duty and political authority remained contentious throughout the eleventh and twelfth centuries, as evidenced by Wulfstan of Worcester's fabled admonition to his fellow bishops, in the midst of a dispute over property rights: 'Dei seruitium, et post agitabimus hominum litigium' (let us first do our duty towards God, and afterwards settle the disputes of men).[55] In La3amon's own Worcester, Bishop Roger's attempt (1164–79) to maintain authority over the church at Wooten Wawen reveals the same clash of political and ecclesiastical issues.[56]

The issue of the conversion of the Saxons, while dropped by Wace, reappears in the *Brut* in an oblique and truncated manner that gives back to the British some of their seemingly lost credibility. After Ælfric – 'for-cuðest alre kinge' [cruellest of all kings] (l. 14878) – seizes Leicester, a delegation of British clergy offers to intercede 'to þan he3en king' (l. 14902). This offer of intercession to the 'high king', despite the clergy's apparent motive of self-preservation, renders moot the question of conversion: the Britons have agreed to intercede with God for the English, and the latter respond with a treacherous attack that would seem to justify persistent British mistrust of the Anglo-Saxons. Rather than marking a shift in sympathies from British to Anglo-Saxon, then, these unexpected Bedan irruptions underscore the conflicts between variant discursive modes of insular historiography. By poetically translating spiritual authorities into secular leaders, La3amon points toward the political motives that compromise ecclesiastical historical translation and that problematize the recovery of 'true' history. Ultimately, the clerical struggle for control over the land becomes emblematic of the irreconcilable conflicts among historical translations. With the land itself at issue, the question of conversion – like that of conquest – becomes a matter of translation.

At stake for Laȝamon, then, is not the relative piety of the two factions, but the struggle for control of translation and of history that plays itself out in the dispute over the land. The slippage from the spiritual to the political realm reveals the perceived sanctification of Dinoot or Augustine as alternative narratives devised by translators. Both Bede and Geoffrey-Wace have, in effect, colonized the narratives for their differing rhetorical purposes. The interpretations they impose on the event translate it into an episode of either British intransigence or Anglo-Saxon treachery. The massacre of the British clerics of Bangor serves as a striking example of the translator's political motives. Although it may be objected that, throughout the *Brut*, direct references to Bede's 'English Book' are extremely rare – the only one that can be directly and exclusively traced to this text is the reference to Pope Gregory's encounter with two slaves of the 'Angles' – Bede's work may inform Laȝamon's reworking of Wace, especially in the latter sections of the text, far more than most previous criticism has realized. As with the 'Marcian Law' episode, this scene dramatizes the power of translation to create history. With irreconcilable differences appearing in the source texts of Bede and Geoffrey, the translator's task itself is further exposed as one of the manipulative devices in the shaping of history. In reducing the doctrinal dispute between the two factions to a territorial struggle, Laȝamon re-conceptualizes Augustine as another colonizer-translator, in the mould of Brutus, Hengest or Æthelstan. In his broader pattern of conquest-colonization as model for translation, his depiction of this event further illustrates the role of translation in shaping history.

Along with narratives of domination, it is impossible to overlook the idea of translation as a dialogue and an exchange; the conqueror-translators are not unaffected by the land they conquer: as the Trojans translate Albion to Britain, they are themselves translated from Trojans to Britons. More dramatically, the place-name changes associated with Hengest and his Saxons paradoxically become narratives of their dishonour and discredit. Nor is the act of territorial translation complete. Never lost in Laȝamon's depiction of geographic translation is the ineradicable mark of the precursor culture – surviving as traces of older names – that hegemonic history seeks to conceal. Laȝamon's recovery of place-names brings to the surface the acts of conflict and suppression that make up insular history, and which are set in an overt parallel with the historian's appropriation of the source text, a process Laȝamon himself perpetuates in the very process of exposing it. Translation of historical texts never erases all traces of the precursor. Indeed, the tropes

166 LA3AMON'S *BRUT*

of desire for the land and desire for the text inform each other in La3amon's surprisingly complex agon of historiographic translation. As we shall see, such acts of translation also affect people, and it is here that we see the most problematic manifestation of La3amon's translation paradigm.

Notes

1 According to Holt, '[I]n Norman family nomenclature in contrast [to Anglo-Saxon practices] the toponymic conveys the sense of belonging, and that in the strongest possible manner: the individual belonged to the place because the place belongs to him' (*Colonial England*, p. 184).

2 'What is found at the historical beginning of things is not the inviolable identity of their origin; it is the dissension of other things. It is disparity' ('Nietzsche, genealogy, history', in *Language, Counter-memory, Practice: Selected Essays and Interviews*, ed. Donald F. Bouchard (Ithaca, 1977), pp. 139–64 (p. 142)).

3 'Erat et ciuitatibus quondam xx et viii nobilissimis insignita, praeter castella innumera quae et ipsa muris, turribus, portis ac seris errant instructa firmissimis' (The country was once famous for its twenty-eight noble cities as well as innumerable fortified places equally well guarded by the strongest of walls and towers, gates and locks); (*Historia Ecclesiastica*, I. i). Bede also documents the five languages – English, British, Irish, Pictish and Latin – without referencing the conflicts that have led to this set of five.

4 Henry of Huntingdon, for instance, credits the Normans for the foundation of religious houses; only Wulfstan's famous lament about the 'piling of stones' at Worcester Cathedral stands as an exception to this tendency.

5 'Human singularity, and hence any originality associated with human endeavor, is a function of the transpersonal laws that make up the patterns (psychological, economic, and intellectual) we call history, which is documented in thousands of written records' (*The Word, the Text, and the Critic* (Cambridge, 1983), p. 134).

6 Francis Ingledew, 'The Book of Troy'.

7 As Otter observes, 'This [Corineus' belligerent activities] is not necessarily a critique of excessive violence, let alone a pacifist sentiment; but even as one may enjoy the drama or the slapstick humor of such scenes, one is not allowed to forget that the conquerors have victims' (*Inventiones*, p. 83).

8 'diuiso tandem regno affectauit brutus ciuitatem edificare' (when the kingdom was divided Brutus built a city) (Geoffrey of Monmouth, *Historia*, I. xvii, p. 251).

9 It is also worth noting parenthetically that La3amon refrains from naming the river Thames since, presumably, it would not have a name until given one by the Trojan exiles.

10 Foucault, 'Nietzsche, genealogy, history', p. 146.

11 Le Saux sees this passage as one of a fairly rare number of instances where Wace's and La3amon's lines correspond to each other: 'In this case, the French

octosyllabic line corresponds almost exactly to the English long line. Both contain two "odes"; had Laȝamon's long line been equivalent to Wace's couplet, the English text ought to have comprised four elements per line – twice of what we actually have' (Le Saux, *Text and Tradition*, p. 28). I concur, in general, but argue that the lexical distinctions between French *vit* and the more nuanced English *bi-heold* represent different understandings of the colonization process.

12 'Concede inquit mihi seruo tu qantum una corrigia posit ambirir infra terram quam dedisti ut ibidem promontorium edifiecem quo me si opus fuerit recipiam' (give to me as much land as I may encircle with a single hide of a bull, and when it is given I can build a fortress where I may defend myself) (Geoffrey of Monmouth, *Historia*, IV. ix, p. 369).

13 A hide was a considerable, but hardly opulent, tract of land. According to Clark-Hall, the amount of land 'varied greatly' but was typically around 120 acres (*Concise Anglo-Saxon Dictionary*, p. 181). *Domesday* refers to a typical baronial manor as having about twenty to thirty hides; Hengest's 'crafty' man must have been able to cut a very thin cord indeed!

14 At least until the twentieth century, Modern Welsh *Saeson* remained a derisive term for a person of English descent.

15 Leckie notes how, in Laȝamon's *Brut*, 'Wace's description of the spread of Anglo-Saxon culture in the wake of the landings now follows, rather than precedes, the background material on Æthelstan' (*Passage of Dominion*, p. 118). Leckie, however, dismisses Laȝamon's treatment as representing 'something of a step backwards where the periodization of Insular history is concerned' (ibid., p. 117). Leckie never considers the importance of Laȝamon's translation of the English ruler into a foundational hero for his own English.

16 The lack of *leod* is no surprise, given the generally less archaic vocabulary of the Otho MS.

17 'In sum, that which would seem to lie at the root of Laȝamon's so-called cultural ambivalence, mistaken patriotism, etc. has been a failure on the part of his critics to recognize the distinction in the poet's mind between the would-be Saxon usurpers who are ultimately banished from Britain during Arthur's reign and "þa ilke þe worn icorne"(14667) – i.e. the Germanic immigrants who, some years later, are invited to assume stewardship of the island in the wake of Gurmund's invasion' (Noble, 'Laȝamon's "ambivalence" reconsidered', p. 181).

18 Stein asserts that 'the Normans are fully present in the passage, for the institutions listed here are for the most part Norman rather than Saxon' ('Making history English', p. 109). Historian Peter Hunter Blair, however, has identified each of the institutions referred to in the *Brut* passage as originating with the Anglo-Saxons (*An Introduction to Anglo-Saxon England* (Cambridge, 1956), p. 296ff.). For instance, Hunter Blair notes that the Anglo-Saxon guild 'was not a merchant guild but a voluntary association which was intended to maintain peace and security in daily life by the apprehension of thieves and the recovery of stolen goods and which also provided spiritual benefits for its members' (ibid., p. 297). Only the 'friõ of deoren', or deer enclosures, are usually associated with William and the Normans, but even these were not

unheard of during the Anglo-Saxon period. See also R. Welldon Finn, *Domesday Book: A Guide* (London, 1973), pp. 71–3. If La3amon were to have had the Normans in mind in this passage, the overall effect would be to efface their contributions to the land in favour of Anglo-Saxon contributions.

[19]   See Alice Sheppard, '"Of this is a king's body made"; lordship and succession in Lawman's Arthur and Leir', *Arthuriana*, 10, 2 (2000), 50–64.

[20]   The loss of British control occurs immediately after the Gurmund donation, coinciding in Wace with the translation of the land from *Bretaine* to *Engleland* (l. 13647). For Wace, of course, the French term maintains its privileged status above both previous insular languages, as he reminds his readers, 'Tant dit Engleterre en franceis' (l. 13649).

[21]   The situation of a privileged language in England reflects that in colonial Ireland, where, as Michael Cronin has observed, translation serves as a metaphor for the displacement of the native Irish: 'Translation at a cultural level – the embrace of English acculturation – is paralleled by translation at a territorial level, the forcible displacement and movement of populations' (*Translating Ireland* (Cork, 1996), p. 49).

[22]   Wace, *Roman de Brut*, ll. 1158–9.

[23]   Le Saux offers an extensive study of Welsh oral sources in the *Brut*, concluding that 'The authority with which the English poet [La3amon] speaks of the Welsh people and customs suggests that he found himself an informant whom he regarded highly, and from whom he gathered some knowledge of Welsh prophetical poetry, especially those prophecies attributed to Myrddin/ Merlin, among which one may postulate a direct influence of *Armes Prydein*. La3amon also gathered elements of the native learned tradition, in the form of triads' (*Text and Tradition*, p. 154).

[24]   According to Margaret Clunie Ross, '*Nið* frequently took the form of poetry in which an aggressor threatened his enemy with actual homosexual rape or with allegations of having been subjected to it' ('Land-taking and text-making in medieval Iceland', in Tomasch and Gilles (eds), *Text and Territory* (Philadelphia, 1998), pp. 159–84 (p. 163)). Read in this context, Norman *nið-craften* might well be a direct affront to English masculinity, as well as to a significantly 'feminized' landscape.

[25]   Ross, 'Land taking in medieval Iceland', p. 163. In *Egil's Saga*, King Egil uses it to expel his rival king Harald from his land. Egil's *nið*, for instance, evokes the land-guardians to avenge him against King Erik:

> Requite him, righteous gods,
> For robbery of my wealth!
> Hunt him away, be wroth,
> High Odin, heavenly powers!
> Foe of his folk, base king,
> May Frey and Njord make flee!
> Hate him, *land-guardians*, hate,
> Who holy ground hath scorn'd!

> (*Egil's Saga*, ed. And trans. Michael Chessnutt (Copenhagen, 2001),
> LVII; emphasis mine)

[26]   The concept was certainly not unknown in England. Richard North suggests
the possibility of a *nið* directed at Byrhtnoth by the Viking commander in 'The
Battle of Maldon' ('Getting to know the General in the *Battle of Maldon*',
Medium Ævum, 60 (1991), 1–15). See Allen Frantzen's argument regarding
this poem (*Before the Closet: Same-Sex Love from* Beowulf *to Angels in America*
(Chicago, 1998), pp. 105–6). T. L. Markey cites a 1272 incident wherein
Scandinavian poachers in Rockingham forest constructed a *niðstang* with
the severed head of a deer, mouth open to the sun, 'in magnum contemptum
domini regis et forestariourm suorum' (in great contempt of the lordship of
the king and of his forests) ('Nordic *niðvisur*: an instance of ritual inversion?',
Medieval Scandinavia, 5 (1972), 7–18 (12)).

[27]   It has been maintained, however, that even Laȝamon's version of the 'Angels/
Angles' story was drawn not from Bede, but from an oral source. And indeed,
Laȝamon's departures are significant: (1) Gregory is already pope, not a bishop
as he is in Bede; (2) Laȝamon drops the other two aspects of Gregory's pun,
'*Ælla/Alleluia*' and '*Deira/De ira*'. It should be remembered, however, that
Wace also has Gregory as pope, so Laȝamon may simply have chosen to defer
to Wace. Regarding Laȝamon's second alteration, Gregory's famous wordplay
would have little meaning to a non-Latinate audience, so Laȝamon's decision
to omit it would be a reasonable one (elsewhere in the *Brut*, Laȝamon is
careful to state when a word or phrase is 'in *Latin*', so we can assume an
audience not very familiar with the language). Therefore, in the absence of
another identifiable source, the safest assumption would be to assume that
Laȝamon meant what he said regarding his sources.

[28]   Alfred's English translation of Bede, the one Laȝamon may have consulted,
reads that Augustine and his followers 'ongunnon heo þæt apostolice lif
þære frymðelecan cyrcan onhyrgan, þæt is, in singalum gebedum 7 in wæccum
7 in fæstenum Drihtne þeodon; 7 lifes word, þæm heo meahton, bodedon 7
lærdon, ond eall þing þisses middangeardes swa fremde forhognodon' (I. 15)
(began to follow the apostolic life of the primitive church, that is, to serve the
Lord in single-minded prayer, vigils, and fasts; and they preached and taught
the Word to all whom they could, and utterly forsook all things of this world).

[29]   *Dream of the Rood*, in *The Vercelli Book*, ed. George Philip Krapp (New
York, 1932), line 78.

[30]   Steiner, *After Babel*, p. 61.

[31]   De Lille overtly comments on the phallic and reproductive possibilities of
the hammer and of the writing pen, *Plant of Naturae*, Book X, prose V. The
phallic nature of the staff is self-evident, and Wace was undoubtedly thinking
of Moses' staff, that draws water from a stone; the psychosexual implications
of the staff are fully explored in the *Roman de la Rose* (Book XII, ll. 21307 ff.)

[32]   Bede, *Historia Ecclesiastica*, I.23.

[33]   Although Laȝamon uses the title less consistently throughout than does Wace,
it hardly seems coincidental that four of the five such references to Augustine
occur before his dispute with other clerics over land. Wace uses the term in
all of his eight references to Augustine.

34   Bede, *Historia Ecclesiastica*, 2. 2, pp. 140–2.

35   Alfred's ninth-century translator would heighten the connection between the
     Britons' spiritual death and their ensuing physical death through synctactic
     parallelism: 'Þa se Godes wer Scs. Augustinus is sægd ðæt he beotigende
     forecwide, gef heo sibbe mid Godes monnum onfon ne wolden, ðæt heo
     wæren unsibbe [and] gefeoht from heora feondum onfon' (2. 2) (Then God's
     man Saint Augustine said and foretold, that if they would not have peace
     with God's friends, then they would have strife and war from their enemies)
     (*The Old English Version of Bede's* Ecclesiastical History of the English People,
     ed. and trans. Thomas Miller (London, 1890, 1898)). Anglican historians,
     such as John Bale and even Milton, would obviate Geoffrey's implications,
     making the Saint the dark-hearted villain of the episode and the British
     monks proto-Protestant martyrs.

36   Bede, *Historia Ecclesiastica*, II. 3. The Old English reads 'Spræcon him
     betweonum: gif he nu us arisen ne wolde, micle ma gif we him underþeodde
     beoð, he us eac for noht gehygeð' (II. 3) (They spoke among themselves: 'if
     he will not arise before us now, how much more will he do if we are under
     him? He will hold us for nought').

37   Regarding the Pelagians, 'convincitur vanitas, perfidia confutatur' vanity is
     turned, heresy confuted); he twice refers to the British monks of Bangor as
     perfidiæ (unbelievers or heretics) (Bede, *Historia Ecclesiastica,* II. 2).

38   Ibid., I. 18.

39   '[T]andem Augustinus iusa necessitate compulsus flecit genua sua ad Patrem
     Domini nostri Iuse Christi, deprecans ut uisum caeco quem amiserat restueret,
     et per inluminationem unius hominis corporalem in plurimorum corde
     fidelum spiritalis gratam lucis accienderet. Nec mora, inluminatur caecus, ac
     uers summae lucis praecox ab omnibus praedicatur Augustinus' (Then
     Augustine, compelled by genuine necessity, prayed, bowing his knees to the
     Father of our Lord Jesus Christ, that he would restore his lost sight to the
     blind man, and through the bodily enlightenment of one man, would bring
     the grace of spiritual light to the hearts of many unbelievers. At once the
     blind man's sight was restored and all acknowledged Augustine to be a true
     herald of heavenly light). The Old English translation renders the passage
     similarly: 'Þa æt nehstan wæs Agustinum mid reohte nedþearfnisse gebæded;
     aras 7 gebegde his cneo; bæd God Fæder ælmihtigne, þæt he þam blindan
     men gesyhðe forgefe, þæt he þurh anes monnes licomlice inlihtnesse in
     monigra geleagfsumra heortan þæs gastlican leohtes gife onbærnde. þa sona
     buton eldnesse wæs se blinda man onlehted 7 gesyhðe onfeng; ond se soða
     boda þæs hean leohtes Agustinums wæs from him eallum bodad 7 hered' (II.
     2) (Then at last Augustine was compelled by righteous need. He arose and
     bowed his knee; he bade God, the Father Almighty, to restore the blind man
     to sight, that he might through one man's bodily illumination kindle the gift
     of spiritual light in many men. This light was soon given to the blind man,
     and he began to see. Then Augustine was acknowledged and declared by all
     as the true bearer of high light).

[40] 'nec mora, adhaerentem lateri suo capsulum cum sactorum reliquiis collo avulsam manibus comprehendit, eamque in conspectu omnium puellae oculis adplicavit, quos statim evacuatos tenebris lumen veritatis implevit' (I. 18) (and straightaway he tore from his neck a little budget. Which he had by his side full of the relics of saints, and seizing it in his hands in the sight of them all put it to the eyes of the maiden, which straight were emptied of darkness and filled with the light of truth). In both instances, failure to restore sight to the afflicted is an obvious sign of spiritual weakness. The failure of the Britons in the Augustine passage to heal a blind Englishman signifies their unwillingness to engage in the conversion of (or bringing of spiritual sight to) the English invaders.

[41] Howe, *Migration and Mythmaking*, p. 69.

[42] Bede, *Historia Ecclesiastica*, II. 2.

[43] See William of Newburgh, II. 13: (When admonished to repent, and become united to the body of the Church, they despised all wholesome counsel. They laughed at the threats kindly held out to induce them to become wise through fear, misapplying the divine expression, 'Blessed are they which are persecuted for righteousness' sake for theirs is the kingdom of heaven', [Matthew V: 10] [. . .] they were conducted to their just punishment rejoicing, their leader preceding with hasty step, singing 'Blessed shall ye be when men shall hate you' [Matthew V: 11] – to such a degree did the seducing spirit pervert the minds of those he had deceived).

[44] [. . .] 'algoris intolerentia, hiems quippe erat, nemine vel exiguum misericordiæ impendente, misere interierunt' (perished miserably from the intolerable cold, for it was winter, and no one would show them the slightest bit of mercy) (ibid., II. 13).

[45] Kristeva defines abjection as 'radically excluded [. . .] [w]hat disturbs identity, system, order. What does not respect borders, positions, rules' (*Power of Horror*, trans. Leon C. Roudiez (New York, 1986), pp. 2–4).

[46] Geoffrey of Monmouth, *HRB*, p. 509.

[47] Although it is tempting to do so, I can offer no direct evidence that Wace's 'Alfred' is a direct affront to the English national hero.

[48] Geoffrey of Monmouth, *HRB*, 12. 1

[49] John Bale, *The First Two Partes of the Actes or Vnchast Examples of the Englysh Votaryes, Gathered out of their Owne Legendes and Chronycles* (London, 1551). Bale is one of the first English writers to accuse overtly Augustine of suborning the massacre.

[50] I. J. Kirby, 'Angles and Saxons in Layamon's *Brut*', *Studia Neophiliologica*, 36 (1964), p. 60.

[51] Wickham-Crowley, *Writing the Future*, pp. 21, 34–6.

[52] Johnson, 'Reading the past', p. 155.

[53] Le Saux, *Text and Tradition*, p. 31. In this passage, Laȝamon refers to the land approximately once every ten lines, as opposed to Wace, who mentions it once every forty lines.

[54] See Wickham-Crowley, *Writing the Future*, p. 36.

⁵⁵ William of Malmesbury, *Gesta Regum Anglorum*, III. 303, p. 539. John of Worcester (entry for 1070) also documents the intrusion of the political into the ecclesiastical realms as it records the efforts of Thomas, the archbishop of York, to subordinate Worcester to his see: 'All the groundless assertions by which Thomas and his abetters strove to humble the church of Worcester, and reduce her to subjection and servitude to the church of York, were, by God's just judgement, entirely refuted and negated by written documents, so that Wulfstan not only recovered the possessions he claimed, but, by God's goodness, and the king's assent, regained for his see all the immunities and privileges freely granted to it by its first founders' (p. 176). Here, we see that the demands of Thomas are much more pernicious than in William's account. It is worthy of note, moreover, that this chronicle portrays Wulfstan of Worcester not as William of Malmesbury's simple, illiterate ('de parua scientia litterarum') and somewhat rustic holy man, but as a literate and sophisticated cleric, more than a match for the Norman-born archbishop of York. See also William's *Vita Wulfstani*.

⁵⁶ See Mary G. Cheney, *Roger, Bishop of Worcester, 1164–1179* (Cambridge, 1989), pp. 7, 79.

4

Translating the people: the body of the king as historian and historical text

Beyond translating text and land, Laȝamon's conception of historiography reveals the effect of historiographic translation upon people. This process often necessitates renaming tribes or ethnic groups in ways that serve the interests of the new conqueror-colonizers. In foundational histories, in particular, narratives of the translation of people – for example, from a multifaceted group of Celtic tribes to a collective entity called 'the Britons' – accompanies the translation of land. Beyond changes in nomenclature, the translation process typically involved translating the characters or natures of people to explain – and often justify – their displacement: Gildas' (and later Bede's) characterization of the Britons as weak and treacherous, and William of Malmesbury's 'translation' of the pre-Conquest English as apostate and 'barbaric' reveal the process of translating people.[1] In both instances, the providential master-narratives in which the historians work demand that the population be depicted as deserving its fate, in the same way that colonialist translation methods translate indigenous inhabitants as either morally depraved or 'backward', and hence benefiting from colonialist enterprises. Obviously, Gildas' characterization of the Britons as cowardly and faithless, which forms the basis of insular history for Bede and Anglo-Norman historians, provides an example of the extremes to which such historiographic revision can go.[2] In contrast to most of his contemporaries and precursors, Laȝamon shows greater affinity for the conquered and displaced, perhaps because of his position as a member of a conquered race who had once been conquerors. Therefore, his concern for the people – including their physical bodies – who undergo translation becomes evident, as it is in his presentation of translating text. In the *Brut*'s narratives of foundation, the power of the founders often depends not only on the reordering of

the topographic details of the land, but also on the physical alteration –
frequently in the form of wounding and mutilation – of the indigenous
inhabitants. What La3amon reveals in his treatment of people is that
acts of conquest and resettlement have human consequences.

As I have previously argued, the translation process transforms populations from active creators of history into passive recipients of the history
of the invaders. The assumption of power by conquerors involves the
prerogative to rename the conquered. Thus, the Britons after their defeat
become the 'Welsh', from the Old English *weallas* (foreigners) – literally
outsiders in their own country. The English remain English after the
Conquest, but the term itself – as Henry of Huntingdon claims, with
emotions apparently as mixed as his own heritage – has become one of
disgrace. The etymology of *Welsh* in all of La3amon's source texts is presented as multifaceted, and hence indeterminate: Geoffrey of Monmouth
states that the name derives either from a previous (unnamed) leader, from
Princess Galoes (mentioned earlier in the *HRB*) or from their barbaric
manners ('barbarie trahentes'); in the last definition one may suspect an
echo of the Anglo-Saxon *weallas*.[3] Wace repeats the first two fictional
genealogies of the term, while omitting the most pejorative. La3amon
omits the folk etymology of the name-change altogether (perhaps out of
personal knowledge that the Britons of Wales never used it), but adds in his
section on Æthelstan that the king had given the (British) inhabitants
English – or Saxon – names: 'and Sexis he gan kenne þa nomen of þan
monnen' (l. 15977) (and he gave the men Saxon names). For La3amon,
the naming, or translation, of indigenous people by outside invaders
completes the conquerors' translation process. Combined with the translation of text and of land, this phase marks the end of a race's or
nation's sense of cultural identity and control of its own history. As we
have seen, La3amon's rulers exercise their authority over territory by
naming and renaming places to preserve their own identity. At the same
time, La3amon reminds us, this activity obscures previous names and
previous histories. New names further conceal contributions of the precursor cultures, as these are translated for the benefit of new conquerors.

Central to the concept of translating people is the body of the ruler,
who serves as an emblem for the body politic, by which I mean as a
symbol for the race or kingdom. William A. Chaney notes the role of
the Anglo-Saxon king as the 'luck' or 'blessing' of the people.[4] In later
medieval cultures, this concept appears to have been transformed into a
conception of the king as the representative of Christ for his people, as
Ernst H. Kantorowicz observes of the twelfth-century understanding of

the ruler's two bodies.[5] Accordingly, the seizure of the king's body, dead or alive, by enemies could well mark the appropriation of their 'luck' and a large portion of their identity by outsiders. In contrast, narratives of the ruler's escape from or elusion of conquerors comes to signify the survival of a displaced ethnic group, and denies closure or totality to the triumphalist histories of the conquerors. This chapter, therefore, examines the translation of people in the *Brut* as a part of translating history: transformation of people and of their rulers, in the form of physical capture and physical transformation of the body, constitutes the third step in Laȝamon's tripartite conception of translating history. Central to my discussion is the figure of Arthur who, for Laȝamon, embodies the ruler both as conqueror-translator and as leader of a people ultimately subject to translation. In this complex figure, standing at the crux of 'history' and 'romance' (or 'fiction'), Laȝamon finds a site for expressing to the fullest extent the concept of history as translation – of text, land and people. Laȝamon depicts the triumphant Arthur as a figure who authors his own history, translating other people in the process; in his departure, as translatable text, he represents the marginal-ization of the Britons, but also embodies their hope for an eventual return to power. In the latter capacity, the fate of Laȝamon's Arthur predicts that of Cadwalader, the last British king, whose sanctified remains – removed out of reach of the conquering Saxons – signify the survival of British culture and the possibility of recovery.

In the *Brut*, the process of translating people is often dramatized through linking violence inflicted upon an indigenous population with the process of translating them from one dominion to another. Incidents of trans-lating the populace are rare, confined to circumstances where some sort of change in the ethnographic make-up of the island is imminent. It occurs only twice: once when the Britons seize the island, destroying the aboriginal giants, who, lacking language or history, scarcely count as a people; the second occurs when the Saxons conquer the island and transform the Britons into 'Welsh'. Hengest's orchestrated slaughter of British nobles is a poignant emblem of this process. Laȝamon's account of the massacre of the British nobles at Ambresbury provides insight into his conception of the translation of people. Although the episode originates with Nennius (*c*.800), whose *Hystoria Brutonum* includes the mock-English command, 'Eu, nimet saxas!', it is Geoffrey of Monmouth who provides the first detailed narrative, including Hengest's capture of Vortigern and the impromptu defence by some of the Britons. At first read, the narrative seems an apt metaphor for the intrusion of an outside language into the land and the catastrophic consequences that can result from the blending of ethnographic groups. Geoffrey heightens dramatic tensions by introducing the motif of a plot, in which Hengest vocalizes his plans to his fellows:

> Et cum colloquium securius tractarent Britones ipse eis hoc daret signum: *Nemet oure saxas*: unde ruquisque abstractis culturis ocuus ipsum jugularet.

> [And when the Britons had gathered among them in security, he would give the sign 'Nemet oure saxas' and which they would draw their knives and cut the Britons' throats.]

Wace follows Geoffrey, albeit with some expansions, notably the means by which the daggers are concealed:

> Henguist ot tuz ses compainuns
> Bien enseinniez e bien sumuns
> Quen jur chauces culteis portassent
> Tels ki de ambes parz tranchassent.
> Quant il as Bretuns parlereient
> E tuit entremellé serreient
> '*Nim eure sexes!*' criereit,
> Qu e nuls des Bretuns n'entendreit;
> Chescuns dunc sun cultel preïst
> e sun procain Bretun ferist. (ll. 7233–42)

[Hengest had brought his companions well clothed and well advised that each carry a knife in his hose, that they might work mischief on the other side, when they spoke to the Britons and were all mingled. 'Nim eure sexes!' he would cry and none of the Britons would understand it. Each would draw out his knife and strike on the British side.]

For Geoffrey, the English language is the appropriate language for the performative act of violence, separate from the Latin prose historical narrative. Wace repeats Geoffrey's deployment of English, although he modifies the verb form to imitate the French imperative. Both texts stigmatize the English vernacular as associated with treachery or barbarism, echoing linguistically William of Malmesbury's character-ization of 'barbaric' pre-Conquest English. The result is a separation of the 'high style' of Latin and French, associated with the 'heroic' Britons and with the Anglo-Norman/Angevin readers, from the 'unsophisticated' and radically different English of the Anglo-Saxons.

Laȝamon follows the Geoffrey-Wace account, but the conception of language is inverted: in both the *HRB* and the *Roman de Brut* the *Saxon* spoken by Hengest and his men is presented as a foreign language, a sort of 'mock' English, unintelligible to the readers or listeners. As a result, the readers of or audience for this text remain in the position of the British victims, who are killed because they cannot understand the command. Beyond the dramatic tension, the differentiation between the language of the previous accounts and the *Sæxisc* of the treacherous Hengest and his followers reinforces the linguistic hierarchy characteristic of colonial England, where the language of the Anglo-Saxons occupied the bottom rung. The English Laȝamon, in contrast, translates the utterance into his own West Midlands dialect: 'Nimeð eoure sexes: sele mine bernes' (l. 7600). His translation, with the English imperative ending restored, places the line in the vernacular, along with the rest of the text. By avoiding a shift in language from the narrative to the performative command, Laȝamon eliminates the bilingualism of the scene; the command would be as intelligible to the English *Brut*'s audience as to the fictional Hengest's fifth-century Saxon warriors. In other words, Laȝamon makes no attempt to differentiate the language of Hengest's Saxons from the English of contemporary Worcester.[6] Laȝamon's 'modernization' of Hengest's English effaces the ethnic and temporal boundaries separating the figures in his source text. Beyond the direct address to his readers or audience, Laȝamon's incorporation of the English utterances into the weave of his narrative transforms the language itself into a site of resistance to the translation of the English people, as effected by Anglo-Norman and Angevin historians. In so doing, he may be advising them to take up their own *Sæxisc* – that is, hold to their English language – to maintain their own ethnic identity and participation in insular history. At the same time, Laȝamon's use of contemporary English to represent what is clearly a 'foreign' language in Wace and Geoffrey reminds his audience that it is their ancestors who are being represented as treacherous, barbaric and dangerous. In so doing, Laȝamon exposes the construction of the Anglo-Saxon people enacted by Geoffrey's and Wace's 'translation' of their own history.

In this context, it is useful to consider this scene in tandem with the earlier 'mead-hall' drinking sequence, wherein Rouwenne initiates the custom of exclaiming 'wæs hal' and 'drinc hal' (ll. 7152–3), bringing a culturally significant custom to England and beginning the process of seducing King Vortigern to paganism; in a second drinking ritual (ll. 7469–83), she poisons Vortigern's son, Vortimer. As with the Ambresbury massacre,

these episodes use differences in language to underscore what Geoffrey
and Wace seem to see as inherent Saxon perfidy; the second scene in fact
corrupts a native English cultural practice. Although Geoffrey may not
have done so on any conscious register, he reworks English ritual as part
of a conception of Saxon treachery. In Geoffrey's account, performance
of the ritual is central to the orchestrated seduction of the British
Christian ruler, initiating Saxon history in the signal act of deceptive
politics. The custom forges a bond of kinship between Hengest and the
British ruler that disrupts the established blood-relations between him,
his sons and his native subjects. In Lévi-Strauss's terms, it initiates the
sort of kinship system that 'lie[s] in an exchange of women between men'.[7]
Geoffrey's (mis)representation of a Germanic custom – which becomes
a divisive, rather than a unifying, ritual – marks the disruption in British
rule through which the Saxons gain temporary control of the island.
Treachery further distances the Anglo-Saxons from the 'honourable' Britons
and Normans, reinforced by the differences in language. As Geoffrey's
narrative progresses, poison is shown as endemic to the Saxons, who
twice resort to it to dispatch British kings. Laȝamon's inclusion of these
scenes may have prompted early critics of the *Brut* to assume that he
enjoyed the condemnation of his own ancestors. Certainly, a reminder
that many foundational narratives are based on acts of treachery would
not be out of character for an English priest. However, it is also possible
that the inclusion of these scenes in West Midlands English further reminds
the *Brut*'s readers that it is their culture that is being 'translated' by non-
English historians. Both Geoffrey and Wace use the genres in which
they work – Latin prose history and French verse history, respectively –
to construct a vision of insular reality in which Saxons are inherently
corrupt, forming what Lefevre terms a textual 'grid' for representing the
past.[8] This grid represents English customs not on their own terms, but
on terms acceptable to their respective audiences – many of whom, we
suspect, would regard the custom as 'quaint'.[9] Their representation of
the English language is presented as equally exotic. In effect, Geoffrey
'poisons' the cup of the English tradition in its textual form, as the drinking
scene forms part of a narrative paradigm of Saxon treachery. When
Laȝamon inherits the narrative of the wassail tradition from Wace, the
poisoning of the cup for the second mead-sharing ceremony may well serve
as a dramatization of the sort of verbal envenoming of the tradition
evident in his source text. In translating the episode, Laȝamon breaks
down the temporal and linguistic barriers, forcing his readers/listeners
to confront English practices on their own terms. Hence, the tale becomes

a further exemplum of the way translation of history can alter people and their customs. Laȝamon thus brings to the surface the traces of his own language, marginalized in his source texts. The English language – a source of mystery, if not anxiety, for Geoffrey and Wace – becomes for Laȝamon a potential source of resistance to colonial translation.

Translating the ruler – translating the people

The persona of the ruler plays a pivotal role in the translation of people that accompanies narratives of conquest and resettlement. The ruler is not only the most prominent figure of a group or nation, he enjoys an iconic status as symbol for the people, their tradition and their history.[10] John of Salisbury, in his twelfth-century *Policraticus*, makes frequent metaphoric associations between the king's body and the body politic.[11] With so much cultural identification vested in the king, it is not surprising that this figure should come to stand for the culture and history of the people he leads, as much of their identity is invested in him. Possession of the king's body, under this rubric, becomes tantamount to possession of the 'soul', culture and history of the people. The seizure of this body may indeed be seen as the secular equivalent of the 'translation' of a saint's relics for the foundation of religious houses. As an example, Chaney notes the appropriation of Oswald's body by his rival Penda as an offering to Odin.[12] This element of translation manifests itself throughout the *Brut* in the linguistic changes endured by the peoples within the text, and in the body of the king itself. The colonialist aims of the Normans in England, and later of Henry II in Wales, involved the possession and control of the body of a previous ruler. When William refused to ransom the corpse of Harold to his mother, preferring instead to inter him in a tomb by the coast as a landscape marker, his jurisdiction over his rival's physical remains affirmed his control over the English landscape and over its people. Similarly, Henry II's efforts to unearth Arthur's tomb were motivated, in part, by a need to control the land and the people, and in part by his need to convince the Welsh that Arthur was indeed dead. The 'discovery' of Arthur's tomb (it was allegedly found in Glastonbury in 1191, a 'find' of dubious historical and archaeological merit) would further signify Henry's control over the insular Britons, making him, in effect, heir to the kingdom of Arthur.[13]

In the *Brut*, then, the fate of the ruler's body mirrors the fate of the entire race: its capture or destruction signifies the loss of cultural self-determination, and its translation into the control of the colonizers signals the translation of the people. In his deployment of the figure of the king as central to a people's cultural identity, La3amon indirectly evokes the Anglo-Saxon concept of a cult of kingship. The account of the late British ruler Caric provides a fitting example of the importance attached to this figure. In Geoffrey and Wace, Caric's defeat signals the overthrow of the Britons; the distribution of Britain among the Saxons by Caric's rival, the African king Gurmund, marks the end of British sovereignty. After the so-called 'Gurmund donation', Geoffrey and Wace write Caric – and hence the Britons – out of insular history. Geoffrey literally erases 'Karedic' from the narrative after his defeat, making no further mention of him.[14] Wace translates Geoffrey directly, adding only 'Ne sai dire que puis avint' (l. 13614) (I don't know what became of him). In both Geoffrey and Wace, what follows Caric's and the Britons' defeat is the establishment of England, with Britain no longer used in reference to the land. La3amon retains the same basic narrative structure. However, the translation of the king himself is accompanied by a general translation of land and people, with the seemingly senseless violence inflicted upon both dramatizing the most pernicious aspects of historiographic translation:

> And Gurmund al þis kinelond walde to his a3ere hond;
> Burges he forbarnde, tunes he forswelde,
> Munekes he forpinede on mani are wise,
> þa riche wif he lette his hired-men makien to horne
> preostes he alle ofslæh alle chirchen he todroh,
> clærkes he aqualde alle þa he funde. (ll. 14534–40)

[And Gurmund had all of this kingdom in his own hand. He burned cities and destroyed towns; he tortured monks in many ways. He let his men use the high-born women as whores. He slew all of the priests and destroyed the churches. He killed all the clerks he could find.]

Unique to La3amon, however, the accompanying alteration of Caric's name occurs as both a personal insult and a commemoration of his defeat, which opens the people to translation:

> Þa wes Karic biswiken al mid heore [the Saxons'] craften.
> Karic auer seoðen Kineric he hehten;
> Al mid hoker-worden þe king heo forhusten. (ll. 14480–2)

[Then was Karic betrayed by the Saxons' craft. Karic was ever after known as Kinric; all derided the king with contemptuous words.]

The etymology of *Kinric* remains obscure, as do the reasons why it might constitute an insult (though it does bear semblance to *kineriche*, or kingdom), but it may be a pun reflecting on the people and the land.[15] It is no accident, I believe, that the deriding of the British ruler coincides with the translation of *Britain* to *England*. As the Saxons advance against the British ruler, they sing songs to his disgrace: 'and euere heo sungen mid hokere of Kinriche þan kinge' (l. 14515) (and everywhere they sang with scorn of Kinric the king). Receiving both a name and a fate imposed by outside elements, Caric – as an emblem of the body of the people – becomes an emblem for the translatable historical text. As Caric escapes the ruin of his last stronghold, Cirencester, Laȝamon adds the humiliating and physical detail that he crept away on his hands and knees 'swulc he mid unsunde, al uorwunded weore' (l. 14630) (as if he were lame or seriously wounded). Laȝamon's depiction of the king's degraded body seems designed to reflect the humiliation suffered by the British people, as Caric's reduction to less-than-regal status signifies the impending denigration of the British people. At the same time, however, Laȝamon maintains the king's escape, and hence leaves open the possibility of British survival, even as his precursors had foreclosed this potential.

The changing of the king's given name is a further indication of the translation process he undergoes, along with the Britons; the severe mutilations inflicted upon them by the invader serve as a direct metaphor for this translation:

And Gurmund wes on heðene mon, and fordud þane Cristindom;
þa þis wes al þus ifare, þæ wes her sorwe and muchel care:
Gurmund falde þa munstres and anheng alle þa munkes;
Of cnihte he carf þe lippes, of madenen þa tittes,
Preostes he blende. Al þis folc he scended,
Ælcne bilifued mon he lette bilimien,
And þus he gon to taken on and fordude al þisne Cristindom.

(ll. 14649–55)

[And Gurmund was a heathen man, and destroyed all Christendom that was here; then there was sorrow and great care here. Gurmund destroyed the monasteries and hanged all the monks; he cut off the lips of knights and the breasts of the maidens, and he blinded the priests. He afflicted all the people, and mutilated all those he spared. And in this way he destroyed all of Christendom.]

The unprecedented and appalling violence in Laȝamon's account of this event reminds the reader that acts of translation have physical consequences. Neither is the nature of the physical mutilation of British bodies coincidental. The wounds Gurmund inflicts deprive the populace of its ability to function as a community. Removing the organs of speech from the secular leaders costs them their authority; young women are deprived of their capacity to nurse children. The priests' loss of sight carries symbolic relevance to their roles as providers of spiritual sight, evidenced by the 'healing of the blind' episodes in Bede's *Historia*.[16] In other words, the attack threatens their status as a cohesive *leod*, in the same way that the translation of history denies the people continued participation in insular history. The overall effect is the translation of people; coupled with the destruction of religious edifices, the physical harm threatens to deprive the Britons of their status as an ethnic group.

After this attack, the land is given to *Angles* of Germany, who rename it *Ænglelond*. In Geoffrey and Wace, as well as in Laȝamon, this section precedes the account of the conversion of the English, and, in spite of a brief recovery under Cadwan, it signals the permanent transition from *Britain* to *England*. The overt linkage between renaming the king's body and the renaming of the land reinforces the association of land and people with the body of the ruler, who comes to stand for both. As further evidence of this historiographic linkage, Laȝamon expresses the destruction of the Britons' last fortress in explicitly textual terms:

> Nes his nohwhar iseid, no a *bocken irad*,
> At æi folc swa faire swa forfare weore
> Swa wes Caric and his genge þe king wes of Bruttene.
>
> (ll. 14623–5; italics mine)

[It is nowhere said nor read in books that any folk so fair as was Caric, who was king of the Britons, and his followers were destroyed in such a way.]

Laȝamon's evocation of textual and oral historiographic traditions reminds the reader (or audience) that the events dealt with are textual traditions, and that the process of creating these traditions may involve the suppression and erasure of previous peoples. Caric's fate – his translation and his marginalization from the narrative itself, in Geoffrey and in Wace – becomes, in this context, an emblem for the process of historiographic translation documented throughout the *Brut*.

Laȝamon, nevertheless, qualifies the narrative of cultural extinction inherited from his precursors, emphasizing to a small degree the continuity of British culture under the dominion of a new group of conquerors. After Caric's defeat by Gurmund, Geoffrey and Wace remove him, along with the Britons, from the narrative. Laȝamon, in contrast, does not write the Britons completely out of his history, although he does maintain Wace's placement of the island's name-change. Concerned with the physical body (be it of persons or of texts), Laȝamon shifts the focus of the narrative to the survival of the traces, both of Caric himself and of the British people. After the sack of Cirencester and the king's escape, the *Brut* leaves open the possibility of his survival and return (possibly echoing twelfth-century accounts of the post-Conquest raids carried out by King Harold's sons):[17]

> And nust naere na man whar Karic hi bicom,
> Buten ænes an ane tide an cniht þer com ride
> And seide Gurmunde of Kariche tidende,
> þat he in Irlonde somnede genge
> and wolde mid fehte æft faren hidere.
> Ah nust nauere na man to whan þe þret him bicom.
>
> (ll. 14633–8)

[And no man knew what became of Caric, but one day a knight came riding, and told King Gurmunde tidings of Caric, that he would raise an army in Ireland and would come and fight, but no man ever knew what became of this threat.]

Although Laȝamon dramatizes the ruler's humiliation, he also allows him, and, by extrapolation, the Britons, a continued history. Indeed, in his depiction of Caric's escape to Ireland, Laȝamon relocates him outside the bounds of orthodox history, and hence beyond the reach of historical translation. The restoration of Caric's original British name and his possible return – both inventions of Laȝamon – disrupt the finality of the translation of both the Britons and their ruler. That he does not return is not as important as what the possibility represents: the viability of the Britons in insular history. Parallel to other traditions of the escaped ruler – accounts of Harold's supposed escape from Hastings come immediately to mind – Caric's body, as a symbol of his culture, becomes an emblem for the endurance of conquered and displaced people. La3amon here resists both the closure imposed on British history by the Wace-Geoffrey narrative and the Britons' complete removal from the stage of insular history by the Bedan Anglo-Norman line. La3amon suggests, in a narrative of defeat and escape, the fact that military defeat need not spell cultural annihilation. Through this narrative move, he challenges the finality of historiographic translation. This trace of British activity comes to emblematize La3amon's resistance to the closure depicted in other historical narratives.

Existing literally on the margins of history, rulers who somehow evade capture come to symbolize the trace of the original text (or land or people) that remains untranslated, untranslatable and, ultimately, beyond the control of the conqueror-translators. The body of a ruler, such as Caric or Arthur, physically absent but present in the form of narrative, emblematizes for La3amon the traces of the original culture and its text that lie beneath the translation. 'Traces' of the past are, as Joachim Knape has observed, the basis for historical writing, as the memorialized traces are reinterpreted and reincorporated into new historiographic contexts.[18] However, the *trace*, in Derridean terms, occurs at the moment of erasure in writing; it is an absence that defines a presence.[19] In translation, such traces provide evidence of precursors as they are appropriated into new texts; evidence of previous texts and the cultures they encode may linger, in spite of the translator's best effort. In Bede, these traces appear as echoes of British history and traditions; in Anglo-Norman histories, they appear as echoes of Anglo-Saxon history, absorbed into the broader patterns of the providential cycle. In Geoffrey and Wace, such traces are evident in the untranslated sections of 'English' that signal its irreducible presence. La3amon differs from most of his contemporaries and precursors in that he brings such traces to the surface and constructs an historiography that dramatizes the process by which these traces re-emerge in history. The metaphor for the untranslatable traces in the *Brut* – the fragments or elements of previous texts and traditions that somehow resist historiographic translation – is the absent or escaped body of the ruler; it avoids translation by the new dominant group and remains beneath the contours of the new culture, hidden but out of its reach. The presence of such traces reminds readers that all historical texts are, to some extent, translations of previous texts. Like the palimpsest, evidence of the previous text, and of the culture that created it, is apparent beneath the surface to the astute reader. For La3amon as a translator, the trace may be a source of anxiety; for La3amon as the author of a text subject to translation, it may also serve as a source of power, a guard against the complete translation and reinscription of his own historical text.

Translating Arthur: the king as text and translator

In the figure of Arthur, Laȝamon makes his fullest statement of the ruler and his relationship to the process of translation. It is difficult to overstate Arthur's importance to Laȝamon's Britons: his birth coming in fulfilment of Merlinian prophecy, Arthur creates a regime that marks the apex of British power and prestige; his reign also marks the epitome of the production of British historical narrative. The figure of Arthur stands in the centre of medieval debates regarding 'true' or 'authentic' history. For Laȝamon, Arthur embodies both historian-translator and translated text, as Laȝamon recasts the legendary British warrior as a potent emblem for the historian, the historical text and the process of translating people.[20] Arthur is an important and intriguing figure in insular historiography as well, not only for Laȝamon, but also for his predecessors and contemporaries. For many historians, such as William of Malmesbury, Arthur occupies a liminal space between 'history' and 'fiction' (or romance) – hence William's lament that Arthur had been remembered in 'idle fiction' when he deserved commemoration in 'authentic history'.[21] Others, such as Henry of Huntingdon, accepted early accounts of Arthur in 'Nennius' without much commentary, while still others, such as William of Newburgh, denounced Arthur as absolute fiction or 'romance'. The reason for such controversy, as Leckie observes, is based on the problems the Galfridian–Arthurian narrative posed for canonical versions of insular history.[22] Even before and after Laȝamon, then, Arthur and the Arthurian narrative were central to debates on the nature of 'true' history. Laȝamon's Arthur occupies a similar space, forming the crux of Laȝamon's own discussion of 'history' and 'fiction'. Accordingly, Laȝamon's Arthur is a figure linked at once to romance or mythology and to history. His birth is attended by elves, but the gifts that they present to him are not the magical items one might expect, but a set of 'historical' virtues associated with good rulership: strength, royal ability and long life (ll. 9608–15). Laȝamon here fuses motifs associated with history and with romance.

When he approaches the figure of Arthur, Laȝamon encounters a figure and a narrative tradition already based on translation. The actual history of the development of the Arthur tradition is itself a narrative of translation and appropriation: by the French for the nascent *fin amour* tradition, by Anglo-Norman Latin historians as a site of debate about 'true' or 'authentic' history, and by the Welsh as a symbol of national unity. In any event, the narrative of Arthur and the Arthur story in the *Brut* becomes upon examination something of an allegory for the process of translating history, specifically, for the process of translating and disseminating Arthurian history. The principal images and motifs that surround La3amon's depiction of the king, including his body and the Round Table, all relate to the translation and the production of history. His extended narrative account of the foundation of King Arthur's celebrated Table – the first version of this event in English – illustrates the complexities of the translation of history. In response to Wace's account, La3amon's narrative engenders a lengthy authorial homily on the way language and narrative may shape – or translate – an individual's reputation, and hence create history:

> Þis wes þat ilke bord þat Bruttes of 3elpeð
> and sugeð feole cunne lesinge bi Arðure þan kinge.
> Swa deð aueralc mon þe oðer luuien con;
> Σif he is him to leof þenne wule he li3en
> and suggen on him wurðscipe mare þenne he beon wurðe;
> ne beo he no swa luðer mon þat his freond him wel ne on.
> Æft 3if on uolke feondscipe arereð.
> an aueræi time bitweone twon monnen,
> me con bi þan læðe lasinge suggen;
> þeh he weore þe bezste mon þe æuere æt at borde,
> þe mon þe him weore lað him cuðe last finden.
> Ne al soh ne al les þat leod-scopes singeð;
> ah þis is þat soððe bi Arðure þan kinge.
> Nes næuer ar swulc king, swa duhti þurh alle þing;
> for þat soðe stod a þan writen hu hit is iwurðen,
> word from þan ænden, of Arðure þan kinge,
> no mare, no lasse, buten alse his la3en weoren.
> Ah Bruttes hine luueden swiðe and ofte him on li3eð,
> and suggeð feole þinges bi Arðure þan kinge
> þat næuere nes iwurðen a þissere weorlde-richen.
> Inoh he mai suggen þe soð wule uremmen
> seolcuðe þinges bi Arðure kinge.

(ll. 11454–75)

[This was that same table, of which the Britons boast, and tell many amazing lies, about Arthur the king. So does every man, who knows how to love another. If he is too dear to him, he will then lie, and speak worship of him, more than he is worthy of. Be he ever so evil a man, his friend will speak well of him. If enmity should arise among a people, or at any time between two men, if one hates the other, he will speak lies about the hated one, even if he were the best man that ever ate at board. The man who finds him hateful knows how to tell lies about him. It is neither all truth nor all lies, the songs the *scops* sing, but this is the truth of Arthur the king. There was never before such a king, so doughty in all things; for it stands in writing, how it befell, from beginning to end, about Arthur the king; no more, no less, but just what his deeds were. But the Britons loved him very much and often lie about him, and say many things about Arthur the king that never happened in this world. One may say enough, if he would tell the truth, of great things about Arthur the king.]

In contrast to Wace, who condemns the *fableürs* who have given every-thing concerning Arthur the appearance of fiction ('Que tut unt fait fable sembler' (ll. 9798)), Laȝamon explains, sympathetically, the process of dissimulating fiction and history about Arthur, and invites reader scrutiny of all accounts. Although the Laȝamonic passage would seem to voice a mere truism about the human tendency to distort facts accord-ing to political biases, it calls attention to what has been a key issue in the *Brut*: the relationship between language and history. For Laȝamon, as for other historians of the period, Arthur serves as a linchpin for the notion of history itself. *Scops* and others circulate stories about Arthur, translating him in the process, just as texts record what they perceive to be his history. In the process of translating Arthur, however, distortions occur, motivated by political and personal interests: the Britons exaggerate their praise for Arthur, and the enemies of the Britons, we may assume, discredit him unfairly. Lost 'in translation' is the 'truth' about Arthur; it may be teased out, but only through a complex hermeneutic process.[23] It may be tempting to see in this passage a differentiation on Laȝamon's part between 'history' – that which is written about Arthur – and 'poetry' or 'fiction' – the work of the *leodscops*, who relate stories about him and exaggerate his deeds in the process. However, if history is translation, as Laȝamon implies throughout the *Brut*, then the process of dissemin-ating Arthurian narrative serves as a model for the transmission of history, in all of its forms, as well as of poetry. Indeed, the faith expressed by Laȝamon in the reliability of textual tradition is undercut by the diffuse and varied textual versions of the Arthur story available to him and to others: one might even make the case that Laȝamon himself participates in this process. In contrast to other historians, who disparage the art of the 'poet' as complete falsehood, Laȝamon allows for a degree of truth to be embedded in the oral poetic accounts of Arthur, in the same way that he invites scrutiny of the written histories.[24] Indeed, Laȝamon himself presents his role as historian and as poet – one who performs in *leofsong* – as equally important. In textual and oral translation of Arthurian material, what occurs is the transformation of the main story through the imperfect art of the translator, and an inevitable change as it passes into a new cultural or aesthetic context. The Arthuriad allows Laȝamon to present the creation and dissemination of Arthurian material as a model for the process of translating history. The 'truth' about Arthur ultimately appears as a matter of translation. Different writers, including Laȝamon, will translate Arthurian narrative to serve different needs. Linked lexically and thematically to Laȝamon's own self-described process of sifting through texts for the *soðere* word, and to his exhortation for the reader to learn the *runes* of his text, this process, like the process of translation itself, is indeterminate. The objective truth of history may exist, but discerning it beneath the layers of variant narrative may prove difficult. In the process of translating Arthur, one thinks, on one hand, of Benjamin's conception of achieving some sort of universal meaning through translation; on the other hand, however, the diffusion of Arthurian material through oral and textual sources introduces the disturbing possibility that translation may be all there is. Colonization of Arthur guarantees the survival of narrative in new and diverse cultural contexts, but it also threatens to destroy by obscurity what may have been the king's 'true' existence. Although he does not naively accept poetic accounts of Arthur and the Round Table, then, Laȝamon shows an awareness that many historians and poets have done to Arthur and the Britons the worst disservice imaginable by translating them out of existence.

In depicting Arthur as a metaphor for historical translation, Laȝamon embodies within the king the dual role of historian, one who consciously works to translate and control historiographic discourse, and of historical text vulnerable to translation. As the object of translation, he represents the stories – textual and otherwise – central to the British people. Initially, Arthur appears as the passive object of historical composition, a text to be appropriated and used by others. The first mention of the legendary king in the *Brut*, Merlin's twice-repeated prophecy of Arthur as a figure for poetry and the historio-poetic tradition, introduces the trope of Arthur as 'sustenance' for poets:

Of him scullen gleomen godliche singen;
of his breosten scullen æten aðele scopes;
scullen of his blode beornes beon drunke. (ll. 9410–12)

[Of him shall the gleemen joyously sing; the noble *scops* shall eat of his
breast; warriors shall be made drunk by his blood.]

Otho inserts *kempes* (warriors) for *scops* (l. 9411), bringing this line into
agreement with the *beornes* in the following line. More important,
however, is the emphasis on the king's body as an emblem for the dissemination of narrative about him. This prophecy is repeated at a pivotal
moment in Arthur's career – the creation of the Round Table – where
his body and blood serve as sustenance for poets and bards, and his own
tongue becomes a fountain of wine:

Swa him sæide Merlin, þe witeȝ wes mære,
þat a king sculde cume of Vðere Pendragune,
þat gleomen sculden wurchen burd of þas kinges breosten,
and þerto sitten scopes swiðe sele
and eten heore wullen ær heo þenne fusden,
and winscenches ut teon of þeos kinges tungen,
and drinken and dreomen daies and nihtes. (ll. 11492–8)

[So Merlin, who was wise and renowned, said about him, that a king should
come from Uther Pendragon; that gleemen would make a board of the
king's breast, and the blessed *scops* would eat their fill before they went away.
And draughts of wine would flow from the king's tongue. And they would
drink and enjoy, both days and nights.]

In Laȝamon's Arthuriad, the king's body becomes a living emblem for
the process of translating and disseminating history. The twice-repeated
prophecy of Arthur's breast as 'food' for *scops* and poets and his blood
as wine for them illustrates the two-sidedness of historical translation: it
passes the Arthur tradition into new languages and new contexts, but at
the same time threatens whatever core of truth may lie beneath the
legends. Not only British stories, but French Arthur narratives also
translate the king from British ruler into the central figure of French
courtly romance and participate in the process of remaking, or translating, the king for their own uses.

Critics have indeed noticed the cannibalistic and eucharistic dimensions of these paired scenes: Otter refers to the image as a 'Eucharist for

bards';[25] Wickham-Crowley, conversely, argues that 'the separate offerings of breast and blood evoke Christian echoes, but the context is otherwise'.[26] Veira's cannibalistic conception of translation as 'murdering' or 'creating a continued existence for the person/text in a different corporeality' certainly seems appropriate to the process of translating Arthurian history by itinerant bards and poets throughout Britain and Europe.[27] This anthropophagous model of translation, which 'moves translation beyond the dichotomy of source/target and sites original and translation in a third dimension where each is both donor and receiver', is useful in conceptualizing La3amon's concept of translating the Arthur story. La3amon certainly employs a cannibalistic motif regarding Arthur, with both the positive and negative implications evident. To consume is also to devour, to destroy the original. In the same way, translating historical text disseminates the material to a wider audience, but also supplants and obscures the original. The violent – if not outright dangerous – implications of the 'love' the *scops* and other admirers express for Arthur resonate with the historian's treatment of his own source texts. In translating these texts, he does, as Veira describes the process, introduce the material into a new and broader context. At the same time, his translation appropriates and obscures the originary material. Through his presentation of Arthur, then, La3amon offers an even more complex exposé of the process of translating history.

The violence implicit in the consumption of Arthur is made explicit in La3amon's narrative of the king's war with the invading Saxon emperor Childric, which becomes as much a struggle for control of language as for control of territory. Taking the rhetorical offensive, Childric's Saxon warriors pledge to appropriate the king's literally fragmented body as a monument to their own ruler:

> Alle dæi heo sungen of Arðure þan kinge,
> and sæiden þat heo haueden hames biwunnen
> þæ scolden heom ihalden in heore onwalden,
> and þer heo wolden wunien wintres and sumeres.
> And 3if Arður weoren swa kene þat he cumen wolde,
> to fihten wið Childrichen, þan strongen and þan richen,
> heo wolden of his rugge makien ane brugge,
> and nimen þa ban alle of aðele þan kinge
> and teien heom togadere mid guldene te3en,
> and leggen i þare halle dure þer æch mon sculde uorðfaren,
> to wurðscipe Childriche, þan strongen and þan riche.
>
> (ll. 10469–79)

[all day they sang of Arthur the king, and said that since they had seized/ occupied his homes, they would hold them in their power and there they would dwell, winters and summers, and if Arthur were so keen (bold) to come to them and fight with Childric the strong and the great, they would make a bridge of his spine and take all the bones of that king and tie them together with a golden chain and lie them on the hall door where men must go forth to honour Childric the strong and the great.]

Laȝamon's imagery in these lines is complex. The dissection of Arthur's body for a bridge seems to reflect – even parody – the piecemeal consumption of the king by poets in Merlin's prophecies, and also serves as a poetic re-enactment of the ingenious act of dissection involved in the Saxons' first stronghold, Thongchester (see p. 136). However, this absorption of Arthur's body is not the potentially life-affirming celebration of history and poetry implied by the Merlinian prophecy, but a violent metaphor for the process of translating history, where the (presumptive) conquerors seek to absorb the historical traditions of their victims. The king's metaphorical identification with the land, furthermore, becomes concrete in Arthur's projected 'translation' into architectural edifice. The 'bridge' serves as an image for the liminal translation of Arthur from a still-living British hero into a static component of Saxon triumphalist history. The conqueror's military violence and the historian's verbal violence thus converge in a single image of the king's dismemberment.

In this respect, the 'consumption' and threatened 'dissection' of Arthur can be seen as analogous to the process of seizing and translating historical material. Read as parallel, Merlin's prophecy and the Saxon bridge illustrate the diametrical extremes of the translation of Arthurian history. Laȝamon mirrors the way the Arthurian tradition itself has passed through different nations and into different languages. On one hand, we see the dissemination of history into different languages and into different traditions as enriching the languages and cultures into which they are translated, metaphorically (and often literally) providing poetic sustenance for poets as they simultaneously glorify Arthur. On the other hand, we see in the Saxons' vainglorious boast the figural dismemberment and mutilation that authors of histories inflict upon the texts and traditions they translate. Laȝamon's reference to the manipulations of Arthur's bones further reflects Anglo-Norman historiographic translations of English material, and may also add a subtle and wry jibe at Henry II's efforts to locate Arthur's tomb.[28] The Saxons' 'singing' about Arthur, a cruel reconception of the oral dissemination of the Arthurian tradition prophesied by Merlin, poetically posits the appropriation of Arthur and of that oral tradition as a public performance intended to initiate the new Saxon historical tradition. By way of comparison, William of Malmesbury cites a dream of Edward the Confessor in which the vital organs of a personified 'England' are devoured by strangers (invaders); Stein observes of this passage that it symbolizes both the destruction of England and its unification with Normandy.[29] From the perspective of Arthur-as-text, the more complex and original images that La3amon attaches to Arthur can be seen as emblems for the process of translating history. Specifically, the motif of Arthur as 'food' for poets becomes a metaphor for the process of reading – 'consuming' and 'digesting' – historical material. La3amon's digestive trope enacts a complex fusion of aesthetics and violence in the process of translation, which Morrison compares to digestion as 'a synonym for a kind of cognition that fuses beauty with violence'.[30] William of Malmesbury's aforementioned 'seasoning' of the *Anglo-Saxon Chronicles* through translation provides an apt example of this process

When Arthur turns the tables on the Saxons, La3amon casts the king as historian; La3amon employs a like trope of dismemberment and translation by converting the mutilated bodies of the Saxon warriors into a poetically inspired 'bridge': 'Þer sunken to þan grunde fif and twenti hundred; / þa al wes Auene stram mid stele ibrugged!' (ll. 10615–6) (There sank to ground five-and-twenty hundred. Then was all of Avon-stream bridged with steel). When Arthur turns the vanquished Saxons into a 'bridge', he can be seen to progress from translatable text to an author capable of appropriating the texts and traditions of others. In La3amon's most striking 'epic' simile, Arthur compares the 'fish' in the Avon to armoured warriors:[31]

> 3urstendæi wes Baldulf cnihten alre baldest;
> nu he stant on hulle and Auene bihaldeð,
> hu ligeð þan stræme stelene fisces;
> mid sweorde bigeorede heore sund is awemmed;
> heore scalen wleoteð swulc gold-fa3e sceldes;
> þer fleoteð heore spiten swulc hit spæren weoren.
> Þis beoð seolcuðe þing isi3en to þissen londe,
> swulche deor an hulle, swulche fisces in wælle!
>
> (ll. 10638–45)

[Yesterday Baldulf was the boldest of knights. Now he stands on a hill and beholds the Avon, how steel fishes, girded with swords, lie in the stream;

their swimming is ruined. Their scales shine like gold-adorned shields. Their fins float as if they were spears. This is a strange thing to see in this land, such beasts on the hill, such fish in the stream!]

This section represents some of Laȝamon's most intricately crafted poetry, an inverted simile, issuing from the mouth of Arthur, that transforms the bodies of the Saxons into fish, which are then compared to mailed warriors. The bridge motif provides Arthur an opportunity to enact the same sort of rhetorical violence on the bodies of his foes that the translator enacts on the source texts and upon the people who produced them. Here, the Saxon bodies are placed in the role of the passive text, providing raw source material for Arthur, who takes on the persona of the historian-*scop* in his own right. Their bodies serve as texts on to which Arthur may inscribe the historical narrative of his own military prowess. As Laȝamon casts Arthur in the role of *scop*, the second element of Merlin's prophecy becomes evident; here 'wine' (poetry) literally drips from the king's own tongue, as he illustrates the capacity to perform his own poetry and translation. This historiographical construct provides a proper context for reading the remainder of Arthur's career as emblematic of historical composition. Arthur's grafting of the now-silenced Saxons onto a nascent Arthurian tradition, as part of a topographical anomaly, recurs in his description of the mysterious Scottish lakes to his kinsman, the Breton king Hoel:

> Bi þisse mære enden, þer þis water wendeð,
> is an lutel wiht mære, monnen to wundre.
> He is endlonge feouwer and sixti munden;
> he is imeten a bræd fif and twenti foten;
> fif foten he is deop – alfene hine dulfen!
> Feower-noked he is, and þerinne is feower kinnes fisc,
> and ælc fisc an his ende þer he his cun findeð;
> ne mai þer nan to oðere buten al swa tacheð his icunde.
> Nes næuer nan mon iboren, ne of swa wise crafte icoren,
> no libbe he swa longe, þe maȝen hit vnderstonde,
> what letteð þene fisc to uleoten to þan oðere,
> for nis þer noht bitwenen buten water clæne!

(ll. 10972–84)

[At the end of this lake, where the water turns, is a smaller lake, a wonder to men. The water is sixty-four hands in length, twenty-five feet in breadth, and five feet deep. Elves dug it. It has four niches, and there live four kinds of fish. And each fish stays in his end where he finds his kin. Nor will any

one go to another, but keeps with his own kind. There has never been a
man born so wise in knowledge, nor may any live so long, that he may
understand what hinders these fish from going to another side, for there is
nothing between them but clear water!]

Laʒamon's implanting of this speech into Arthur's mouth furthers the
role of the king as historian in his own right: Gildas and Bede begin
their histories with descriptions of the topography of Britain. Arthur's
geographical aside about the island is a prelude to his control of the
landscape, analogous to the historian's control of the text he translates.

Laʒamon's configuration of Arthur as author of his own history
culminates in the *Brut*'s rather disturbing narration of the foundation of
the Round Table. The written account of the Table's establishment originates with Wace, where the *Roman de Brut* expressly cites its currency in
folk tradition. Wace, however, treats the invention of the Round Table
mainly as a symbol for the harmony of Arthur's 'international' court,
and as a figure for the relatively new code of chivalry:

> Pur les nobles baruns qu'il out,
> Dunt chescuns mieldre estre quidout,
> Chescuns se teneit al meillur,
> Ne nuls n'en saveit le peiur,
> Fist Artur la Roünde Table
> Dunt Bretun dient mainte fable.
> Illuec seeient li vassal
> Tuit chevalment e tuit egal;
> A la table egalment seeient
> E egalment servi esteient;
> Nul d'els ne se poeit vanter
> Qu'il seïst plus halt de sun per,
> Tuit esteient assis meain,
> Ne n'i aveit nul de forain.
> N'esteit pas tenuz pur curteis
> Escot ne Bretun ne Franceis,
> Normant, Angevin ne Flamenc,
> Ne Burguinun ne Loherene
> De ki que il tenist sun feu,
> Des occident jesqu'a Muntgeu,
> Ki a la curt Artur n'alout
> E ki od lui ne sujurnout,
> E ki n'en aveit vesteüre
> E cunuissance armeüre

> A la guise que cil teneient
> Ki a la curt Artur serveient.
>
> (ll. 9747–72; italics mine)

[Because of the noble barons he [Arthur] had, with each seeking to be the best, each holding himself better than the other, and none wishing to consider himself lower, Arthur made the Round Table, of which the Britons have made many fables. Each of his vassals held the other as chivalrous and entirely equal. And those at the table stand as equals and are served equally; no one could boast that he was higher than his peer, for all who sat to eat, none was considered foreign. No one was held to have courtesy, neither Scot nor Briton, nor Frenchman, nor Norman, nor Angevin, nor Fleming, nor Burgundian nor Lorrainian, or any who held his fief, from the west of Montgieu, if he had not gone to Arthur's court and had not sojourned there, and did not have the vestments, the appearance, armour and the guise of those who served Arthur.]

This passage seems to support the idea that Wace was deliberately representing Arthur as a parallel for Henry II, as the denizens of Arthur's court reflect those of Henry's Angevin Empire; in this respect, Wace's expanded translation of Geoffrey and (presumably) of oral sources represents the sort of translation and appropriation Laȝamon hints at in his version of this event. The purpose of the Table in Laȝamon's precursor is to provide a sense of shared identity among members of a chivalric community that transcends national identity, and to provide a sense of unity and harmony for Arthur's distinctly 'international' court. This is something that Laȝamon's experience as a member of a people who had seen conquest and the marginalization of their language would, in all likelihood, not allow him to accept unconditionally. Further, although Laȝamon depicts stories of Arthur circulating through French provinces, the French themselves make no appearance at Laȝamon's Round Table. It could be that Laȝamon is replicating the process of suppression and alteration identifiable in Wace, but it could also be an effort on Laȝamon's part to recover what he perceives as an older, pre-Romance history of Arthur. In either event, Laȝamon shows awareness of the changes and omissions that inevitably accompany the translation of history. Further, the languages of 'chivalry' and 'courtesy' that appear in embryonic form in Wace remain untranslated in Laȝamon. Laȝamon translates the French *curteis* as 'deden itald oht' (l. 11481) (deeds held for nothing), concretizing the French term which, we may suspect, is untranslatable in Laȝamon's English. Likewise, the courtly mimicry of

Arthurian dress, again reminiscent of 'courtly' customs of the twelfth
century, is translated as *knowledge* of the appearance of Arthur and his
men, and, more importantly for Arthur's context, the ability to speak
and *sing* about them: 'suggen and singen of Arðure þan ginge' (l. 11484)
(speak and sing of Arthur the young).

It is this awareness of language and its power that characterizes
Laȝamon's innovation of transforming the Round Table into an emblem
of the historical translator's craft. We must remember that in Laȝamon's
Brut the Table is brought into being only after bloodshed. The blending
of multiple people and multiple tongues proves dangerous, for the unity
Wace envisions, like the continuity of Anglo-Norman historical texts,
can be achieved only through the suppression of rival voices. Offering a
more elaborate – and seemingly more realistic – account of the events in
Arthur's court that precipitate the Table's construction and foundation,
Laȝamon brings to the surface the clashes that remain potential and below
the surface in Wace's *Roman de Brut*. As in Wace, Arthur's reputation in
Laȝamon has earned him an international retinue: 'Folc com to hirede
of feole cunne þeode; / widen and siden folc wes on selen' (ll. 11332–3)
(folk came to serve him, folk of numerous countries; from far and near,
the people were happy). However, in the *Brut* this fact is not so much a
credit to the king as an ominous foreboding of the violent episode that
is to shatter Arthur's twelve-year peace:

> Ich mai sugge hu hit iwarð, wunder þæh hit þunche.
> Hit wes in ane ȝeol-dæie þat Arður in Lundene lai;
> þa weoren him to icumen of alle his kinerichen,
> of Brutlonde, of Scotlonde, of Irlonde, of Islonde,
> [. . .]
> þer weoren seouen kingene sunes mid seouen hundred cnihten icumen
> wiðuten þan hired þe herede Arður.
> Ælc hafede an heorte leches heȝe
> and lette þat he weore betere þan his iuere.
> Þat folc wes of feole londe; þer wes muchel onde
> for þe on hine talde hæh, þe oðer muche herre.
>
> (ll. 11345–8, 11351–6)

[I may say how it was, though it seems a wonder. It was on a Yule day when
Arthur lay in London. There had come to him people from all his kingdoms
– from Britain, from Scotland, from Ireland, from Iceland [. . .] There were
seven kings' sons with seven hundred knights, not counting the household
men who served Arthur. Each had great pride in his heart and believed that
he was better than his comrades. The folk was of many lands; there was

much strife. For if one would consider himself high, the other thought himself higher.]

A fierce brawl follows this dispute, which disturbance the king punishes by having the perpetrator drawn and quartered and tossed into a bog, and the heads of his male relations and the noses of his female relatives severed, while pledging to exterminate the man's entire family: 'and swa ich wulle al fordon þat cun þat he of com' (l. 11400) (and so will I completely destroy that kin from whence he came). As with the poetically commemorated Saxons, the bodies of opponents here form the foundation of Arthur's authority. Laȝamon's translation of Arthur may be viewed from two perspectives. In concretizing Wace's conception of French *curteis* as deeds, including speaking and singing, Laȝamon in effect peels back the layers of French chivalric or courtly tradition, calling attention to the cultural ramifications of translating the king into different contexts.[32] In this respect, the violence underlying the foundation of the Table itself (apart from serving as a brutally realistic detail) may well serve as part of a larger metaphor for the violence that underlies the foundations of new orders and new textual traditions: suppressed or reduced to a 'trace' in Wace, Laȝamon brings these violent acts to the surface. At the same time, however, in dramatizing the process through which stories of Arthur spread and distort the actions of the 'real' king, Laȝamon reminds his readers/listeners that his Arthuriad is another retelling of the story that may be open to scrutiny. In 'colonizing' the Geoffrey-Wace Arthuriad for an English audience, Laȝamon adds another narrative layer, this time concealing traces of the 'courtly' tradition beneath its surface.

Laȝamon's depiction of Arthur's extermination of an entire clan, here made to include the textually significant act of facial mutilation, betrays a desire to control by limiting the means of translating historical material; the prevention of reproduction by the offending family symbolizes the halting of one line of a narrative tradition. Such facial mutilation has precedence in English law, as a punishment for adultery. An intriguing literary analogue to this mutilation is to be found in Marie de France's *lai* 'Bisclavret', which concludes with an adulterous wife having her nose bitten off by her betrayed werewolf-husband, whereupon she and her erstwhile lover – banished from acceptable society – produce a race of noseless women.[33] Whether Laȝamon had read this *lai*, whether he and Marie were working from common British (or Welsh) oral fables, or whether the act of mutilation is an appropriately grotesque punishment for the respective crimes, remains open to question, but the symbol is a powerful one. The enigmatic workman (La3amon's original addition) who proposes to build the Table makes his offer to Arthur because he has heard news of the brawl – 'neowe tidende' (ll. 11428) – beyond the sea. The spread of news about Arthur's inability to control his own people compromises his status as an effective leader; the Table, as depicted by La3amon, provides a remedy to what could be perceived as weakness. Assuring him that no similarly humiliating narratives about his apparent weakness will be spread in the future, the table serves as an emblem for Arthur's control of his own history. Unity and harmony in La3amon's depiction of Arthur's court seem to rest on acts of mass execution and mutilation – one even twelfth- and thirteenth- century readers would likely consider excessive – transformed into an aesthetic construct whose apparent inclusiveness conceals the violence underlying its own hege-monic foundation.[34] Warren argues that the Round Table 'signifies the moment when the violence of group boundary formation cedes to the peace of boundless hegemony'.[35] True, but it is important to remember that this hegemony depends upon Arthur's ability to control discourse and to author his own discourse, by force, if necessary. Appropriately, it is at this very moment that Arthur may be seen to seize control of his own history.

It is the very political, even nationalistic, nature of translating history that La3amon addresses in his discussion of the Round Table. If history is seen as the property of conquerors, a process of translation achieved by the appropriation and suppression of other traditions, then any claim about locating truth underneath the layers of translated narrative becomes problematic. Through these narrative innovations, La3amon exposes the seeming unity of historical writing as dependent upon translation and retranslation of previous texts and tradition, bringing to the surface acts of violence that the providential historiographic matrices of his period exclude. Founded on genocide, the Round Table provides a temporary, if not false, sense of unity in Arthur's court, just as the historiographic master-narratives of the twelfth century had imposed a seemingly unified system on human events, and suppressed the very acts of violence upon which they were founded. Arthur's response to the threat of the loss of control of discourse is to inflict similar violence upon his own rivals, reversing his status as text to be inscribed, and becoming a translator who authors his own narrative. In a similar vein, La3amon, as an English historical poet working with French and Latin sources, exposes and reverses the predominant process of translating Anglo-Saxon historical traditions into Anglo-Norman historical texts.

Throughout the narrative of Arthur's Roman campaign, which becomes an account of the king's drive to regulate historical discourse, Laʒamon remains intensely aware of the importance of language in determining history. Arthur's demand – unprecedented in Geoffrey or in Wace – that the vanquished giant of Mont-Saint-Michel relate his lineage and, specifically, disclose his kinship, further highlights his desire for control of discourse:

> Tel me of þine cunne and whar beo heore beonste,
> and wha þe weore on uolde fader oðer moder ihalde,
> and of whulche londe þu art iliðen hidere.
>
> (ll. 13021–23)

[Tell me of your kin, and from what stock you come, and who in the world might be counted your father or your mother, and which country you are from.]

Knowledge of the giant's ancestry will enable Arthur to appropriate him and his history for his own ends, and in this sense he echoes the foundational violence and suppression of the aboriginal giants of Albion by Britain's eponymous founder, Brutus. Because the giants lack a written or a spoken history, they are liable to cultural eradication at the hands of Brutus and the Britons. Having no historical tradition, the giant – like his predecessors in Britain – suffers the permanent status of being acted upon and written about. Arthur punishes the giant's reticence with decapitation; the destruction of his body pushes him beyond the margins of recordable history, the very condition facing Arthur in his early career, and the one confronting Laʒamon as a member of the post-Conquest English.

Laʒamon later depicts the linguistic violence that underlies translation and the actual violence inflicted upon the bodies of adversaries. When the challenge issued to the Roman emperor by Arthur's surrogate, Gawain, reduces the Roman leader to silence – 'aset þe kaisere swulc he akimed weore / and andsware nauer nan no aʒæf þissen eorlen' (the emperor sat as if he were struck dumb and made no sort of answer to these earls) (ll. 13153–4) – the act becomes a verbal assault.[36] In Gawain and the emperor's ensuing rhetorical duel, each evokes rival claims to historical precedence – with references to the rival conquerors Julius Caesar and Brennes – in asserting rival territorial claims. When the rhetorical struggle between historical traditions escalates into actual violence, the bilingual Gawain – 'Walwain cuðe Romanisc, Walwain cuðe Bruttisc' (l. 13099)

(Gawain knew Latin; Gawain knew British) – equates the teaching of
'British speech' to the Romans with the Britons' physical assault:

> and þas word sæide Walwain þe sele:
> 'Marcel, far to helle, and tel heom þer spelles,
> and wune þer toȝere mid Quenceline þin ifere,
> and haldeð þer unker rune; betere inc weoren inne Rome,
> for þus we eou scullen techen ure Bruttisce speche!'
>
> (ll. 13244–8)

[And Gawain the blessed spoke these words: 'Marcel, go now to Hell, and
relate tales there. And dwell there together with Quincelin your comrade,
and hold counsel with him. Better the two of you were in Rome, for thus we
shall teach you our British speech!']

The unprecedented linguistic dimension Laȝamon gives Gawain makes
him the 'translator' of his Roman adversaries, as he transforms them into
passive objects of British history through the same sort of violent action
inflicted upon the Saxons and upon Arthur's unruly courtiers. Gawain's
assault also forecloses the historiographic debate, demonstrating that
questions of historical precedence may ultimately be decided by brute
force. Laȝamon's rather grotesque metaphor of slayer as language teacher
underscores this violent aspect of historical composition; Gawain's
apostrophe to the fallen Marcel signals the latter's removal from active
participation in history. In this way, the *Brut* imitates the process the
English had undergone under a century of Anglo-Norman occupation.

Elsewhere in the text, Arthur's men fear becoming objects of translation, should they offer a negative interpretation of his first dream: 'Ne
durste þer na cniht to ufele ræcchen na wiht / leoste he sculden leosen
his leomen þat weoren him deore' (nor dared any knight reckon any evil
in any way, lest he lose the limbs that were dear to him) (ll. 12792–3).
Even the messenger sent to tell Arthur of Modred's treachery is reluctant
to deliver his message for fear of Arthur's wrath. Arthur's carefully constructed narrative of desire and fulfillment concerning his own queen,
Guinevere, and his projected conquest of Rome – a discourse that refuses
to entertain any counter-version – has been shaped to reflect the process
of translating history, which likewise seeks to construct a singular narrative of the past. The need to silence opponents and opposing voices
intensifies, reaching its most poignant expression in Arthur's brutal
massacre of the citizens of Winchester as retribution for their support
of Modred. It seems that, once history has eluded Arthur's control,

violent acts simply beget more violent acts. For Arthur, as for Laȝamon, historical translation may ultimately be a matter decided by the sword.

Laȝamon's depiction of Arthur's dual role of history-producing subject and object of history becomes more complex in the final 'dream' sequence (MS Caligula, ll. 13977–14015), where Laȝamon again assigns Arthur the role of passive, yet this time untranslatable, text. At first glance, the dream marks a retreat or withdrawal from history. After the destruction of Arthur's hall, the traditional symbol of royal authority – by Modred and Guinevere – Laȝamon posits the king alone on a bleak, almost Dantesque, landscape, where the images he encounters, 'gripes and grisleche fules' (l. 14006) (griffons and hideous birds), a golden lion and a fish, offer multiple interpretative possibilities. The fish, a Christian icon, obliquely associates Arthur with the wounded Fisher King of the Grail legend, but there is no overt link to any system of icons, Christian or otherwise.[37] The free interpretative play and multiple meanings heighten the sense of mystery of the dream vision. Events in the dream move beyond Arthur's control as ruler, as the king remains passive throughout the second section of the vision; his self-representation finally suggests nothing more than a newborn infant: 'Þa wes ich al wet and weri of sorwen and seoc' (l. 14015) (Then I was all wet, weary of sorrow and sickness). Readers versed in the Arthurian legend (and even those not so well versed) might see Arthur's sea voyage as a reference to his removal to Avalon, but this reading is not forthcoming in the text, and even if it were so, it would leave the mysterious beasts – as well as the king's sorrow upon his arrival – unexplained. The coast on which Arthur finds himself is not identified as a place of healing and resurrection. The enigmas surrounding Arthur's prophetic dream contrast with his self-assured authorship of his own history, and also with the self-assurance with which translators approach his life. By defying interpretation (and hermeneutic systems), the dream defies translation.

Coupled with the narrative of the wounded Arthur's escape from the battlefield of Camlann, the mysterious dream marks how the king and his narrative tradition prove uncontainable by interpretative models. Beyond the confines of conventional history and in the milieu of legend and myth – literally outside of time – Arthur's body remains unreachable by his enemies. Arthur's death is uncertain, as are the time and place of his return: '[Merlin] bodede mid worde – his quiðes weoren soðe – / þat an Arður scule ȝete cum Anglen to fulste' (ll. 14296–7) (Merlin prophesied with words – his sayings were true – that an Arthur should yet come to help the English). The consolation offered to Arthur by his dream, then, is an escape from the mortality demanded by history. From this perspective, the aphorism Laȝamon assigns to the messenger who first hears of the dream, 'ne sculde me nauere sweuen mid sorwen arecchen' (l. 14023) (no one should ever reckon dreams with sorrow), carries more significance than its teller realizes. This passage calls into question the finality of translation. Arthur's uncertain end encapsulates Laȝamon's construct of the king's body as cultural emblem. Its survival signals the possibility of some sort of survival for the British people.

Situating Arthur as a creator of history in his own right, as well as a subject of the history of others, Laȝamon lays out what could be termed a theory of historiography as a construct of language, wherein the appearance of historical truth is achieved by the translation and appropriation of rival historical texts and traditions. Arthur's struggle to resist the territorial displacement of the Britons by foreign invaders and the replacement of British history by foreign history comes to reflect Laȝamon's own challenge to the historiographic paradigm used by Anglo-Norman historians in their attempts to legitimize the marginalization of the English – a paradigm that depended upon the appropriation and translation of English historical material. Simultaneously, the genuine love and admiration Laȝamon expresses for Arthur and his story – which he received from Wace's French text and from Welsh oral sources – seems indicative of the desire of the colonized and the colonizers for the texts and traditions of the Other. The Arthuriad encapsulates the odd mixture of love and aggression that typifies Laȝamon's historiopoetics, as expressed throughout the *Brut*. His earlier admonition about the political motives for spreading stories about Arthur thus constitutes not only a challenge to dominant historiographic paradigms, but also an invitation to scrutinize Laȝamon's own claims to historical 'truth'. Thus, while Laȝamon reconstructs the life of Arthur, he remains aware that he, too, may be engaging in the same process of appropriation and suppression he identifies as underlying insular history.

The escaped ruler and the untranslatable trace

The escape of a ruler, such as Caric or Arthur, or his evasion of conquerors denies closure to his defeat and to any conquest itself, even if the ruler is not in a position to threaten imminent return, and hence problematizes the finality of the translated text itself. The defeated but uncaptured king has a similar iconic function for the colonized people, representing their lingering hopes for recovery, or at least for survival. In death, the ruler's body may be transformed into a sort of secular relic, and the presence of a ruler's remains – entombed – in the land itself signifies continuity of the dynasty. The enduring tradition of Arthur's return to medieval Wales (and, of course, in the *Brut* itself) and the Anglo-Saxon tradition of Harold's escape, documented in the late twelfth-century *Vita Haroldi*, become points of resistance to the dominant culture, as the sanctified body of the ruler remains out of reach of the aggressors. The bodies of Arthur and Cadwalader remain beyond the reach of *literal* translation (at least until the fulfilment of certain prophecies). As a result, the British people remain viable as forces in insular history. What mattered was the symbolic value of the successful concealment of those bodies from the conquerors; as cultural symbols, the inviolability of the rulers' bodies preserves to an extent the cohesiveness of the ethnic groups they led.

The body of Cadwalader, in the final section of the *Brut*, becomes a symbol of the prophecy of the Britons' eventual return to power, and for the incompleteness of the translation process. The Laȝamonic narrative is itself a translation of Wace's and Geoffrey's references to the translation of unspecified relics that will precede the prophesied British recovery. The vulgate version of Geoffrey's *Historia* refers to the retrieval of saints' relics, but not explicitly to Cadwalader's body: 'Nec id tamen prius futurum quam britonum reliquie que propter paganorum inuasionem abscindiute fuerant amissum regnum recuperarent' (Not until the relics that were removed because of the pagan invasion are returned will the Britons recover the realm). The *Variant* adds 'Nec id tamen antea futurum quam Britones reliquiis corporis sui potiti illas in Britanniam a Roma asportarent' (Not until the Britons take the relics of the body from Rome and bring them to Britain).[38] Wace offers a fairly close translation, which likewise leaves the nature of the relics indeterminate:

> Desi la que li tens vendreit
> Que les reliques de sun cors
> De sepultres traites fors,
> Serreient de Rome aportees
> en Breatine presentees

(ll. 14796–800)

[Not until the time came when the relics of his body, taken from his tomb, would be brought back from Rome and presented in Britain.]

As Judith Weiss notes, it is not even clear whether the remains are those
of Cadwalader or Merlin.[39] Further, the passage could refer to artefacts
the deceased has on his person, and not to the body itself. Laӡamon
expands this line, naming the body as Cadwalader's and richly enshrining
his bones:

> þenne sculle Bruttes sone buӡen to Rome
> and draӡwn ut þine banes alle of þene marme-stane,
> and mid blissen heom uerien uorð mid heomseoluen
> in seoluere and in golde into Brutlonde.

(ll. 16023–6)[40]

[Then shall the Britons go to Rome and draw out all of your bones from
the marble tomb, and with bliss bring them with themselves, encased in
silver and in gold, into Britain.]

Laӡamon directly associates their retranslation with the restoration of
British rule. As he does with texts in his prologue, Laӡamon dwells upon
the material artefact itself, concretizing the French *reliques* as *banes* –
bringing to the surface the physical features glossed over or, in this case,
abstracted by the French and Latin texts. Here, Cadwalader's corpse
becomes a secular relic. His body is linked lexically to the process of
translation through use of *uerian* (l. 16025), a term whose present-day
English reflex is 'ferry' and whose Latin cognate is *fero* – to bring, bear,
win or carry off, the root of 'transfer'.[41] Further, the reappearance of the
place-name *Brutlonde* in conjunction with the future *Bruttes* predicts the
retranslation both of the land and of the landscape. The elusiveness of
Cadwalader's body thus serves the Britons in much the same way, one
suspects, as the tradition of Harold's escape from Hastings served the
Anglo-Saxons. In both instances, translation remains incomplete and
the possibility – however remote – of future return remains intact.
Laӡamon's second reference to Cadwalader's entombment directly and
lexically links the king's body to the metaphorical sealing of Merlin's
prophecy in text:

> His ban beoð ilokien faste in guldene cheste,
> And þer heo scullen wunie þat daӡes beon icumene
> þa Merlin ine iurn-daӡen vastnede mid worden.

(ll. 16076–8)

[His bones will be locked fast in a golden chest and there they shall dwell in
the coming days that Merlin set fast with words.]

Drawn from Wace's rather sparse reference to the entombment – 'Le cors fud mult bel cunreez / En terre cors saint posez' (ll. 14839–40) (The corpse was handsomely entombed, and the holy corpse was buried in the earth) – Laȝamon both concretizes the passage and heightens the importance of the king as cultural icon. In the English *Brut*, the king's body carries with it anthropological significance for the kingdom as a whole. Hence, in the post-Conquest period, the emphasis on the translation of saints' relics by Norman and Saxon clergy gained importance. Laȝamon here enacts a narrative of disclosure and concealment of Cadwalader's body, corresponding to the earlier prophetic act of uncovering and eventual return of the king's body, which itself is to coincide with the return of the Britons to power. Concerning the physical act of translating – *trans-ferring* or *uerian* – from Rome to Britain, Laȝamon adds a sequence of literal translation, paralleling the acts of figural translation that would presumably presage renewed British control of history as well. The return of the king, even his corpse, for Laȝamon revivifies the notion of *leod*, as a unification of land, people and language, all associated with the body of the king.

In the *Brut* and in the texts of Laȝamon's contemporaries, the king's body becomes something of a totem, representing the collective consciousness of the culture. Kantorowicz notes in the eleventh-century Norman Anonymous the dual natural (*natura*) and sacred function of the king as a temporal ruler, but also as a 'shadow' or imitator of Christ:

> The kings of the New Covenant no longer would appear as the 'fore-shadowers' of Christ, but rather as the 'shadows', the imitators of Christ. The Christian ruler became the *christomimetes* – literally the 'actor' or 'impersonator' of Christ – who on the terrestrial stage presented the living image of the two-natured God.[42]

What this evidence indicates is that, as the signifier of Christ, the king's body comes to represent the grace or divine sanction of the people. Keeping it out of the hands of invaders in effect preserves the divine sanction – and hence part of the cultural identity – of the people who maintain it. They avoid the rewriting, or the literal translation, of this facet of their history.

In presenting the escape and preservation of the ruler outside the hands of conquerors, Laȝamon firstly dramatizes how historical translation affects people – not only collective groups, but the rulers who govern them and reflect their culture and interests. Second, he presents a vision of history as translation that remains open and indeterminate. The return of repressed or marginalized people remains possible as long as the symbols of their collective identity remain intact. It is not a difficult leap, from this point, to see the ruler's body as analogous to the historical text: representing the collective history of a people, its translation into the language of the conquerors signifies their conquest of a new history. However, just as the ruler's body may be kept safe from outside translation either by concealment or by escape, parts of the target texts remain untranslatable. We have seen such occurrences in Henry of Huntingdon's reworking of *Brunanburh*, in the French and Latin abstract nouns that La3amon could not (or would not) find English equivalents for, and in the culturally encoded English terms (such as *scop*) that La3amon embeds in his own text. Beyond the reach of the historian-translator, these elements preserve fragments (or traces) of the precursor language and its culture. Such traces exist in the texts, but also in the land itself (in the form of elements of prior place-names) and in the collective memories of the people. Occupying a liminal point between translator and writer of a text subject to translation, parallel to his membership of a conquered people that had once been conquerors, La3amon expresses in the *Brut* the ambiguous possibilities of historical translation. It makes history available to a broader audience, but at the same time threatens to appropriate and conceal its own source text(s).

Conclusion

Where La3amon differs from his immediate source – and from his less immediate sources – is in his intense concern for the translation of land and people that accompanies territorial conquest. His own turning of the *Roman de Brut* into the indigenous vernacular simultaneously exposes the appropriative nature of this process in Wace and seeks to reverse it, by translating the history of the *English* as *English* history. With the English language and the English translator-author still viable, La3amon seems to tell us, English literature and culture may avoid complete erasure. His emphasis on the land and on the people displays what could accurately (if anachronistically) be termed 'post-colonial' consciousness: an awareness of the sort of cultural repression that accompanies translation by social and political groups. Collectively, instances of textual, territorial and human translation constitute a subtext to the *Brut* that presents history as a matter of translation. Control of discourse is, further, closely linked with control of territory, as conqueror-colonizers rewrite previous insular history for their own uses. Rulers may in turn become the objects of later historians' translation. Returning to Laȝamon's prologue, the reader is invited to scrutinize even Laȝamon's claim to 'truth'. After all, the prologue instructs the reader to say the truer (*soðere*) words together, but at the same time, Caligula-*Brut* tells them to learn the *runen*, or 'secret counsels'. There is, thus, an invitation to read beneath the surface of the *Brut* itself.

Although it is difficult to assess Laȝamon's influence beyond his immediate period, I believe it is more productive to see Laȝamon as the beginning of a tradition (Middle English) rather than as the end of one (Old English).[43] It is evident from the two manuscript traditions that someone in the Middle Ages was reading the *Brut*. Certainly, Laȝamon's fingerprints are evident in such works as the alliterative *Morte d'Arthur*. What Laȝamon offered to medieval English historiography, and offers to readers today, is an exposure of history as a construct of language, and of ways in which historiographic translation functions in the 'post-colonial' environment of Norman and Angevin England. In this environment, Laȝamon apparently worked to revivify the English language as an apt vehicle for the recording of history. In so doing, he instituted the process of linguistic rehabilitation that would come to fruition in the fourteenth century with the alliterative revival, and with the works of Geoffrey Chaucer.

Notes

1 William of Malmesbury, *Historia Regum Anglorum* (cited in ch. 1).
2 Gildas, *De Excidio Brittaniae* (cited in ch. 1).
3 *HRB*, XII. 19, p. 535. Geoffrey never explains the definition; perhaps he has some limited familiarity with the English term.
4 William A. Chaney, *The Cult of Kingship in Anglo-Saxon England: The Transition from Paganism to Christianity* (Berkeley, 1970).
5 Ernst H. Kantorowicz, *The King's Two Bodies, A Study in Mediaeval Political Theology* (Princeton, 1957).
6 Laȝamon's re-Anglicization of this line is also closer to Geoffrey of Monmouth's 'Nemet oure saxas'.
7 Lévi-Strauss, *Elementary Structures of Kinship*, trans. James Harle Bell et al. (Boston, 1969), p. 171. See also Gayle Rubin, 'The traffic in woman: notes on the "political economy: of sex"', in Rayna R. Reiter (ed.) *Toward an Anthropology of Women* (New York, 2000), pp. 157–210; Carol Parrish Jamison, 'Traffic of women in Germanic literature: the role of the peace pledge in marital

exchanges', W*omen in German Yearbook: Feminist Studies in German Literature and Culture*, 20 (2004), 13–36.

[8] Lefevre states, concerning the grid, that 'certain texts are supposed to contain certain markers designed to elicit certain reactions on the reader's part, and that the success of communication depends on both the writer and the reader of the text agreeing to play their assigned parts in connection with those markers' ('Composing the Other', p. 76). Through use of these grids, Lefevre further argues, 'Western cultures "translated" (and "translate") non-Western cultures into Western categories to be able to come to an understanding of them, and therefore, to come to terms with them' (ibid., p. 77).

[9] Quaint, or even morally questionable; see Anglo-Norman depictions of *wassailing* by Harold's men on the eve of Hastings (Orderic, William of Malmesbury and Wace's *Le Roman de Rou*).

[10] According to Chaney, '[W]hen the light of history and tradition falls on Germanic kingship of the age of migrations, the king is leader of the war-hosts but also the charismatic mediator with the divine, the sacral holder of the tribal "luck"' (*The Cult of Kingship*, p. 96). This view of king as emblem of the people further reflects the controversial Christian doctrine of king as shadow of Christ. Ernst Kantorowicz addresses the possibility that 'the king's impersonal and immortal super-body appeared, during the earlier Middle Ages [. . .] embedded in the very idea of his spiritual character resulting from the clericalization of the royal office p. 45). In other words, the king's body serves as both a secular surrogate for the Godhead and as a symbol for the collective soul of the populace. With the gloss of Anglo-Saxon *leod* as prince or leader, the king in La3amon can be seen to combine the elements of land, people and even language.

[11] Citing Plutarch, John compares the ruler to the 'head' of the state (*Policraticus*, ed. Cary J. Nederman (Cambridge, 1990), VI. i); elsewhere, he cites an anecdote in which the Emperor Trajan, when advised to punish severely a potentially disloyal senator, responds that one would be insane to gouge out rather than seek to cure a bleary eye, and that sharp nails are to be cut rather than torn away (ibid., IV. viii).

[12] Chaney, *Cult of Kingship*, p. 96.

[13] See Giraldus Cambrensis, *Journey through Wales and the Description of Wales*, trans. Lewis Thorpe (Harmondsworth, 1978).

[14] HRB, XI. 11, pp. 506–7.

[15] Wickham-Crowley (*Writing the Future*, pp. 50–1) offers a survey of the etymology of *Kinric*. Although Caric is linked reliably to the Welsh Triads, the origin of the name *Kinric* and the reasons it would be taken as an insult remain obscure. One possibility is a pun on the Saxon leader Kinric, who suffered a minor defeat at the hands of the Britons at Beranbyrig. While the suffix *ric(he)*, with the obvious meaning of realm or kingdom, is a common second element in English given-names, *Cin-* (or *cine-* or *cyne-*) is difficult to pin down: none of its possible meanings – *kin* or *family*, *chin*, *parchment*, *chink/cavern*, or *kine* – seems appropriately pejorative for La3amon's context;

however, a name suggesting a ruler of 'paper', 'caverns' or 'cattle' might be
enough of an insult.

16 Discussed in chapter 3.

17 The *Anglo-Saxon Chronicle* ('D' text) documents two such (unsuccessful) raids,
    in 1067 and 1068. 'Florence' of Worcester includes both in his chronicle,
    although he moves the dates forward by one year.

18 Knape, 'History as rhetoric', p. 117.

19 See *Writing and Difference* (Chicago, 1978), pp. 278–80.

20 I accept Hanning's definition of 'emblem': 'a symbolic artefact or character
    within a narrative that transcends its role as an emblem of the fiction in which
    it appears and becomes a powerful comment on the artistic enterprise of the
    creator' ('Poetic emblems in medieval narrative texts', in Lois Ebin (ed.),
    Vernacular Poetics in the Middle Ages (Kalamazoo, 1984), pp. 1–18 (p. 1)).

21 William of Malmesbury, *Gesta*, I. 8. 2, p. 26.

22 Leckie, *Passage of Dominion*, pp. 67–72.

23 Bryan reads the above-cited passage about Arthur's Round Table as a
    metaphor for the possibility of recovering historical truth: 'Layamon offers a
    claim to truth and an image (the Round Table) that both destabilizes some
    others' claims to truth and enables the concept of storytelling that somehow
    finesses human bias born of political loyalty. In inviting the reader to
    contemplate the image of Arthur's marvelous Table and to consider what it
    might mean to have "the whole story", Layamon's *Brut* positions the reader
    to engage in the process of sorting out the accretion of stories. Unlike Wace,
    Layamon uses the Round table to cheer on the search for Truth' ('Truth and
    the Round Table in Lawman's *Brut*',*Quondam et Futurus*, 2, 4 (1992), 34). I
    agree with her overall assessment, though I find that the political biases
    surrounding the Arthurian narrative make the search more problematic and
    more ideologically charged; in short, I don't find as much optimism in
    Laȝamon about the prospects of recovering the 'truth'.

24 E.g. William of Newburgh; Spiegel further cites the anonymous *La mort Aimeri
    de Narbonne*, in which the author completely denounces the 'lies' associated
    with the *chansons de geste* (*Romancing the Past*, pp. 60–1).

25 Otter, *Inventiones*, p. 91.

26 'Cannibal cultures and the body of the text in Laȝamon's *Brut*', in Allen,
    Perry and Roberts (eds), *Laȝamon, Contexts, Language and Interpretation*
    (London, 2002), pp. 351–69 (p. 356).

27 Viera, 'Haroldo de Campos' poetics of transcreation', p. 97.

28 According to Giraldus Cambrensis, Arthur's tomb was discovered under
    Glastonbury, according to a 'prophecy' (remarkably similar to Layamon's
    Merlin's archaeological activity). *De principis instructione*, trans. Joseph
    Stevenson, (Felinfach, 1991), I. 20.

29 William of Malmesbury, *Historia Regum Anglorum*, 2. 27; Stein, 'Making history
    English', p. 101.

30 Karl Morrison, *History as Visual Art in the Twelfth Century Renaissance*
    (Princeton, 1990), p. 36.

31 For a detailed discussion of epic similes in the *Brut*, see H. S. Davies, 'Laȝamon's similes', *Review of English Studies*, 11, 42 (1960), 129–42.

32 Laȝamon's translation process is here tangential to the process Donoghue identifies as translating Wace's British knights into Saxon foot-soldiers ('Layamon's ambivalence').

33 Dolores Warwick Frese argues that the mutilation 'serves to direct aesthetic attention to Marie's underlying issue of reproductive authenticity in the transition from oral to written poetics' ('The marriage of woman and werewolf: poetics of estrangement in Marie de France's "Bisclavret"', in Alger Nicholas Doane and Carol Braun Pasternack (eds), *Vox Intexta: Orality and Textuality in the Middle Ages* (Madison, 1991), pp. 183–202 (p. 196)).

34 Indeed, some of Arthur's actions come close to John of Salisbury's definition of tyranny. See *Policraticus*, Book IV. iv.

35 Warren, *History on the Edge*, p. 93.

36 My translation of *akimed* as 'struck dumb' follows that of Barron and Weinberg. Allen's version, however, may come closer to the spirit of the situation of a ruler reduced to silence in his own court: 'The emperor went on sitting there just like a moron, / And no response whatever did he return to these earls' (ll. 13153–4). As an analogue, we may consider the humiliation Arthur suffers in *Sir Gawain and the Green Knight* when his court is reduced to silence.

37 Each could be a symbol of resurrection; the lion is often a Christ-figure, though it may also represent pride (Dante) or unrestrained violence; for discussion of the Latin-Christian origin of these symbols, see Gloria Mercanti, 'Some rhetorical devices of the Latin tradition in Layamon's *Brut*', in Allen, Perry and Roberts (eds), *Layamon, Contexts, Language and Interpretation* (London, 2002), pp. 241–50 (pp. 245–8).

38 Geoffrey, *Historia Regum Britanniae*, 12. 17, p. 533; *Variant*, 205, p. 190.

39 *Roman de Brut*, 371, n. 5.

40 Equivalent Otho passage destroyed.

41 Its Latin synonym is *lato*, the root of *translatio*.

42 Kantorowicz, *The King's Two Bodies*, p. 47.

43 James I. McNelis III traces an extensive line of definite, probable and possible Laȝamonic influences through the later Middle Ages ('Laȝamon as *Auctor*', in Le Saux (ed.), *Text and Tradition,* pp. 253–69). See also Bryan, 'The two manuscripts of Laȝamon's *Brut*: some readers in the margins' (ibid., pp. 89–102).

Bibliography

Primary Sources

Alfred, King of England, *King Alfred's West-Saxon Version of Gregory's* Pastoral Care, ed. Henry Sweet, EETS 45, 50 (London: Early English Text Society, 1872).

Alan of Lille, *Plaint of Nature*, trans. James J. Sheridan (Toronto: Pontifical Institute of Medieval Studies, 1980).

Alan de Lille, *De Planctu Naturae*, in Thomas Wright (ed.), *The Anglo-Latin Satirical Poets and Epigrammatists of the Twelfth Century*, 2 vols (London, 1884; repr. Lessingdruckerei Wiesbaden, Germany: Krauss, 1964).

Andreas Capellanus, *On Love*, ed. and trans. P. G. Walsh (London: Duckworth, 1982).

The Anglo-Saxon Chronicle According to the Several Original Authorities, ed. Benjamin Thorpe (London: Longman, 1861).

Anglo-Saxon Riddles of the Exeter Book, trans. Paull F. Baum (Durham: Duke University Press, 1963).

Augustine of Hippo, *City of God*, trans. Marcus Dods (New York: Modern Library, 1950).

——, *Confessions*, trans. Henry Chadwick (Oxford: Oxford University Press, 1991).

Bale, John, *The First Two Partes of the Actes or Vnchast Examples of the Englysh Votaryes, Gathered out of their Owne Legendes and Chronycles* (London, 1551).

Bede, *Ecclesiastical History of the English History*, trans. Bertram Colgrave and R. A. B. Mynors (Oxford: Oxford at the Clarendon Press, 1969; repr. 1992).

——, *The Old English Version of Bede's* Ecclesiastical History of the English People, ed. Thomas Miller (London: Early English Text Society, 1890, 1898).

Boethius, *The Consolation of Philosophy*, trans. Richard Green (Indianapolis: Bobbs-Merrill, 1962).

Chaucer, Geoffrey, *Riverside Chaucer*, 3rd edition, ed. Larry D. Benson (New York: Houghton-Mifflin, 1987).

de Bury, Richard, *The Philobiblon* (Berkeley: University of California Press, 1948).

Dream of the Rood, in *The Vercelli Book*, ed. George Philip Krapp (New York: Columbia University Press, 1932).

Egil's Saga, ed. and trans. Michael Chessnutt (Copenhagen: Viborg, 2001).

'Exeter Riddle 26', in *The Exeter Book*, ed. George Philip Krapp and Elliott Van Kirk Dobbie (New York: Columbia University Press, 1936).

Gaimar, Geffrei, *L'Estoire des Engleis*, ed. Alexander Bell (Oxford: University of Oxford Press, 1960).

Geoffrey of Monmouth, *Historia Regum Britanniæ*, ed. Anton Griscom (New York: Longmans, 1929).

——, *Historia Regum Britanniæ, First Variant Version*, ed. Neil Wright (London: Brewer, 1988).

Gildas, *The Ruin of Britain and Other Works*, ed. Michael Winterbottom (London: Phillimore, 1978).

Giraldus Cambrensis, *Journey through Wales and the Description of Wales*, trans. Lewis Thorpe (Harmondsworth: Penguin, 1978).

——, *The History and Topography of Ireland*, trans. John O'Meara (Atlantic Highlands, NJ: Humanities Press, 1982).

——, *Opera*, J. S. Brewer (Nendeln: Krauss, 1966).

Guillaume de Lorris and Jean de Meun, *Le Roman de la Rose*, ed. Armand Strubel (Paris: University Press of France, 1984).

——, *The Romance of the Rose*, trans. Charles Dahlberg (Hanover, NH: University Press of New England, 1983).

Guthlac, Saint, *Felix's Life of Saint Guthlac*, ed. and trans. Bertram Colgrave (Cambridge: Cambridge University Press, 1956).

Guy of Amiens, *Carmen de Hastingae*, eds and trans. Catherine Morton and Hope Muntz (Oxford: Oxford at the Clarendon Press, 1972).

Henry of Huntingdon, *Historia Anglorum*, ed. and trans. Diana Greenway (Oxford: Oxford at the Clarendon Press, 1996).

John of Salisbury, *Policraticus*, ed. Cary J. Nederman (Cambridge: Cambridge University Press, 1990).

John of Worcester, *Chronicle of John of Worcester*, eds R. R. Darlington and P. McGurk; trans. Jennifer Bray and P. McGurk (Oxford: Clarendon Press, 1995).

La3amon, *Brut*, eds W. R. J. Barron and S. C. Weinberg (Harlow, Essex: Longmans, 1995).

——, *Brut*, eds G. L. Brook and R. F. Leslie, London, EETS 250, 276 (Oxford: Oxford University Press, 1963).

——, *Lawman's Brut*, trans. Rosamund Allen (London: Dent, 1992).

——, *Layamon's Brut: A History of the Britons*, trans. Donald G. Bzdyl (Binghamton, NY: Medieval and Renaissance Texts and Studies, 1989).

Life of Edward the Confessor, Cambridge University Library MS Ee.3.59.

Nennius, *British History and Welsh Annals*, trans. John Morris (London: Phillimore, 1990).

The New Oxford Annotated Bible, Revised Standard Version, eds Bruce M. Metzger and Roland E. Murphy (New York: Oxford University Press, 1991).

Orderic Vitalis, *Ecclesiastical History*, ed. Marjorie Chibnall (Oxford: Oxford at the Clarendon Press, 1980).

Orosius, *Seven Books of History Against the Pagans, the Apology of Paulus Orosius*, trans. Irving Woodworth Raymond (New York: Columbia University Press, 1936).

Sir Gawain and the Green Knight, ed. W. R. J. Barron (Manchester: Manchester UP, 1998).

Ussher, James, *Britannicarum Ecclesiastica Antiquitates* (London, 1639).

Virgil, *Eclogues, Georgics, The Aeneid, The Minor Poems*, 2 vols, ed. and trans. H. Rushton Fairclough (London: William Heinemann, 1932).

Vita Haroldi, The Romance of the Life of Harold, King of England (London: Stock, 1895).

Wace, *Roman de Brut, A History of the British*, ed. and trans. Judith Weiss (Exeter: University of Exeter Press, 1999).

——, *Le Roman de Rou*, ed. A. J. Holden (Paris: A. and J. Picard, 1970).

William of Jumièges, Orderic Vitalis and Robert of Torigni, *Gesta Normannorum Ducum*, ed. and trans. Elisabeth M. C. Van Houts (Oxford: Oxford at the Clarendon Press, 1992).

William of Malmesbury, *Gesta Regum Anglorum*, eds and trans. R. R. Thomson and M. Winterbottom (Oxford: Oxford University Press, 1999).

William of Newburgh, *Historia Rerum Anglicarum* (London, 1856).

——, *The History of William of Newburgh*, trans. Joseph Stevenson (Lampeter, Wales: Llanerch, 1996).

Wulfstan, *Sermo Lupi ad Anglos*, ed. Dorothy Whitelock (London: Methuen, 1963).

Secondary Sources

Albu, Emily, *The Normans in their Histories: Propaganda, Myth and Subversion* (Suffolk: Boydell and Brewer, 2001).

Barnstone, Willis, *The Poetics of Translation: History, Theory, Practice* (New Haven: Yale University Press, 1993).

Bassnett, Susan and Harish Trivedi, 'Introduction: of colonies, cannibals, and vernacular', in Susan Bassnett and Harish Trivedi (eds), *Post-Colonial Translation: Theory and Practice* (New York: Routledge, 1999), pp. 1–18.

Benjamin, Walter and Steven Rendall (trans.), 'The translator's task', *TTR: Traduction, Terminologie, Rédaction: Études sur le texte et ses transformations*, 10, 2 (1997), 151–65.

Bennett, Matthew, 'Poetry as history?: the *Roman de Rou* of Wace as a source for the Norman Conquest', *Anglo-Norman Studies*, 5 (1982), 21–39.

Bernstein, David J., *The Mystery of the Bayeux Tapestry* (Chicago: University of Chicago Press, 1987).

Bhabha, Homi K., 'Postcolonial criticism', in Stephen Greenblatt and Giles Nunn (eds), *Redrawing the Boundaries: The Transformation of English and American Literary Studies* (New York: MLA, 1992), pp. 437–65.

Biddick, Kathleen, 'Bede's blush: postcards from Bali, Bombay, Palo Alto', in John Van Engen (ed.), *The Past and Present of Medieval Studies*, (South Bend: University of Notre Dame Press, 1994), pp. 16–44.

Borges, Jorge Luis, 'The innocence of Layamon', in *Other Inquisitions*, trans. Ruth L. C. Simms (New York: Washington Square, 1966).

Brehe, Stephen Karl, 'Reassembling the *First Worcester Fragment*', *Speculum*, 65 (1990), 521–36.

Breisach, Ernst, *Classical Rhetoric and Medieval Historiography*, Studies in Medieval Culture 19 (Kalamazoo: Western Michigan University Press, 1985).

Bryan, Elizabeth J., *Collaborative Meaning in Medieval Scribal Culture: The Otho Laȝamon* (Ann Arbor: University of Michigan Press, 1999).

——, 'Truth and the Round Table in Lawman's *Brut*', *Quondam et Futurus*, 2, 4 (1992), 27–35.

——, 'The two manuscripts of Laȝamon's *Brut*, some readers in the margins', in Françoise Le Saux (ed.), *The Text and Tradition of Laȝamon's* Brut (London: Brewer, 1994), pp. 89–102.

Camille, Michael, 'The book as flesh and fetish in Richard de Bury's *Philobiblon*', in Dolores Warwick Frese and Katherine O'Brien O'Keeffe (eds), *The Book and the Body*, University of Notre Dame Ward-Phillips Lectures in English Language and Literature 14 (Notre Dame: University of Notre Dame Press), pp. 34–77.

Chaney, William A., *The Cult of Kingship in Anglo-Saxon England: The Transition from Paganism to Christianity* (Berkeley: University of California Press, 1970).

Cheney, Mary G., *Roger, Bishop of Worcester, 1164–1179* (Cambridge: Cambridge University Press , 1989).

Clark-Hall, J. R., *A Concise Anglo-Saxon Dictionary* (Toronto: University of Toronto Press, 1894; repr. 1960).

Copeland, Rita, *Rhetoric, Hermeneutics, and Translation in the Middle Ages: Academic Traditions and Vernacular Texts* (Cambridge: Cambridge University Press, 1995).

Crick, Julia C., *The* Historia Regum Britanniae *of Geoffrey of Monmouth*, IV, *Dissemination and Deception in the Later Middle Ages* (London: Brewer, 1991).

Cronin, Michael, *Translating Ireland: Translation, Languages, Cultures* (Cork: Cork University Press, 1996).

Curtius, Ernst Robert, *European Literature and the Latin Middle Ages*, trans. Willard R. Trask (Princeton: Princeton University Press, 1953).

Davies, H. S., 'Layamon's similes', *Review of English Studies*, 11, 42 (1960), 129–42.

Derrida, Jacques, *Writing and Difference* (Chicago: University of Chicago Press, 1978).

——, and Joseph F. Graham, 'Des Tours de Babel', in Joseph F. Graham (ed.), *Difference in Translation* (Ithaca: Cornell University Press, 1985), pp. 165–248.

Dinshaw, Carolyn, *Chaucer's Sexual Poetics* (Madison: University of Wisconsin Press, 1989).

Donoghue, Daniel P., 'Laȝamon's "Ambivalence"', *Speculum*, 65 (1990), 537–63.

Dumville, David, '"Nennius" and the *Historia Brittonum*', *Studia Celtica*, 10 (1976), 78–95.

Ellis, Roger and René Tixier, *The Medieval Translator* (Belgium: Brepols, 1996).

Fenster, Thelma, 'Preface: why men?', in *Medieval Masculinities: Regarding Men in the Middle Ages*, Clare A. Lees (ed.) (Minneapolis: University of Minnesota Press, 1994), pp. ix–xiv.

Fernie, E. C., 'Church architecture in Anglo-Norman England', in David Bates and Anne Curry (eds), *England and Normandy in the Middle Ages* (London: Hambledon, 1994), pp. 103–15.

Finke, Laurie and Martin Shichtman, *King Arthur and the Myth of History* (Gainesville: Univeristy of Florida Press, 2004).

——, 'The Mont-Saint-Michel Giant: sexual violence and imperialism in the chronicles of Wace and Layamon', in Anna Roberts (ed.), *Violence Against Women in Medieval Texts* (Gainesville: University Press of Florida, 1998), pp. 56–74.

Finn, R. Welldon, *Domesday Book: A Guide* (London: Phillimore, 1973).

Flint, Valerie I. J., 'The *Historia Regum Britanniae* of Geoffrey of Monmouth: parody and its purpose: a suggestion', *Speculum*, 54, 3 (1979), 447–68.

Foucault, Michel, 'Nietzsche, genealogy, history', in *Language, Counter-memory, Practice: Selected Essays and Interviews*, ed. Donald F. Bouchard (Ithaca: Cornell University Press, 1977), pp. 139–64.

Frantzen, Allen J., *Before the Closet: Same-Sex Love from* Beowulf *to* Angels in America (Chicago: University of Chicago Press, 1998).

Frese, Dolores Warwick, 'The marriage of woman and werewolf: poetics of estrangement in Marie de France's "Bisclavret"', in Alger Nicholas Doane and Carol Braun Pasternack (eds), *Vox Intexta: Orality and Textuality in the Middle Ages* (Madison: University of Wisconsin Press, 1991), pp. 183–202.

Friedlander, Carolynn VanDyke, 'Early Middle English accentual verse', *Modern Philology*, 76 (1979), 219–30.

Fries, Maureen, 'Women, power, and (the undermining of) order in Lawman's *Brut*', *Arthuriana*, 8, 3 (1998), 23–32.

Gillespie, Francis Lylte, 'Layamon's *Brut*: a comparative study in narrative art', *University of California Publications in Modern Philology*, 3 (1916), 361–510.

Gillingham, John, *The English in the Twelfth Century* (Woodbridge, Suffolk: Boydell, 2000).

Glowka, Arthur Wayne, 'Masculinity, male sexuality, and kingship', in Rosamund Allen, Lucy Perry and Jane Roberts (eds), *Laȝamon, Contexts, Language and Interpretation*, King's College London Medieval Studies 19 (London: King's College London Centre for Late Antique and Medieval Studies, 2002), 413–31.

Godard, Barbara, 'Culture as translation', in Shantha Ramakrishna (ed.), *Translation and Multilingualism, Post-Colonial Contexts* (Delhi: Pencraft, 1997), pp. 157–82.

Gransden, Antonia, *Historical Writing in England c.550 to c.1307* (Ithaca: University of Cornell Press, 1974).

——, *Legends, Traditions and History in Medieval England* (London: Hambledon, 1992).

Grant, Lindy, 'Architectural relations between England and Normandy, 1100–1204', in David Bates and Anne Curry (eds), *England and Normandy in the Middle Ages* (London: Hambledon, 1994), pp. 117–29.

Hanning, Robert W., 'Poetic emblems in medieval narrative texts', in Lois Ebin, (ed.), *Vernacular Poetics in the Middle Ages*, Studies in Medieval Culture 16 (Kalamazoo: Medieval Institute Publications, 1984), pp. 1–18.

——, *The Vision of History in Early Britain, from Gildas to Geoffrey of Monmouth* (New York: Columbia University Press, 1966).

Harford, Thomas A., *A Comprehensive Study of Layamon's* Brut, Studies in Mediaeval Literature 21 (Lewiston, NY: Mellen, 2002).

Hinckley, H. B., 'The date of Layamon's *Brut*', *Anglia*, 56 (1932), 43–57.

Hollister, C. Warren, *The Impact of the Norman Conquest* (New York: Wiley, 1969).

Holsinger, Bruce, 'Medieval studies, postcolonial studies, and the genealogies of critique', *Speculum*, 77 (2002), 1195–227.

Holt, J. C., *Colonial England 1066–1215* (London: Hambledon, 1997).

Howe, Nicholas, *Migration and Mythmaking in Anglo-Saxon England* (Notre Dame: University of Notre Dame Press, 1989).

Howlett, David, 'The literary context of Geoffrey of Monmouth', *Arthuriana*, 5, 3 (1995), 25–69.

Hunter Blair, Peter, *An Introduction to Anglo-Saxon England* (Cambridge: Cambridge University Press, 1956).

Ingham, Patricia Clare and Michelle R. Warren, 'Introduction: postcolonial modernity and the rest of history', in Patricia Clare Ingham and Michelle R.

Warren (eds), *Postcolonial Moves: Medieval through Modern* (New York: Palgrave-Macmillan, 2003), pp. 1–18.

Ingledew, Francis, 'The Book of Troy and the genealogical construction of history: the case of Geoffrey of Monmouth's *Historia regum Britanniae*', *Speculum*, 79 (1994), 665–704.

Jamison, Carol Parrish, 'Traffic of women in Germanic literature: the role of the peace pledge in marital exchanges', *Women in German Yearbook: Feminist Studies in German Literature and Culture*, 20 (2004), 13–36.

Johnson, Lesley, 'Reading the past in Layamon's *Brut*', in Françoise Le Saux (ed.), *The Text and Tradition of Layamon's* Brut (London: Brewer, 1994), pp. 140–61.

Kantorowicz, Ernst H., *The King's Two Bodies, A Study in Mediaeval Political Theology* (Princeton: Princeton University Press, 1957).

Karkov, Catherine E., '"Tales of the Ancients": colonial werewolves and the mapping of Postcolonial Ireland', in Patricia Clare Ingham and Michelle R. Warren (eds), *Postcolonial Moves: Medieval through Modern* (New York, Palgrave-Macmillan, 2003), pp. 93–110.

Keith, W. J., 'Layamon's *Brut*, the literary differences between the two texts', *Medium Ævum*, 29 (1960), 161–72.

Kirby, I. J., 'Angles and Saxons in Layamon's *Brut*', *Studia Neophilologica*, 36 (1964), 51–62.

Knape, Joachim, 'History as rhetoric', in Erik Kooper (ed.), *The Medieval Chronicle II* (Amsterdam: Rodopi, 2002), pp. 117–29.

Kolodny, Annette, *The Lay of the Land: Metaphor as Experience and History in American Life and Letters* (Chapel Hill: University of North Carolina Press, 1975).

Kristeva, Julia, *Power of Horror: An Essay on Abjection*, trans. Leon S. Roudiez (New York: Columbia University Press, 1982).

Kurath, Hans (ed.), *Middle English Dictionary* (Ann Arbor: University of Michigan Press), 1952.

Leckie, R. William Jr., *The Passage of Dominion: Geoffrey of Monmouth and the Periodization of Insular History in the Twelfth Century* (Toronto: University of Toronto Press, 1981).

Lefevre, André, 'Composing the Other', in Susan Bassnett and Harish Trivedi (eds), *Post-Colonial Translation, Theory and Practice* (New York: Routledge, 1999), pp. 75–94.

Lerer, Seth, *Boethius and Dialogue: Literary Method in* The Consolation of Philosophy (Princeton: Princeton University Press), 1985.

Le Saux, Françoise H. M., *Layamon's Brut: The Poem and its Sources* (Cambridge: Brewer, 1989).

——, 'Paradigms of evil: gender and crime in Layamon's *Brut*', in Françoise Le Saux (ed.), *The Text and Tradition of Layamon's* Brut (London: Brewer, 1994), pp. 193–206.

Lévi-Strauss, Claude, *The Elementary Structures of Kinship*, trans. James Harle Bell et al. (Boston: Beacon Press, 1969).

Loomis, Roger Sherman, *Arthurian Literature in the Middle Ages* (Oxford: Oxford at the Clarendon Press, 1959).

MacDougall, Hugh A., *Racial Myth in English History* (Hanover: University Press of New England, 1982).

McNamarra, Jo Ann, 'The *Herrenfrage:* the restructuring of the gender system, 1050–1150', in Clare A. Lees et al (eds), *Medieval Masculinities: Regarding Men in the Middle Ages* (Minneapolis: University of Minnesota Press, 1994), pp. 3–30.

McNelis, James I. III, 'Layamon as *Auctor*', in Françoise Le Saux (ed.), *Reading the Past in Layamon's* Brut (London: Brewer, 1994), pp. 253–69.

Markey, T. L., 'Nordic *niðvisur*: an instance of ritual inversion?', *Medieval Scandinavia*, 5 (1972), 7–18.

Mercanti, Gloria, 'Some rhetorical devices of the Latin tradition in La3amon's *Brut*', in Rosamund Allen, Lucy Perry and Jane Roberts (eds), *La3amon: Contexts, Language and Interpretation*, King's College London Medieval Studies 19 (London: King's College London Centre for Late Antique and Medieval Studies, 2002), pp. 241–50.

Minnis, Alastair J. (ed.), *Chaucer's Boece and the Medieval Tradition of Boethius* (Cambridge: Brewer, 1993).

——, *The Medieval Theory of Authorship: Scholastic Literary Attitudes in the Later Middle Ages*, 2 edition (Philadelphia: University of Pennsylvania Press, 1988).

Morrison, Karl, *History as Visual Art in the Twelfth Century Renaissance* (Princeton: Princeton University Press, 1990).

Morse, Ruth, *Truth and Convention in the Middle Ages: Rhetoric, Representation, and Reality* (Cambridge: Cambridge University Press, 1991).

Mossé, Fernand, *A Handbook to Middle English*, trans. James A. Walker (Baltimore: Johns Hopkins University Press, 1952).

Neubert, Albrecht and Gregory M. Shreve, *Translation as Text* (Kent, OH: Kent State UP, 1992).

Niranjana, Tejaswini, *Siting Translation: History, Postcolonialism, and the Colonial Context* (Berkeley: University of California Press, 1992).

Noble, James, 'Layamon's "ambivalence" reconsidered', in Françoise Le Saux (ed.), *The Text and Tradition of Layamon's* Brut (London, Brewer, 1994), pp. 171–82.

North, Richard. 'Getting to know the General in the *Battle of Maldon*', *Medium Ævum*, 60 (1991), 1–15.

Otter, Monika, *Inventiones: Fiction and Referentiality in Twelfth-Century English Historical Writing* (Chapel Hill: University of North Carolina Press, 1996).

Partner, Nancy, *Serious Entertainments: The Writing of History in Twelfth- Century England* (Chicago: University of Chicago Press, 1977).

Patterson, Lee, *Chaucer and the Subject of History* (Madison: University of Wisconsin Press, 1991).

Rener, Frederick, *Interpretatio: Language and Translation from Cicero to Tytler* (Amsterdam: Rodopi, 1989).

Rider, Jeff, 'The fictional margin: the Merlin of the *Brut*', *Modern Philology*, 87, 1 (1989), 1–12.

Ringbom, Håkan, *Studies in the Narrative Technique of* Beowulf *and Lawman's* Brut (Åbo: Ekenas Tryckeri, 1968).

Robinson, Douglas, *The Translator's Turn* (Baltimore: Johns Hopkins University Press, 1991).

Ross, Margaret Clunie, 'Land-taking and text-making in medieval Iceland', in Sylvia Tomasch and Sealy Gilles (eds), *Text and Territory, Geographical Imagination in the European Middle Ages* (Philadelphia: University of Pennsylvania Press, 1998), pp. 159–84.

Rubin, Gayle, 'The traffic in woman: notes on the "political economy: of sex"', in Rayna R. Reiter (ed.), *Toward an Anthropology of Women* (New York: Monthly Review Press, 2000), pp. 157–210.

Said, Edward W., *The World, the Text, and the Critic* (Cambridge: Harvard University Press, 1983).

Sedgwick, Eve Kosofsky, *Between Men, English Literature and Male Homosocial Desire* (New York: Columbia University Press, 1985).

Sheppard, Alice, '"Of this is a king's body made", lordship and succession in Lawman's Arthur and Leir', *Arthuriana*, 10, 2 (2000), 50–64.

Shichtman, Martin B., 'Gawain in Wace and Layamon, a case of metahistorical evolution', in Laurie Finke and Martin Shichtman (eds), *Medieval Texts and Contemporary Readers* (Ithaca: Cornell University Press, 1987), pp. 103–19.

Simon, Sherry, 'Introduction', in Sherry Simon and Paul St. Pierre (eds), *Changing the Terms, Translating in the Postcolonial Era* (Ottawa: University of Ottawa Press, 2000), 1–15.

Spiegel, Gabrielle M., *Romancing the Past, The Rise of Vernacular Prose Historiography in Thirteenth-Century France* (Berkeley: University of California Press, 1993).

Stanley, E. G., 'The date of Layamon's *Brut*', *Notes and Queries*, 213 (1968), 85–8.

——, 'Layamon's antiquarian sentiments', *Medium Ævum*, 38 (1968), 23–37.

Stanton, Robert, 'The (m)other tongue, translation theory and Old English', in Jeanette Beer (ed.), *Translation Theory and Practice in the Middle Ages* (Kalamazoo: Western Michigan University Press, 1997), pp. 33–46.

Stein, Robert M., '"Making history English", cultural identity and historical explanation in William of Malmesbury and Layamon's *Brut*', in Sylvia Tomasch and Sealy Gilles (eds), *Text and Territory: Geographical Imagination in the European Middle Ages* (Philadelphia: University of Pennsylvania Press, 1998), pp. 97–115.

Steiner, George, *After Babel: Aspects of Language and Translation* (London: Oxford University Press, 1975).

Stock, Brian, *The Implications of Literacy: Written Language and Models of Interpretation in the Eleventh and Twelfth Centuries* (Princeton: Princeton University Press, 1983).

Tatlock, J. S. P., *The Legendary History of Britain* (Berkeley: University of California Press, 1950).

Tiller, Kenneth J., '"Romancing history", masculine identity and historical authority in Layamon's prologue (Cotton MS Caligula A.ix, ll. 1–35)', in Rosamund Allen, Lucy Perry and Jane Roberts (eds), *Layamon, Contexts, Language and Interpretation*, King's College London Medieval Studies 19 (London: King's College London Centre for Late Antique and Medieval Studies, 2002), pp. 371–84.

——, 'The truth "bi Arðure ðan kinge"; Arthur's role in shaping Lawman's vision of history', *Arthuriana*, 10, 2 (2000), 27–49.

Veira, Else Ribeiro Pires, 'Liberating Calibans: readings of antropofagia and Haroldo de Campos' poetics of transcreation', in Susan Bassnett and Harish Trivedi (eds), *Post-Colonial Translation, Theory and Practice* (London: Routledge, 1999), pp. 95–113.

Visser, G. J., *Layamon: An Attempt at Vindication* (Assen: Van Gorcum, 1935).

Vitz, Evelyn Birce, *Medieval Narrative and Modern Narratology: Subjects and Objects of Desire* (New York: Columbia University Press, 1989).

Warren, Michelle R., *History on the Edge: Excalibur and the Borders of Britain* (Minneapolis: University of Minnesota Press, 2000).

——, 'Making contact: postcolonial perspectives through Geoffrey of Monmouth's *Historia regum Britannie*', *Arthuriana*, 8, 4 (1998), 115–32.

White, Hayden, *Metahistory: The Historical Imagination in Nineteenth-Century Europe* (Baltimore: Johns Hopkins University Press, 1972).

Wickham-Crowley, Kelley M., 'Cannibal cultures and the body of the text in Layamon's *Brut*', in Rosamund Allen, Lucy Perry and Jane Roberts (eds), *Layamon, Contexts, Language and Interpretation*, King's College London Medieval Studies, 19 (London: King's College London Centre for Late Antique and Medieval Studies, 2002), pp. 351–69.

——, *Writing the Future: Layamon's Prophetic History* (Cardiff: University of Wales Press, 2002).

Windschuttle, Keith, *The Killing of History: How Literary Critics and Social Theorists are Murdering our Past* (San Francisco: Encounter, 1996).

Wright, Neil, 'Angles and Saxons in Layamon's *Brut*, a reassessment', in Françoise Le Saux (ed.), *The Text and Tradition of LaΣamon's* Brut (London: Brewer, 1994), pp. 161–170.

Wyld, Henry Cecil, 'Layamon as an English poet', *Review of English Studies*, 6 (1930), 1–30.

Index